Thinking Cis

Thinking Cis

Cisgender, Heterosexual Men, and Queer Women's Roles in Anti-Trans Violence

alithia zamantakis

ROWMAN & LITTLEFIELD
Lanham • Boulder • New York • London

Rowman & Littlefield
Bloomsbury Publishing Inc, 1359 Broadway, New York, NY 10018, USA
Bloomsbury Publishing Plc, 50 Bedford Square, London, WC1B 3DP, UK
Bloomsbury Publishing Ireland, 29 Earlsfort Terrace, Dublin 2, D02 AY28, Ireland
www.bloomsbury.com

Published by Lexington Books
An imprint of The Rowman & Littlefield Publishing Group, Inc.
4501 Forbes Boulevard, Suite 200, Lanham, Maryland 20706
www.rowman.com
86-90 Paul Street, London EC2A 4NE

British Library Cataloguing in Publication Information available

Library of Congress Cataloging-in-Publication Data

Names: zamantakis, alithia, 1994– author.
Title: Thinking cis : cisgender, heterosexual men, and queer women's roles in
    anti-trans violence / alithia zamantakis.
Description: Lanham: Rowman & Littlefield, [2023] | Includes bibliographical references
    and index. | Summary: "An analysis of the social construction of cis-ness, a political,
    discursive, and social manifestation that shapes how we think about race, gender,
    sexuality, and who we consider worthy of living"—Provided by publisher.
Identifiers: LCCN 2023037367 (print) | LCCN 2023037368 (ebook) |
    ISBN 9781538177624 (hardback) | ISBN 9781538177631 (epub)
Subjects: LCSH: Gender identity. | Cisgender people—Psychology. | Transgender
    people—Public opinion. | Transphobia.
Classification: LCC HQ18.55 .Z36 2023 (print) | LCC HQ18.55 (ebook) |
    DDC 305.3—dc23/eng/20230901
LC record available at https://lccn.loc.gov/2023037367
LC ebook record available at https://lccn.loc.gov/2023037368

This book is dedicated to the unnamed and unknown trans women who fought and continue to fight for a new world.

Contents

Acknowledgments

This book is the product of a collective labor. Like any other scientific work, it relied on the hours of support, critique, and labor of countless mentors, friends, and family members.

I would like to thank my dissertation advisor, Dr. Katie Acosta, and my dissertation committee, Drs. Veronica Newton and Wendy Simond, for the innumerable hours of work they poured into me and this book. Thank you to my sister scholars and best friends, Dresden Lackey and Monisha Jackson, for being my rocks throughout grad school and life. Thank you to my platonic soulmate and best friend, Margarita Ruíz Hernández, for letting me vent to you, gassing me up, and inspiring me to do and be my best. You make life livable.

Thank you to my best friend and mother, Misty, for crying with me through the pains of this research and for always fighting for me. Gracias a mi mamá transgénero, Lí An (Estrella) Sanchez, por ayudarme a afirmar todo lo que soy y por inspirarme a seguir luchando. Thank you to my friends and chosen family, Tabitha Ingle, Kara Tsukerman, Andy Chang, Ella and Amanda Blanchard-James, Kira Kiko Lian, Nico Climaco, Jasmine Deskins, Artur Queiroz, Pablo Zapata, and so many more unnamed for supporting me and loving me along the way. Thank you to my comrades for keeping me grounded in organizing, guerilla intellectualism, and revolutionary optimism.

Thank you to the Southeastern Women's Studies Association for the 2019 Dissertation Fellowship that enabled me to compensate my participants, making it possible to complete my research in the time I did. Thank you to Georgia State University for the Provost Dissertation Fellowship that allowed me to survive while having the time to focus on my dissertation. The editing and tailoring of this manuscript were also supported by a training grant from the National Institute of Mental Health (T32MH130325; PI: Newcomb).

During the formative stages of this book, many reviewers provided invaluable criticism for which I'm incredibly grateful, including:

Chris Barcelos, *University of Massachusetts, Boston*
Tristan Bridges, *University of California, Santa Barbara*
Cary Costello, *University of Wisconsin–Milwaukee*
Chloe Goldbach, *Southern Illinois University Carbondale*
Shanna Kattari, *University of Michigan*
Douglas Knutson, *Oklahoma State University*
Adam Messinger, *Northeastern Illinois University*
Max Osborn, *Villanova University*
Emily Via, *University of Illinois–Chicago*
Terrell Winder, *University of California, Santa Barbara*

Finally, thank you to each of my participants for your vulnerability, honesty, and willingness to answer the questions of a stranger.

Introduction

In season 2, episode 9 of the Emmy-awarded show *Pose*,[1] a group of Black trans women friends go on a girls' trip to a beach house outside Manhattan. Sitting at a table in a country club, Blanca (MJ Rodriguez), the main protagonist of the show, explains to the other girls that the lifeguard at the beach earlier that day just asked her to take a walk with him. Elektra (Dominique Jackson), Blanca's mother,[2] responds, "You obviously said no."

Blanca: No, I said yes. That man is fine. Plus, it's been a cute minute since I had a man show me that kind of kindness.

Angel (Blanca's daughter; played by Indya Moore): Take it for the team.

Elektra: You're insane! It's unsafe for girls like us to walk in the middle of the night with a stranger. You know you can't trust a man once the sun goes down.

LuLu (Blanca's sister; played by Hailie Sahar): That's true!

Angel: Oh, I didn't think about that.

Blanca: That doesn't make any sense!

Angel: Yes, it does. You know these men are afraid of their desires for us. They take it out on us all the time.

Elektra: That's probably what happened to Candy [one of Elektra's daughters who had previously been murdered by one of her johns]. They don't kill us because they hate us. They kill us because they hate what it means to love us.

Blanca: So, am I supposed to just live in fear for the rest of my life? Die without ever knowing love?

LuLu: Maybe you could just meet him for coffee or something before we head back.

Angel: Yeah girl.

Blanca: Where's the passion in that? Listen, I know y'all care for me, but I have to trust my instincts on this one. I'm going.

Elektra: Wait! If you're going to go, at least take this.

At this point, Elektra hands Blanca a switchblade. Angel then proceeds to remove brass knuckles from her purse for Blanca, and LuLu hands her a taser. Fortunately for Blanca, the man she meets does not come to harm her and does not feel bothered by her trans-ness. Instead, he finds her the most desirable woman he's come across yet as a lifeguard.

As a trans woman, I know all too well the risks of dating and interacting with cisgender heterosexual men (henceforth cis-het men). Today, I am mostly assumed to be a cisgender woman, but countless times prior to this, I have been threatened by cis-het men who yell in my face demanding to know "what I am," who are disgusted by my presence and threaten to physically harm me, who so despise me that they threaten to kill me. I, too, like Elektra, LuLu, and Angel, always carry with me a knife, taser, and pepper spray. While many women may fear for their physical safety when out in public, those fears are often heightened for trans women, Black women, other women of color, and those intersectionally marginalized according to race, class, and gender.

In the scene above, Elektra highlights that it is not mere transphobia that gives rise to murders of trans women. She argues instead that cis-het men kill trans women not out of a hate of trans-ness but, instead, out of a fear and hatred for what it means when others see them desiring trans women. Indeed, in my interviews with cis-het men and cis-lesbian, bisexual, and queer (LBQ) women, participants highlighted how interactions with a trans woman not only repelled or confused them but changed how others would see them. Being with a trans woman does not simply highlight that a person desires this individual woman. Instead, being with a trans woman elicits questions regarding one's manhood and heterosexuality, and for others their woman-hood and lesbian identity. Violence functions to reconstitute one's gender identity and sexual orientation—to place one back in a "straight orientation" in the words of Ahmed[3] or an "upright position" in the words of Strauss[4] and Salamon.[5] Violence also enables one to renew their position within hierarchies of masculinities[6] and ensure that their manhood remains confirmed and validated by other men.[7]

Salamon explicates this in her phenomenological analysis of the murder of Latisha King. Salamon notes, "In the trial of Brandon McInerney, the cis-het, White student who murdered [Latisha King], it became clear that Brandon's murderous rage toward Larry [*sic*] was being described as a defense not of Brandon's person or body, but of the integrity of his sexual identity."[8] Latisha was described by Brandon, his girlfriend, staff and teachers at the high school, and others as provoking a response from others by dressing in "women's" clothing, walking in heels, donning makeup, and requesting to be referred to as Latisha. Latisha's very being provoked and taunted the cis-het, White student body, staff, and faculty of her school. Brandon McInerney felt compelled to get rid of her to, in his words, "make everyone's life better."[9]

Latisha's life as a Black trans girl became a problem to solve, and the solution lay in murdering her without apology. Brandon McInerney is not alone in these sentiments nor have these sentiments faded away in the decade since Latisha's murder. In my interviews, it was not uncommon for cis-het men participants to state that certain situations justified the murders of trans women. While no cis-LBQ woman sought to justify the situation, many spoke of trans women as deceptive, dishonest, and duplicitous, and discursively shifted the blame onto trans women.

Often, anti-trans homicides within the United States are framed as an epidemic. However, Laurel Westbrook, a sociological scholar of gender, has shown that trans people do not necessarily experience more fatal violence than cisgender people.[10] While the murders of trans women are not an epidemic, I, and I dare say most, would argue that one life lost to anti-trans, anti-Black violence is one life too many. Though the rates of murders of trans people, as a whole, are less than murders of cisgender people, research has found that young, Black, and/or Latina trans women and transfeminine individuals are at a higher risk of murder than their cisgender counterparts.[11] Further, murders of individuals for being cisgender or for not disclosing their cisgender identity are not known to occur, while murders of individuals for being transgender or for not disclosing their transgender identity have been known to occur, as I highlight throughout this book. Thus, a need arises to better understand the social and cultural conditions that give rise to violence against Black trans women, including homicide.

In a *New York Times* editorial, author Amanda Hess asks, "When did our national discourse become so consumed with the state of our national discourse?"[12] Hess ends the article highlighting that these "squabbles over whose rhetoric is out of line and who started it . . . makes the political discourse louder, but not any clearer." Hess's point is that we need to move beyond a focus on discourse to the material reality surrounding us, yet the reality is that words do shape our very lives. Although popularly described as "debate and arguments" taking place on Twitter, discourse does not refer to "hot takes," "bad takes," or online discussion. Instead, analyses of discourse are focused on how language functions as a mechanism of social reproduction. Words are not tangible realities, yet they do constrain, shape, and/or enable our tangible realities. Words construct policies, which construct barriers or facilitators to accessing work, health care, education, and justice. Words allow us to understand the similarities and differences between one person's life and another's, and words give meaning and justification to our actions. Words are not tangible realities, but words enable us to analyze *the structuring of tangible realities*. The opposite is also true that material reality shapes culture and language. Thus, the two—language/culture and material reality—are interconnected.

xiv   *Introduction*

In this book, I discuss how the thirty-two participants I interviewed make sense of gender, sexuality, and violence as it relates to transgender people. It is important to note, though, that this book is not one about trans people. *Thinking Cis* is a book about thirty-two cisgender people—their words, their body language, and the ways they make sense of trans lives and trans deaths. This book is also not about *all* cisgender people. My aim is not to produce generalizable knowledge, but to further scientific explorations into social, cultural, and (albeit not a focus of this book) the structural mechanisms through which anti-trans, anti-Black violence is perpetuated. Queer theorists remind scholars that the task of queer theory is not to formulate a theory about queers, but to analyze, critique, and rethink the "knowledges and social practices that organize 'society' as a whole" vis-à-vis the politics of sexuality.[13] Trans Studies, too, takes its role as such—to analyze, critique, and rethink the epistemological, ontological, and material mechanisms through which gender shapes and is shaped by the social world. Trans Studies seeks not to construct a theory of trans/nonbinary people but to analyze the sociopolitical and historical "conditions that cause transgender phenomena to stand out in the first place, and that allow gender normativity to disappear into the unanalyzed, ambient background."[14] In other words, Trans Studies is (or should be) as much a study of cis-ness as it is a study of trans-ness.

CRITICAL CIS-NESS STUDIES

Trans Studies, in recent years, has begun to expand within the field of Sociology. The Sociology of Trans Studies, however, remains quite limited in terms of breadth of empirical research and the scope of existing research. Schilt and Lagos note in the *Annual Review of Sociology* that the Sociology of Trans Studies currently falls into three main categories:

> Research that explores the diversity of transgender peoples' identities and social locations, research that interrogates transgender peoples' experiences within institutional and organizational contexts, and research that presents quantitative approaches to transgender peoples' identities and experiences.[15]

Save for work such as that by Pfeffer[16] and Ward,[17] both of whom analyze how cisgender people negotiate gender and sexuality while in relationships with trans people, much of the Sociology of Trans Studies focuses on understanding the lives of trans people. However, little work within the Sociology of Trans Studies examines the ways in which cis-ness is constituted, constructed, and maintained through interpersonal and/or institutional means. I situate this book within a subfield of "Critical Cis-ness Studies," which aims to interrogate cis-ness as a political, discursive, and social manifestation. To do so I explicate how gender, itself, is a manifestation of cissexism (i.e., the systemic and institutional oppression of transgender, nonbinary, and gender-nonconforming individuals), which functions in tandem with white supremacy and heterosexism and is a product of capitalism and colonialism.

Gender is a relational project, replicating itself through discursive and material interactions between individuals. Sociologists and feminist theorists have long argued that gender is an action and not an inherent quality of an individual.[18] Social forces (e.g., religion, the economy, the family) and cultural schemas shape an individual's gender presentation(s) and organize gender around culturally legible ideas of manhood and womanhood. In doing gender, individuals hold themselves and others accountable to "proper" ways of being and interacting.[19] These particular ways of manhood and womanhood to which individuals are held accountable are not arbitrarily determined. Rather, contemporary ideas of "proper" manhood and "proper" womanhood form out of a white supremacist heteropatriarchy. Notions of a gender binary evolved out of a patriarchal system "in which only two genders exist, one dominating the other."[20] Masculinities scholar Raewyn Connell notes that current, Western notions of masculinity (and I would add femininity) are a "fairly recent historical product" developing out of European colonialism, capitalism, imperialism, and (neo)liberalism.[21] Heterosexuality and homosexuality, co-invented and -invested with meaning through the scientific racist practices that aimed to justify white supremacy and colonization in the United States, map themselves around the non-White body.[22]

The colonization/genocide of Indigenous peoples and the enslavement of African peoples, as projects of White, capitalist expansion,[23] relied upon this binary, heteropatriarchal order to deem particular bodies (Indigenous and Black bodies) as primitive for their "lack" of a two-gender, heterosexist system of love, marriage, family, and gender expression.[24] The imposed "primitivity" of Black and Indigenous bodies, then, became a part of the logic and justification for their forced assimilation, genocide, removal, and enslavement. Marx noted:

> The individual comes into the world possessing neither capital nor land. Social distribution assigns him at birth to labor. But this situation of being assigned is itself a consequence of the existence of capital and landed property.[25]

These social assignations that Marx wrote of include gender, race, ethnicity, and other statuses created to divide working and oppressed individuals, provide the basis for a gendered and racialized division of labor, and justify the ongoing exploitation and oppression of working and oppressed people by the ruling class.[26] Heterosexism, cissexism, and racism rely upon one another to serve larger projects of the capitalist class. This is evident in the Moynihan Report's pathologizing of the Black family and its placement of blame upon the "deviant" Black family for high rates of poverty in Black communities.[27] Cissexism as a product of class society cannot be sidelined in this discussion. As discussed later, class, socioeconomic status, race, and gender are each core to understanding the totality of conditions that give rise to violence against Black trans women, as well as to developing solutions to mitigate and end this violence.

Heterosexism and cissexism are analytically distinct categories, yet they remain mutually imbricated in actual practice.[28] Heterosexuality serves as the lynchpin of the gender binary, "yet the relationship between heterosexuality and gender oppression remains under-theorized in social science research."[29] The present, "natural" order of a two-gender system relies upon men and women existing as different, complementary counterparts that are attracted to one another and reproduce the heteropatriarchal system through marriage and childrearing. In addition to the role of heteronormativity in gender oppression, homonormativity,[30] the normalization of White gay and lesbian individuals and communities has relied upon attachments to normative ontologies of gender and a political and social distancing from trans-ness and gender nonconformity.[31] Cis-lesbian women, radical feminists or not, have long conceptualized trans women's (potential)[32] penises as physical threats to their identity and community. Janice Raymond, transphobic Women's Studies scholar and author, wrote, "Because transsexuals have lost their physical 'members', does not mean that they lost their ability to penetrate women—women's mind, women's space, women's sexuality."[33] The threat of patriarchy is coded onto the penis, but even when it is absent, a trans woman's body and identity remain threats as a form of discursive rape and penetration.

At the 2018 London Pride Festival, a group of White (and/or White-passing), cis-lesbian women protested trans women's inclusion in lesbian/women's spaces and events. *Pink News* journalist asked one protestor, "Would you like trans people banned from women only spaces?" The protestor responded, "Definitely, we want women-only spaces for women only and a trans person cannot be a woman."[34] A leaflet distributed by the group read:

> With the recent development of trans politics an increasing number of lesbians are reporting pressure from their "LGBTQ" community to change their sexual orientation. . . . **Bullying, harassing, threatening or forcing lesbians into accepting penises into their sex lives is pure COMPULSORY HETEROSEXUALITY AND RAPE CULTURE.** The situation is alarming: lesbians are back to a situation where we have to spend our energy defending our own sexual boundaries from men. (emphases are original)

The declaration that trans women's call for acceptance of their bodies as female bodies, whether or not they have a penis, is received as rape culture propaganda. Accepting trans women is viewed as accepting the end of lesbianism and promoting the rape of cisgender women. In this way, homonormativity mirrors heteronormativity's attachment to the gender binary fostered through White constructions of manhood and womanhood.

My interest in pulling together these theoretical frames is to analyze how the maintenance of gender relies upon the victimization and murder of Black trans women. Discursive and physical violence functions to constitute cisness as gender. Gender is never "done" alone.[35] Rather, to be gendered is to be interpreted as a particular gender by others. Individuals attribute gendered meaning to acts, behaviors, body parts, and inanimate objects. We also gender ourselves. To say, "I am a woman," is to say I am not another gender. My gender is made legible through relationality and negation of the Other.

Cis-ness, too, is constituted through relationality. Cis-ness comes into being through separation from and devaluation of trans-ness, and, as Butler argues, the self is constituted by vulnerability, violence, and relationality.[36] For cis-het men, violence often functions symbolically to assert one's masculinity and empower an individual above others. For cis-lesbian women, discursive regulation of womanhood also functions as a symbolic maneuver to empower one above another. To be with trans women, though (be it sexually, romantically, platonically, and/or in solidarity), is to allow oneself to be touched by trans-ness—to be "undone," in Butler's words, by the Other. Trans-ness destabilizes popular understandings of gender and sexual binaries, but violence against trans women can function to re-stabilize these binary understandings. Violence against trans women because they are trans women is a process of negation—it is an assertion that trans women "are not really" women—and self-constitution relies upon negation.

White supremacy, cissexism, and heterosexism, distinct in the ways they enact power, rely upon one another. In addition, they rely upon the death of trans women of color in order to maintain the White, cis-heteropatriarchal order. The violence used to absent trans women of color from the social world does not solely include physical violence. The consequences of doing gender outside of accountable conduct relies as much upon physical violence as it does upon discursive aggression, or the ways in which "communicative acts are used in a social interaction to hold people accountable to social and cultural-based expectations."[37] To refuse to accept trans women as women is to claim the power to define womanhood. "Holding someone accountable to expectations is claiming power" to decide what is accountable conduct.[38] There is no physical violence enacted by merely stating that trans women rape and penetrate women's spaces, bodies, and minds. However, to do so, as Raymond does above, is to define who counts as a woman. Doing so lies tangentially next to the physical aggression used by cis-het men to hold trans women accountable for "deceiving" them or "aggressing" against them by merely existing. The two forms of violence are different, yet the justifications and arguments used by both rely upon White, cis-heteropatriarchal notions of which bodies are allowed to exist and which must be absented.

CRITICAL TRANS STUDIES

In the introduction to the *Transgender Studies Reader*, Susan Stryker notes the role of transgender studies in understanding the social forces that "allow gender normativity to disappear into the unanalyzed, ambient background" and gender non-normativity to appear hypervisible, distinct, different, and potentially dangerous.[39] While transgender studies has the capacity to do so, many trans of color critique theorists have simultaneously noted the whiteness perpetuated within White Trans Studies analyses, as well as the colonizing force of whiteness within readings of trans-ness "cross-culturally."[40] The whiteness that haunts and invades White Trans Studies disallows for analyses of the ways "not all queer [and/or trans] bodies 'matter' the same way."[41] I aim to understand the ways in which trans women of color's bodies seemingly do not matter in terms of the lives lost, yet paradoxically do matter in terms of the ways in which "trans death opens up political and social life" for cisgender and White transgender individuals.[42] I will flesh this out more thoroughly in the following section; however, I raise this point, here, as I frame my work within a critical trans politic that attends to the "contingent and contradictory mobilizations of race, class, disability, sexuality and other ideologies of morality and stock."[43]

Dean Spade, critical trans legal theorist and activist, in *Normal Life* fleshes out a critical trans politic that focuses in on "the distribution of life chances."[44] Spade argues against a (neo)liberal notion of equality adherent to homonormative and transnormative[45] politics. The critical trans politic that Spade fleshes out is informed by the work of Critical Race Theorists and Critical Race Feminists. I frame my analyses with these theories to attend to the racialized, gendered, and classed forces that shape how violence is culturally and interpersonally understood and enacted. I focus on the sociocultural narratives of desirability that cis-het men and cis-LBQ women construct vis-à-vis the gendering and sexing of bodies that normalize the disposability of trans women of color. While one could argue that all trans women are rendered disposable in this process, the murders of trans women, transfeminine people, and/or people assumed to be trans women disproportionately affect Black trans women/transfeminine people. My aim, thus, is to understand how cis-het men and cis-lesbian women come to "mark" Black trans women, and trans women in general, within their narratives of desirability to understand what role the disposability of Black trans women and trans women of color serves.

White supremacist, cis-heteropatriarchy creates intersecting vulnerabilities for trans women of color. These intersecting vulnerabilities leave trans women of color in a precarious position as regards violence. Much research focusing on trans women's experiences of violence, though, are analyzed vis-à-vis particular forms of violence and/or situations of hyper-vulnerability, such as while incarcerated,[46] engaging in sex work,[47] or experiencing domestic violence,[48] leaving everyday forms of violence unexamined. In this book, I utilize Mbembe's theory of necropolitics to center the ways in which life and death metaphorically "stick" to Black trans women. I argue that the Black transfeminine body is disposed of through a necropolitical framework that requires death and disposability to maintain white supremacist, cis-heteropatriarchy.

I utilize Mbembe's articulation of necropower and necropolitics to theorize the ways in which cis-ness and cisgender sexualities are produced through the disposing of the Other. Mbembe notes that power "continuously refers and appeals to exceptions, emergency, and a fictionalized notion of the enemy."[49] The reference to emergency and a fictionalized enemy is evidenced in the numerous attempts to pass bathroom legislation to keep trans people, largely trans women, from accessing the bathroom that corresponds with their gender. In 2018, the Alliance For Defending Freedom (ADF), a conservative Christian group, asked the US Supreme Court to hear a case they lost in an appellate challenge to "Boyertown Area High School's policy that allows transgender students to use the bathrooms and locker rooms matching their gender identity."[50] The AFD argues that gender-affirming polices for transgender kids amount to "a novel—and dangerous—experiment," highlighting the risk of sexual assault of girls and women as potential problems that would arise.[51] Groups like the AFD view trans women using women's restrooms as the impetus for a gendered and sexualized emergency. Such groups conceptualize trans women as deceptive for "pretending" to be women with penises between their legs. In response, cis-het men who feel "duped" by the trans women with whom they have (or attempt to have) sex have reacted with physical violence, sometimes resulting in death of the trans woman of color. These men feel that "their masculinity is challenged as they feel 'raped' and feminized" by having sex with a trans woman.[52] Black and Indigenous trans women experience the vast majority of these murders.[53] The result of each of these states of emergency is a vast and disproportionate murder rate for Black transgender women/transfeminine individuals.

In the words of Goffman, Black trans women and trans women of color become stigmatized through "abominations of the body" and "blemishes of individual character." The penis itself is conceptualized as a "physical deformity" upon trans women, and their trans-ness is perceived as denoting "unnatural passions, weak will . . . and dishonesty."[54] Elliot and Lyons highlight, "The function of a phobic object is to specify and contain a general-ized threat."[55] The phobic object, in this case, becomes women of color's bod-ies with or without a penis. In an edited selection of quotes and discussions of trans-ness by cis-lesbian women, a cis woman states, "S. told me what the operation involved. And I guess if she hadn't told me that—that it is the penis and it's been inverted—then maybe I wouldn't have reacted the way I did. But my reaction was, 'Oh my God, that is a cock.' And I just didn't want to be anywhere near it."[56] Even with post-gender affirmation surgery, trans women remain "tainted" by the presence/inversion of a once-penis. Irrational fears of emasculation, rape by trans women, gender/sexual confusion fold in around the object of the penis. However, the presence of the penis, as with any phobic object, "then evokes the anxiety thereby contained" within it.[57] In situations where cisgender individuals are confronted with disruptions to gender/sex essentialism, they may work to "frantically reassert" the binary. Westbrook and Schilt term this reaction a "gender panic," but through analy-sis of policy controversies regarding trans bodies, they note that "'gender panics' might more accurately be termed 'penis panics,'" due to the perceived danger imposed upon the individual with a (potential) penis.[58]

The doing of gender is a relational process. Gender, sexuality, and sex binaries are constructed through these relations, and they simultaneously require the abjection of those bodies that reveal the fiction of binary logic. Trans-ness blurs what exactly constitutes men and women, heterosexuals and homosexuals. Trans bodies come to serve "as the border that determines the necessity and impossibility of the difference" between trans bodies and cis bodies.[59] The very creation of the word cisgender occurred out of a need to better linguistically differentiate non-trans bodies from trans bodies after transgender itself was already established as a word. Trans-ness surrounds cis-ness, delimiting its borders.

Stigma, disgust, and difference, though, are "sticky objects." To "touch" the stigmatized is to become stigmatized. Stigma, disgust, and difference are "intimate and involve the feeling of recoiling from something threatening and close."[60] Ahmed elaborates, "The stranger is produced as a figure that is dis-tinct from the . . . body only through a process of expulsion."[61] The stranger, the deviant, the "transsexual" must be expelled from a cissexist society to maintain racial and gender coherence.

In this elaboration of abjection and the constitution of cis-ness/trans-ness, it remains critical to understand that not all differences are equal (i.e., cissex-ism functions differently for White, Black, and other trans people of color). To return to Mbembe, "The politics of race is ultimately linked to the politics of death."[62] I seek to interrogate the ways in which "trans [of color] death opens up [cis] political and social life."[63] In doing so, I ask, what constitutes cis-ness vis-à-vis sexuality? What gendered and racialized patterns emerge in cis-het men's and cis-lesbian's conceptualizations of desirable bodies? And how do the desirability discourses of cis-lesbian women and cis-heterosexual men enact necropolitical boundaries around trans women's subjectivity?

CENTERING CIS-NESS

Few studies on trans people's intimate experiences exist outside a pathological, medical, and/or public health approach. Further, very few researchers focus on cisgender subjects and how they understand their cis-ness. I do not view the data of the participants' responses as representative of a particular cisgender subject or of a particular sample of cisgender subjects. Rather, my aim is to discursively analyze the constitution of "cis-ness." Writing in response to Sandy Stone's "Posttransexual Manifesto," Halberstam notes, "The post in posttranssexual demands . . . that we examine the strangeness of all gendered bodies."[64] Influenced by Ingraham's *Thinking Straight,*[65] I argue that cis-ness is about much more than the bodies it clings to or the bodies who cling to it. Rather, cis-ness is political, discursive, and social manifestation that disburses beyond the individual body.

Cis-ness proliferates within bills filed in various states across the United States, such as Utah's Vital Statistics Act Amendment (HB 153), that would define male and female as biological realities that are "innate and immutable . . . [and] established at conception and . . . confirmed before or at birth."[66] Executive legislation, as well, further perpetuates cis-ness through the Trump administration's defining of gender as biological, binary, objective, and predetermined.[67] Both forms of legislation function to make concrete a more abstract understanding of gender. Cis-ness functions as a binary ontology that claims there exist "two—and only two—separate and distinct" genders and sexes.[68] A social order is constructed that results in consequences, pushbacks, and policing for those that challenge or refute cis-ness. Labeling cisgender feminists who perpetuate transphobic ideas as trans exclusionary radical feminists, for example, becomes viewed as a slur rather than a mere descriptor.[69]

Cis-ness imbues social thought, interaction, and existence, framing trans women using the women's restroom as predatory men seeking entrance to women's spaces in order to sexually assault women. "Gender reveals" grow in number to celebrate the assigned sex of a fetus, despite the harm such assignments cause trans, nonbinary, and/or intersex individuals. Cis-ness goes beyond the assignation and/or self-determination of identity; it affects who gets jobs and who does not; who is protected by the government and who is not, and who is criminal and who is the victim.

Cis-ness operates in tandem with whiteness, producing a misunderstanding of reality as inherently sexed and naturally and binarily gendered. This misunderstanding of reality relies upon the ability of cis-ness to remain closed off from other (a)gendered realities. Just as whiteness extends beyond White bodies and includes the perpetuations of whiteness by people of color, so too does cis-ness extend beyond cis bodies. Binary transgender individuals, for example, have reacted to nonbinary identities by stating, "'Pick a side' or 'Nonbinary is an insult to my experience.'"[70] Cis bodies, trans bodies, and all bodies otherwise can perpetuate cis-ness; however, only the capitalist class—who use cis-ness to divide the oppressed among themselves—benefits from cis-ness.[71] These statements that one must be a man or a woman or that a nonbinary person's refusal and/or inability to exist as a man or a woman is an affront on others are rooted in cis-ness. Core to cis-ness is gender essentialism: that biologically, psychologically, and emotionally, one is inherently a man or a woman. Cis-ness, thus, is a politic and a lens rather than the particular attributes of any cisgender population or individual.

In working to understand what constitutes cis-ness, it is critical to simultaneously understand the linkage of whiteness and cis-ness. Whiteness and cis-ness, as noted earlier, share early connections within origins of capitalism and colonialism in the West. Inherent within white supremacist and colonialist logic are binary oppositions and fixed categorizations/demarcations of bodies. The gender binary evolves out of its origins within US/European white supremacy, for, as much as the Black/White binary is central to such logic, so too is the female/male binary. Gender essentialism not only posits that men and women are biologically and fundamentally different but that varying races express fundamentally different manhoods and womanhoods.[72] Thus, I intersectionally analyze the racialized and gendered patterns in how participants made sense of and/or perpetuated cis-ness.

SETTING THE SCENE

Atlanta, a city of just over 500,000 and a metropolitan area (MSA) of 5.6 million, is home to radical, transgender organizers of color, long struggles for racial justice, and entrenched, structural racism and cissexism. Atlanta is home to four historically Black colleges and universities: Morehouse College, Spelman College, Clark Atlanta University, and Morehouse School of Medicine. The city has been named by some as "the Black Mecca,"[73] with Black residents making up 32.4 percent of the MSA and the city being only second to New York City in rates of Black home ownership.[74] 4.6 percent of the city's inhabitants openly identify as LGBTQ.[75]

While Democrats have historically retained control of the city proper, the suburbs of Atlanta are more politically mixed. Looking at results of the 2016 presidential elections, the city of Atlanta and immediate surrounding suburbs, including Panthersville, East Point, Tucker, and Lithia Springs, voted for Hillary Clinton.[76] Suburbs furthest away from the city proper, including Acworth, Kennesaw, Buford, and South Fulton, voted for Donald Trump, while others like Marietta, Sandy Springs, and Lilburn were split by neighborhood. In the mid-1900s, White flight produced a predominantly Black city surrounded by predominantly White suburbs.[77] However, gentrification and a rising cost of living have reversed that trend, with White suburbanites returning to the city and Black residents being pushed out to the suburbs.

A recent analysis of Atlanta's racial demographics identified counties as "historically Black," "nearing majority black," "diversifying" (or having a recognizable minority of Black residents), and the "remainder."[78] The City of Atlanta is primarily located in Fulton County, with a small segment next door in DeKalb County. Atlanta is immediately surrounded by DeKalb, Clayton, and South Fulton Counties, three historically Black counties, as well as Cobb County, a "nearing majority Black" county and, slightly, North Fulton County, a "diversifying" county. While Atlanta and some cities within North and South Fulton, Dekalb, and Cobb Counties have protections against discrimination vis-à-vis sexual orientation and gender identity, suburbs in other surrounding counties do not.[79] Only 12 percent of the entire state currently is protected in this regard, with most of such protections existing within aforementioned counties, and protections against conversion therapy are banned across the entire state.

Atlanta, like other urban cities across the United States, has been home to major queer clubs. From 1975 to 2004, Backstreet, the Studio 54 of the South, was the largest LGBT dance club in the city, open 24/7.[80] Backstreet was located in Midtown, an Atlanta neighborhood once populated by marginalized individuals, hippies, and working-class individuals that quickly became home to middle- and upper-class individuals and families in the late 1990s and early 2000s. Backstreet originally served a White, cisgender, gay male clientele, excluding women without an escort and overcharging Black LGBTQ individuals to prevent them from entering. Over time, the club ceased its exclusionary policies and its demographics shifted; that is, until Backstreet's liquor license was denied in 2004 due to complaints of "drugs and prostitution" by newly arrived White, middle-, and upper-class residents.[81]

Atlanta has also been the site of numerous murders of Black trans individuals. In 2017, TeeTee Dangerfield, a Black trans woman, was shot and killed. She was found with multiple gunshot wounds in her vehicle.[82] In May 2018, Nino Fortson—who also went by the last names Starr and Blahnik—was shot in Atlanta during an argument. Nino was part of the House of Blahnik in the Atlanta ballroom scene, where he frequently walked in the category of "Butch Realness."[83] In 2021, Bianca "Muffin" Bankz, a Black trans woman, was killed in a suspected murder-suicide.[84] Muffin, who had long lived without housing, received support to access an apartment shortly before her murder. Just a month before, Bonaire "Bonnie" Black, a Black trans teenage girl who was experiencing homelessness, was found dead. Her body was found in a parking garage in the neighborhood of Midtown. *Project Q* quoted a local Atlanta housing activist, Marshall Rancifer, saying, "What we're hearing is that a guy at the party, they got in some argument, and he broke her neck."[85] In May of 2021, Sophia Arrieta Vasquez, a thirty-six-year-old transgender Latina, was shot dead at her apartment in Brookhaven, a northeastern suburb of Atlanta.[86] Forty minutes outside Atlanta in the suburb of Canton, Kathryn "Katie" Newhouse, an Asian American transgender teenager girl and activist was murdered in 2022 by her father before he took his own life.[87]

Alongside these murders exists a breadth of activism and community organizing across the city of Atlanta. Southern Fried Queer Pride, the Solutions not Punishment Collaborative (SnapCo), Southerners on New Ground (SONG), TRANScending Barriers, La Gender, and Community Estrella are Black and/or Latinx trans-run organizations that span the gamut of cultural work, abolition, migrant justice, racial justice, and housing justice. In collaboration with my trans mother, Lí An Sanchez, founder and director of Community Estrella, the Atlanta branch of the Party for Socialism and Liberation (PSL), has demonstrated against the detention, abuse, and deportation of migrants at Stewart Detention Center, south of the city.[88] Growing out of a photography project and a GoFundMe, both of which sought to uplift the lives of Black trans women experiencing homelessness in the city, the Trans Housing Coalition (THC) was born. The online fundraiser quickly ignited into something much larger, raising over three million dollars in less than a year.[89] Operating from a housing first model built on a coalition of aforementioned organizations, as well as the Trans Housing Atlanta Program (THAP), THC now provides case management services, emergency funds, temporary shelter, and permanent housing.

Agencies like Someone Cares provide sexual health services, hormone replacement therapy, and behavioral health programming to a predominantly Black trans clientele just west of the downtown area. Someone Cares is not alone as a health agency in providing for trans individuals throughout Metro Atlanta. Grady Hospital, one of the primary hospitals in the city, houses the Gender Center, Feminist Women's Health Center provides services to people of all genders, and Emory University's healthcare system is home to a transgender clinic on the east side of the city.

Atlanta is no stranger to trans people, struggles for intersectional trans justice, and the provision of life-sustaining trans healthcare. Atlanta, like all urban centers across the United States, is a complex, nuanced space in which murders of mostly Black trans women exist alongside these organizations, high rates of homelessness for LGBTQ youth, especially Black trans youth, exists alongside weekly trans nights at Tokyo Valentino, a dance club on the city's infamous Cheshire Bridge Road,[90] and historic legacies of systemic racism and cissexism that are continuously reified in the present exist in tandem with Atlanta's historic legacy of resistance and cultural transformation. DuBois wrote in 1903, "South of the North, yet north of the South, lies the City of a Hundred Hills, peering out from the shadows of the past into the promise of the future,"[91] and it is in the City of a Hundred Hills that I sat and spoke with participants, in coffee shops and libraries, office rooms and city streets.

SITUATING THE AUTHOR WITHIN THE WORK

Before outlining the chapters of this book, it is important to situate myself within this work. I conducted this research as a White, often "cis-passing," trans woman—meaning that, in daily life, I am often treated and viewed as a cisgender woman by cisgender people. While I experience violence, vulnerability, and harm due to (cis)sexism, I am also often protected from violence and granted entryway to spaces, such as academia, that are often closed to trans people of color due to barriers within academia as well as economic, social, and political barriers outside academia. I center Black trans women within my work, thus, to ensure that, as better understandings of cis-ness are gained, pathways to liberation can be mapped from these knowledge productions that include all of us and not just some of us (i.e., White people). While I do so, I also acknowledge that no Black trans women or other trans women of color were involved in this research. Community-embedded research is critical to the development of knowledge, but so too is paying community members for their time, experience, and labor involved in such work. I did not have the funds to engage anyone other than my sample of participants in this work. While this does not negate the limitations of not engaging Black trans women in this work, all royalties I earn from this book will be redistributed.

I believe that my White, trans womanhood shaped the interviews and subsequent focus groups differently than were a cis person to conduct this research. Throughout the interview process, only one cis-het man visibly acknowledged that I am a woman of trans experience. One other cis-het man knew me through a graduate school colleague and thus knew I was a trans woman. Two asked if I was transgender, but only after having voiced their attraction to me and then seeing the pictures I showed them. The pictures of trans women made me "suspect" to them momentarily, but once I told them I was not trans to protect my safety, they returned to flirting and wanting to have sex. As I will document later in chapter 6, many cis-het men openly spoke to me of their disgust, discomfort, and/or confusion regarding trans women.

Further, my whiteness undoubtedly shaped my readings of interview data, analyses of my participants' body language, and the research process itself. While I situate the work within Critical Race, Black feminist, and intersectional theoretical frameworks and connect to broader literature on race, gender, and sexualities, my own lens remains shaped (and mis-shaped) by my whiteness. Through feedback from my mentors and other scholars, I have attempted to minimize this. However, it ultimately is not possible to disconnect this book, these data, and my analyses from my whiteness.

During interviews, I paid attention to participants' body language. Part of what I paid attention to was their comfort or reticence to discuss various topics with me. Men told me that they understood the murders of Black trans women, the feelings of being overwhelmed, "raped," and/or "feminized" by sexually and/or romantically interacting with trans women, and indeed, some told me they, themselves, would kill trans women. While doing so, their body language remained open and comfortable with their legs spread wide, their backs leaned back against their chairs, and their eyes meeting mine. With cis-het men of color, participants became uncomfortable at points discussing whiteness, and I had to develop trust with them so that they could feel comfortable speaking to me as a White woman. In comparison, I did not have to do this with any of them regarding trans-ness. With cis-LBQ women, I am unsure who knew and did not know I was trans. One participant afterward asked me, "I don't know if I can ask, but are you trans?" When I asked how she knew, she said it was about my "energy." This happened as well with one other woman participant. One cis-queer woman participant knew me through a former coworker and thus knew I was of trans experience. Amy, a White, Brazilian, cis-lesbian woman, spoke repeatedly of a "gay energy" she felt from queer, and sometimes trans women, and it is possible that my trans-ness was more visibly readable by queer women who saw me as "one of them." My body stood in stark contrast with some cis women participants. I am a six feet tall, "thick" woman and about half were between five feet and five feet, five inches tall. My body, thus, may have appeared more "trans" to some cisgender women than others.

Throughout my research, I kept field notes about the ways in which individuals responded to me, vis-à-vis body language. I did not share that I am a trans woman with any cis-het man participant. I did with two cis women participants who asked. I chose not to share with the two cis-het men participants who asked due to risks to my safety.

My final sample of participants was predominantly Black. This is an uncommon result for White researchers. With two Latina participants, I

shared my mixed, Latina/Greek ancestry, as a way of connecting and opening myself up to them, as I was asking them to open themselves up to me.
However, if I had not noted this, they would not have known. Participants
often acknowledged that I am White, and this was most emphasized with cis-
het men participants.

Most cis-het men participants were recruited through flyers I passed out
at grocery stores and placed on cars. As I did so, it was not uncommon for
cis-het men to stop and ask me for a flyer, to call me to their car for a flyer,
or in the case of one man, to ask why I skipped past his car—I had done so
because I did not feel comfortable putting flyers on the windows of cars with
people sitting in them. This excitement to know what I was doing was uncommon to me as a researcher. In previous projects, I did not have the same ease
in recruitment, nor did I have this same ease in recruitment with cis-lesbian
women. Thus, numerous factors (my own identities, how I recruited, and
participants' identities and experiences) shaped both who participated in my
ultimate sample and how I analyzed the data.

METHODS

To analyze the constitution of cis-ness and the interpersonal mechanisms
through which violence against trans women is justified and enacted, I
utilized in-depth interviews, focus groups, and photo elicitation methods.
Eligibility was limited to women who were assigned female at birth and
experience solely or primarily attraction to other women, as well as men who
were assigned male at birth and experience solely or primarily attraction to
women. I limited participation to cis-het men and cis-LBQ women to focus
on those politico-sexual groups that are most likely to come into intimate
contact with trans women. Between May 2019 and March 2020, I conducted
thirty-two interviews with seventeen cis-LBQ women and fifteen cis-het men
in the Metro Atlanta area. The interviews ranged from 30 minutes to 100 minutes, with the 30-minute interview being cut short for safety reasons. After
that experience, I applied for an IRB amendment (approved in January 2020)
to recruit participants through the Atlanta Pre-Arrest Diversion Program
(PAD). PAD works with the Atlanta Police Department to "divert people
subject to arrest" in parts of the city to their organization, which "provides
case management, linkage to care, and participant advocacy" to challenge the
racist, capitalist, and ableist foundations of the criminal legal system. Out of
the total sample of thirty-two participants, six were recruited through PAD.

My participants were mostly Black (twenty-two out of thirty-two participants, or 69 percent of the sample), with one participant who was Black and
Portuguese, one who was Haitian, one who was Moor, and nineteen who

were African American. Six participants (19 percent) were non-Latinx White. Two (6 percent) were Latina, including one White Latina and one non-White Latina. One participant was Middle-Eastern American, and a final participant was Southeast Asian American. Fourteen of the fifteen cisgender men participants were heterosexual with one heteroflexible—this participant, however, only ever had relationships with women. Seven of the seventeen cisgender women participants were bisexual/queer with primary attractions to women, one was homoflexible (however she had only had relationships with women), and the rest were lesbian. Slightly under half of all participants (14/32) fell between the ages of eighteen and twenty-four. Another twelve were between twenty-five and thirty-five, and the remaining six were over thirty-six. While the vast majority of participants (27/32) had completed some college education or more, a similar majority (24/32) simultaneously fell within what the Pew Research Center terms a "low income" or "below/near poverty."[92] For complete demographic information, additional demographics, and a full discussion of methods and methodologies, see appendices 1, 2, and 3.

At the end of each interview, I also asked participants if they would be interested in participating in a focus group at a later point in time. I planned to hold three focus groups, each consisting of three cis-het men and three cis-lesbian women, as a way of better analyzing the patterns that emerge between their discourse of desirability, as the focus groups would allow their conversations to play off one another and would also give a chance for them to disagree and/or agree with others' sentiments. In order to elicit focus group participation, I compensated participants twenty dollars for their time. During the duration of the study, only one focus group took place. I originally planned one focus group of White/White-passing participants (due to the small sample size of White participants), one of Black participants under thirty-five, and one of Black participants over thirty-five. The distinction in age for Black participants was to assess whether age shaped differences in discourse, understanding, and anti-trans sentiments. While I was able to organize and execute the White focus group, the other failed to occur. I attempted to hold the other two focus groups twice each, but each time participants cancelled last minute, did not respond to emails or texts about the focus group, or simply did not show up. Each time only two participants showed up, who I compensated for arriving, but I was unable to hold a focus group with only two people.

I am not sure if my failure to execute the focus groups was due to an inability to develop the connections necessary to recruit interview participants to continue in the study or other reasons. Black participants were more likely to tell me they had more than one job, were in school and working, or had parental responsibilities in addition to work and/or school compared to White/White-passing participants who had more resources even when living on a lower-income. Thus, it was also difficult to find a time that worked for multiple Black individuals compared to finding a time that worked for others. Ultimately, while I cannot compare focus group data comparatively, having a focus group of White/White-passing participants aided in fleshing out their interviews since Whites comprised only a small percentage of my sample. This included one cis-het man and three cis-lesbian women (*see* appendix Three for focus group demographics).

Finally, I additionally utilized photo elicitation to understand how cis-het men and cis-LBQ women conceptualize desirability. Using publicly available photos from *Shutterstock*, an open-source stock photo library, I provided interview participants with photos of trans women—including those who visually "pass" as cisgender, those who do not, and those categorized on the site as White, Black, Latina, and Asian (*see* chapter 1 for photos). Using these photos, I asked participants to rate their levels of desire to each of the women in the photos, asking for reasons as to their rating process. As participants rated each of the women, they did not know that the women are transgender. I utilize photo elicitation in the interviews as a way of entering into questions of desirability, race, gender, and sexual attraction. In addition, the photos served to ask participants to reflect on hypothetical reactions to the women they are most interested in revealing that they are transgender.

FINAL CAVEATS

As I analyzed participant responses vis-à-vis racialized cissexism and the murders of Black trans women, I actively reflected on how my identities, body, and recruitment shaped my data. Participants who shared overtly cissexist responses, including open acknowledgment of their disposition to killing trans women, were primarily Black. However, this does not mean that Black people, and Black, cis-het men in particular, are more cissexist and more murderous than Whites or non-Black people of color. If my sample of participants would have been more racially mixed, my results would have been different. It is possible that my results would have included more racially representative proportions of participants who would and would not kill trans women. Further, many men who openly stated their attraction to me may have displayed overt transphobia as a way of signaling their masculinity, bravado, and power to me as a mechanism of heterosexual attraction. This is not to deny that Blackness and whiteness differentially shape racial groups' transphobic discourse and behaviors. Legacies of emasculation, lynching, and castration of Black men place cis-het, Black men in a different position in response to trans-ness than cis-het, White men.[93] I work to attend to these differences without making a monolith of cis-het, Black men, essentializing

Blackness, or conflating Blackness and transphobia. The legacies of cissexism woven through all racial communities are products of whiteness and must be tackled through the abolition of whiteness in all spaces.

Finally, in analyzing how my sample of cisgender participants justified and understood violence against Black trans women and trans women in general, my aim is not to foster division between cisgender and transgender people or to point blame at cisgender people for cissexism. To tackle the problems discussed in this book, a united, organized, and militant front of cisgender, transgender, and all other working and oppressed peoples is needed to fight against the capitalist ruling class that fosters bigotry and oppression between members of the working class. The Spanish project Rojo del Arcoíris writes in *Towards a Queer Marxism*:

> We know the capitalist class wants us atomized, as Marx and Engels taught us: "Wage-labor rests exclusively on competition between the laborers." They use our sexual dissidence to keep us apart. They corrode the solidarity between us to the shouts of "Faggot!". But the cisheteronormative working class receives no benefit from the oppression of queer people.[94]

To ultimately get at the roots of cissexist, racist oppression of Black trans women and trans people in general goes beyond the scope of this book, as doing so would require a materialist analysis of the economic, social, and political conditions that come together to perpetuate such oppression under capitalism.[95] This is not to discount that working class and oppressed people internalize the racism, cissexism, and heterosexism fostered by the ruling class. We all must work to undo the ways in which we have internalized such manifestations of oppression. However, it is to say that we must also adequately place the blame for cissexist, racist violence on those from whom it originates and who benefit from it (i.e., the ruling class).

Thinking Cis is ultimately an examination of how thirty-two individuals make sense of violence against Black trans women and trans women in general. Understanding how people make sense of violence allows for development and adaptations of anti-violence interventions, programs, policies, and initiatives targeting the cultural and interpersonal mechanisms through which such violence is enacted and experienced.

OUTLINE OF THE BOOK

Chapter 1, "A Natural Woman," questions what it means to be a "natural woman." The desire for the "natural" pervades numerous facets of society: makeup, hair, beauty culture, and debates over who counts as a "woman."

It is important to ask, though, what exactly is "natural"? Here, I turn to the work of radical feminists, scholars of performativity, and the sociology of race and the body in analyzing participants' discourse regarding what they like (sexually and romantically) in a woman. I discuss how white supremacy, (cis)sexism, heterosexism, and classism each play into social and cultural understandings of the "natural."

Chapter 2, "That's a Guy," homes in on data from the photo elicitation methods I utilized. I examine how participants ranked various photos of trans women as regards their desirability and how those rankings were shaped by education, class, gender, and other factors. I then turn to Queer of Color Critique to detail how cis-centricity and Eurocentricity are bound together in cis individuals' desires for women. In doing so, I highlight the roles of gender-nonconformity and race in terms of the murders of Black trans women by analyzing how participants responded differently to White and Black women, as well as gender-nonconforming and "cis-passing" women. Finally, I end with a discussion of how several participants expressed a lack of desire for gender-nonconforming women through coded language, body language, and microaggressions.

Chapter 3, "Cisgender Women Thinking Cis," looks solely at cis-LBQ women participants. Within popular feminist discourse, as well as academic scholarship, there is a dichotomy between trans-exclusionary radical feminists (TERFs) and trans-inclusive feminists. This dichotomy, though, does not reflect the many ways in which cis-ness is perpetuated beyond overt, explicit hate. Indeed, none of my participants fell into a conceptualization of TERF logic. Instead, they used TERFs as a point of comparison, to detail how they were different. I explicate three categories of what I term "thinking cis." These include "Conditionally Accepting Cis-ters," who were TERF-adjacent, "Casual Transphobes," and "Critically Cis" women. I end with this chapter as it provides a glimpse into how cis-LBQ women are not only perpetuating cis-ness but also how they are strategically challenging it.

In chapter 4, I tease apart the tensions between desire and disgust, as well as desire and symbolic violence. I utilize data from interviews and focus groups to build on Connell's work on masculinities, Schippers's work on feminini-ties, and Bourdieu's work connecting masculinities and symbolic violence. My focus in this chapter is on what violence elicits, or in other words, how violence functions to reconstitute one's masculinity and/or lesbian identity. I name this chapter after a quote from the scene in *Pose* that I began this introduction with, "They hate what it means to love us." I intentionally chose to do so, as this quote reflects what participants explained regarding violence against trans women—that this violence is not born of hate of trans women but a hate of what it means to be with trans women.

In chapter 5, "I Might Just Kill You," I detail how participants made sense of the murders of Black trans women. I extend theoretical arguments around masculinities and femininities from chapter 4 and connect these arguments with scholarship on necropolitics and Critical Race Theory. I show that participants' responses fell into four groups: (1) those who would not kill but understand why cis-het men do; (2) those who would kill Black trans women; (3) those who find the murders wrong but perpetuate the same cissexist rhetoric as those in the two previous groups; and (4) those who challenge the necropolitics of cis-ness. Finally, I explicate how challenging the necropolitics of cis-ness is a challenging of gender *and* racial orders.

I conclude this book by attending to what is to be done to mitigate or work against racist, cissexist violence. I turn to a literature on anti-violence interventions within sociology and public health, as well as socialist interventions against violence. As elaborated in this introduction, white supremacist, colonialist, capitalist violence birthed cissexism. As such, in countering the violence of the present, we must look to other futures—ones in which the government is made of the people to protect the people. If the death of the oppressed opens up life for others, then there is also power in the survival of the oppressed to open up a new life.

Thinking Cis is not meant to be another foray into the pain and oppression of existing within a cisgender world. I do not aim to write an academic trauma pornography analyzing the despair that some trans people feel as they fight to survive and thrive. Instead, *Thinking Cis* is a deep dive into the meaning making of cisgender people. This book is an interrogation of how cisgender people think and how they create the world in their image through their words.

NOTES

1. Developed by Ryan Murphy, Brad Falchuk, and Steven Canals, and produced by Janet Mock, *Pose* follows a group of Black trans women and queer men in the 1980s house and ball scene. The show is fictional but relies on actual events that took place in the lives of trans people.

2. Here, mother refers to an individual who serves the role of a chosen mother as well as a mentor in the balls. The balls are events where Black and/or Latinx queer/trans people "walk" categories, such as "Face," "Body," and "Executive Realness," among others and compete to be legendary (or among the best). Mothers not only mentor their children within the balls but also provide housing, food, and a family for children who otherwise have been forced to leave their family of origin or were kicked out for being queer and/or trans.

3. 2006, "Orientations: Toward a Queer Phenomenology."

4. 1952, "The Upright Posture."

5. 2018, *The Life and Death of Latisha King*.

6. Connell and Messerschmidt, 2005, "Hegemonic Masculinity." Pascoe, 2007, *Dude, You're a Fag*.

7. Bourdieu, 1998, *Masculine Domination*.

8. 2018, *The Life and Death of Latisha King*, 5.

9. 2018, *The Life and Death of Latisha King*, 153.

10. Westbrook, 2021, *Unlivable Lives*.

11. Dinno, 2017, "Homicide Rates of Trans Individuals."

12. 2017, "America is Struggling."

13. Seidman, 1996, *Queer Theory/Sociology*, 13.

14. Stryker, 2006, "(De)Subjugated Knowledges," 3.

15. 2017, 146.

16. 2016, *Queering Families*.

17. 2010, "Gender Labor."

18. Butler, 1990, *Gender Trouble*. Butler, 2004, *Undoing Gender*.

19. West and Zimmerman, 1987, "Doing Gender."

20. Smith, 2006, "Heteropatriarchy and the Three Pillars of White Supremacy," 5.

21. 1995, *Masculinities*. I place neoliberalism *and* liberalism here to problematize both in relation to gender. Neoliberalism is well discussed in academic literature regarding the ways it regulates bodies and functions ideologically. Classic liberalist theories, as well though, constitute citizenship vis-à-vis white manhood with hegemonic masculinities serving as the signifier of proper manhood (*see* Glenn 2002).

22. Sommerville, 2000, *Queering the Color Line*.

23. Rodney, 1972, *How Europe Underdeveloped Africa*.

24. Lugones, 2007, "Heterosexualism and the Colonial/Modern Gender System." Mogul, Ritchie, and Whitlock, 2011, *Queer (In)Justice*. Driskill, 2016, *Asegi Stories*. Gossett, 2016, "Žižek's Trans/gender Trouble."

25. 1858, *The Grundrisse*, 233.

26. Marx, 1858, *The Grundrisse*. Feinberg, 1998, *Trans Liberation: Beyond Pink or Blue*.

27. 1965.

28. Jackson, 2005, "Sexuality, Heterosexuality and Gender Hierarchy."

29. Schilt and Westbrook, 2009, "Doing Gender, Doing Heteronormativity," 141.

30. Homonormativity refers to the upholding and sustaining of heteronormativity LGBQ individuals and/or organizations "while promising a demobilized gay constituency and a privatized, depoliticized gay culture anchored in domesticity and consumption" (Duggan 2003: 179).

31. Vitulli, 2010, "A Definining Moment in Civil Rights History?"

32. I use "potential" here and elsewhere to highlight that the presence of a penis is assumed, not a known fact.

33. 1979, *The Transsexual Empire*. Nataf, 1996, *Lesbians Talk*.

34. Voss, 2018, "Anti-Trans Lesbian Protest."

35. Butler, 2004, *Undoing Gender*.

36. 2004, *Undoing Gender*.

37. schuster, 2017, "Punctuating Accountability."

38. schuster, 2017, "Punctuating Accountability."

39. 2006, 3.

40. Towle and Morgan, 2002, "Romancing the Transgender Narrative." Snorton and Haritaworn, 2013, "Trans Necropolitics."

41. Shakhsari, 2014, "Killing Me Softly with Your Rights," 104.

42. Snorton and Haritaworn, 2013, "Trans Necropolitics," 106.

43. Haritaworn, 2012, *The Biopolitics of Mixing*, 12.

44. 2011, 32.

45. Transnormativity refers to a "regulatory normative ideology that structures interactions in every arena of social life" (Johnson 2016: 466; Miller 2018).

46. Wilson et al., 2012, "You're a Woman, a Convenience, a Cat, a Poof, a Thing, an Idiot."

47. Ristock et al., 2017, "Impacts of Colonization on Indigenous Two-Spirit/LGBTQ Canadians." Rev and Geist, 2017, "Staging the Trans Sex Worker."

48. Dank et al., 2014, "Dating Violence Experiences."

49. 2003, "Necropolitics," 13.

50. Hall, 2018, "Boyertown Students Ask U.S. Supreme Court to Hear Appeal."

51. Kramer, 2018, "Should Ideology Trump Biology in Schools?"

52. Schilt and Westbrook, 2009, "Doing Gender, Doing Heteronormativity."

53. Human Rights Campaign, 2018, "A National Epidemic."

54. 1963, *Stigma*, 4.

55. 2017, "Transphobia as Symptom," 364.

56. Nataf, 1996, *Lesbians Talk*, 37.

57. Elliot and Lyons, 2017, 365.

58. 2013, "Doing Gender, Determining Gender," 48.

59. Ahmed, 2000, *Strange Encounters*.

60. Aizura, 2014, "Trans Feminine Value."

61. 2000, *Strange Encounters*, 57.

62. 2003, 17.

63. Snorton and Haritaworn, 2013, "Trans Necropolitics," 66.

64. Halberstam, 1994, "F2M," 226.

65. 2003.

66. 2019, "Utah Vital Statistics."

67. Goodnough, Green, and Sanger-Katz, 2019, "Trump Administration Proposes Rollback."

68. Wade and Ferree, 2015, *Gender*, 10.

69. *See* Morris, 2016, *The Disappearing L*.

70. Bergner, 2019, "The Struggles of Rejecting the Gender Binary."

71. Feinberg, 1998, *Trans Liberation Beyond Pink or Blue*.

72. Frankenberg, 1993, *White Women, Race Matters*. Ferber, 2010, "Constructing Whiteness."

73. Hobson, 2017, *The Legend of the Black Mecca*.

74. Pooley, 2015, "Segregation's New Geography."

75. Conron, Luhur, and Goldberg, 2021, "LGBT Adults in Large US Metropolitan Areas."

76. Cox and Merwin, 2016, "How Every Neighborhood in Metro Atlanta Voted."

77. Pooley, 2015.

78. Pooley, 2015.

79. Movement Advancement Project, "Georgia's Equality Profile."

80. Eldredge, 2020, "Backstreet."

81. Cofield, 2021, "Queer Urban Space Beyond the Gayborhood."

82. Human Rights Campaign, 2017, "A National Epidemic."

83. Human Rights Campaign, 2018, "A National Epidemic."

84. Hennie, 2021, "Transgender Woman Shot to Death."

85. Hennie, 2021, "Transgender Teen Found in Midtown."

86. Proctor, 2021, "Trans Woman Shot and Killed.

87. Assunção, 2022, "Friends Hold Vigil."

88. Green, 2022, "Support Urgent Immigrant Hunger Strike."

89. Willis, 2021, "A Trans Housing Movement." More information available at https://www.transhousingcoalition.org/our-story.

90. Cheshire Bridge Road is host to several strip clubs, including gay men's strip clubs, gay nightclubs with male go-go dancers, BDSM nightclubs, and cruising scenes.

91. *The Souls of Black Folk*.

92. Below/Near Poverty is less than $20,000. A low income falls between $20 and $44,999.

93. Yanagina, 2020, "The Psychoanalysis of Murderous Violence."

94. 2022. Here, working class does not refer to bourgeois ideas of class that are reduced to income. Instead, the working class constitutes all members of capitalist society who are forced to work to survive and who do not own the means of production.

95. Those interested in such analyses and discussions can look to Artyukhina, 2020, "Our Armies Are Rising," available at https://www.liberationschool.org/our-armies-are-rising-sylvia-rivera-and-marsha-p-johnson/, Liberation School, 2014, "Leslie Feinberg," available at https://www.liberationschool.org/leslie-feinberg-revolutionary-communist-transgender- warrior-2/, and Feinberg, 1998, *Trans Liberation Beyond Pink and Blue*.

Chapter 1

"A Natural Woman"

How Cissexism, Classism, and White Supremacy Permeate the Desire for a "Natural" Look in a Woman

Since at least the writing of West and Zimmerman's "Doing Gender,"[1] sociologists have understood gender to be both a politically constructed axis of power and a socially constructed identity. Gender is not something one is born; rather, it is something one does at the risk of being held accountable for "improper" doings of gender. Prior to the emergence of gender as a sociological subfield, women's studies scholars and women's liberationist activists have long also critiqued the idea that gender and sex are something one is born. French feminist theorist Simone de Beauvoir argued that "one is not born, but rather becomes, a woman."[2] A few decades after de Beauvoir, Women's Studies scholar Monique Wittig argued that the idea of womanhood is a heterosexual construction. She explained, "It would be incorrect to say that lesbians associate, make love, live with women, for 'woman' has meaning only in heterosexual systems of thought and heterosexual economic systems. Lesbians are not women."[3]

For Wittig, to be a lesbian meant to exist outside the bounds of heteronormativity, resulting in no longer living according to a sex-gender binary. The idea of "woman," she argued, was something constructed by men to legitimize and institutionalize hegemonic masculinities and hegemonic femininities—the subordination of women to men. Butler later took up Wittig's postulation, arguing that gender and sex are not natural, innate components of a body or mind. Instead, Butler conceptualizes gender and sex as performative constitutions that are produced through repetition and interpretation. Further, she writes, "Genders can be neither true nor false, neither real nor apparent, neither original nor derived."[4] Oyěwùmí later elucidated how the conceptualization of gender was not simply born of heteropatriarchy but also of White, Western ontologies.[5] Further, Oyěwùmí contrasted Western ontologies of gender to pre-colonial Yorùbá societies in which gender did not exist.[6] In doing so, she deepened sociological and historical analyses of gender as something other than biological and/or innate.

Despite the work of Women's Studies and Sociology scholars, gender and sex continue, in the United States, to be culturally connected to an essentialist idea of nature and naturality. This became evident in the interviews I conducted with cis-het men and cis-lesbian, bisexual, and/or queer (LBQ) women. Repeatedly, participants noted a desire for a "natural" woman or a "natural" look in a woman. This varied from a desire for "natural" genitals as opposed to "surgically constructed" genitals to a desire for "natural" makeup, "natural" hair, or a "natural" body (i.e., thin and abled). It additionally included a desire for a "natural" feminine aesthetic as compared to a hyperfemininity. In participants' discussions of their desire for naturalness and a mute aesthetic, there arose, simultaneously, a disdain or disliking of the "artificial" and "excess."

In this chapter, I flesh out participant discourse about what attracts them to a woman and analyze how the desire for a "natural" woman is embedded within racism and cissexism. In the desire for "naturality," trans-ness, queerness, and Black aesthetics are constructed as excess. Here, excess is that which goes beyond what is wanted. It is too much. It is the superfluity of what is otherwise human and desirable. Thus, I connect to queer/trans of color critique, Black feminist theory, and Trans Studies to elucidate how participants' desires for particular women are shaped by White, cissexist ideas of what constitutes the natural, proper, desirable woman. I first analyze participant discourse vis-à-vis "naturality" and makeup, hair, and aesthetics. I then discuss participant discourse regarding genitalia. Finally, I explicate the relationship between genitalia, hair, and race throughout my interviews.

"WHEN A BLACK WOMAN MAKES THEIR HAIR STRAIGHT, IT MAKES ME MORE ATTRACTED TO A WHITE WOMAN": RACE, GENDER, AND STYLIZATIONS OF THE BODY

Hair, makeup, and aesthetics have historically and presently been framed within racialized logics. How one styles the body is, even if not intentional, racialized and sexualized. It shapes how one is perceived and treated in the workplace,[7] intimate relationships,[8] education,[9] and everyday life.[10] In my interviews with cis-het men and cis-LBQ women, nearly all participants (28/32) emphasized a desire for a natural look in a woman as regards hair and makeup and a desire for a muted or toned-down expression. It is important to ask, though, what constitutes a natural look? Does a natural look include wearing minimal, skin tone makeup? Does it include using only moisturizers, exfoliators, and cleansers but not wearing makeup? Or does a "natural look" refer to a completely unadulterated face—hair, pimples, and all? This list of question continues to grow when shifted to "natural hair."

I include within this category of natural hair and natural makeup a discussion of a desire for a muted or toned-down expression, as participants expressed a desire to see women in their "natural" element without bold aesthetics, makeup, or hair. The desire among participants for a muted aesthetic and natural hair/makeup connects around racialized and gendered views of how the body is stylized and expressed. As regards aesthetic, hair, and makeup, participants detailed a disdain for that which is deemed "excessive." What does it mean, though, for certain ways of looking, acting, and being to be considered excess and others to be considered natural? I attend to these natural-unnatural, muted-excessive binaries by interrogating and critiquing notions of the "natural." In doing so, I think together queer and trans of color critique scholarship regarding excess, surplus, and queer/trans of color aesthetic and Black studies scholarship. Throughout the chapter, I use the term "cis-ness" to refer to a political, discursive, and social manifestation that creates a misunderstanding of reality as naturally and binarily gendered and sexed and of trans people as deviant and/or pathological. I use the term "cis-sexism" to refer to the institutionalization of cis-ness, or the establishment of cis-ness as a taken-for-granted norm within individuals' discourse, behavior, decision-making, and social relations.

Nails

At the start of each interview, I asked participants, "What do you like in a woman?" They would begin to share two or three things they look for in a woman. I, then, asked further questions about whether hair, makeup, gender expression, genital appearance, and so forth. At this point, participants often stated what they desired and then concluded with a comparison of what was unattractive. This was the case with Sheila, a cis-bisexual, Black woman, as she discussed the appearance of nails on a woman. Sheila told me:

> I love nails done, sometimes. I don't . . . um . . . I feel like I like them when they're simple, because it says a lot about, it kinda says who you are, what you do. Even though I'm an entrepreneur, we can do whatever we want. I know a lot of people are, when you're in certain industries, you can't have ghetto nails. Like it's, it's uh . . . I can't do ghetto nails.

Sheila preferred shorter nails with more subtle coloring, as compared to longer, flashier, "ghetto" nails. Sheila, and other participants who shared her sentiment. highlighted how class shapes desire. Sheila's desire for a

Table 1.1   Descriptions of The Eight Photos Participants Were Provided

Photo	Description
Woman A	A "cis-passing," light-skinned, Black woman wearing a business attire black dress. She has her hair in braids draped over one side while speaking on the phone.
Woman B	A "more visibly trans," high femme, Latina woman. She is wearing a variegated body contour dress with long sleeves, a wig with bangs, and has on bright red lipstick, and has long, brown hair.
Woman C	A "cis-passing," Asian American woman in a blue blouse. She is standing confidently before a river with her arms crossed. She has long brown hair and light makeup.
Woman D	A "more visibly trans" Asian American woman in a snow white costume. She is leaning forward with one hand on her leg and the other up in a rocker pose. She has on a long black wig with bangs and is wearing bright red lipstick.
Woman E	A "cis-passing," Latina woman in a black leather jacket wearing a chain necklace. Her hair is long and black and is draped over one shoulder with the sun cutting across her face.
Woman F	A "more visibly trans," masculine, Black woman. She has a side shave with a black over-comb. She is wearing an off-white sweater over a white dress shirt with her arms behind her head.
Woman G	A "more visibly trans," White woman. She is wearing a reflective, silver dress with a studded choker. She has long brown, ombre hair and has on bright pink lipstick, dark eye shadow, colored eyebrows, and false eyelashes.
Woman H	A "cis-passing," White woman in a forest green tank top. She has long blonde hair, is smiling at the screen, and is wearing minimal makeup.

woman whose nails appear professional was not only shaped by classist logic, though, but also racialized logic. Nails are embedded with racial meanings, with "clean," pastel, French manicures attaching themselves to White, middle-class womanhood, and professionalism. In comparison, expressive art, acrylics, bright colors, and long nails symbolically attach to Blackness, working-class identity, lack of professionalism, and excess.[11]

Clothing, Makeup, Hair, and "Passing"

In addition to a lack of desire for "excessively" styled nails, participants often highlighted a desire for a more muted aesthetic in terms of clothing, makeup, and hair. During interviews, I asked participants to rate various photos of women, all of whom, unbeknownst to participants, were trans (See Table 1.1 and Figure 1.1). Participants rated these photos from one to ten, with one being highly undesirable and ten being highly desirable and explained their reasoning. Each of the six photos of women of color were unfortunately of lighter-skinned women, and all eight women were slender. The lack of widespread availability of publicly available stock photos of trans women limited

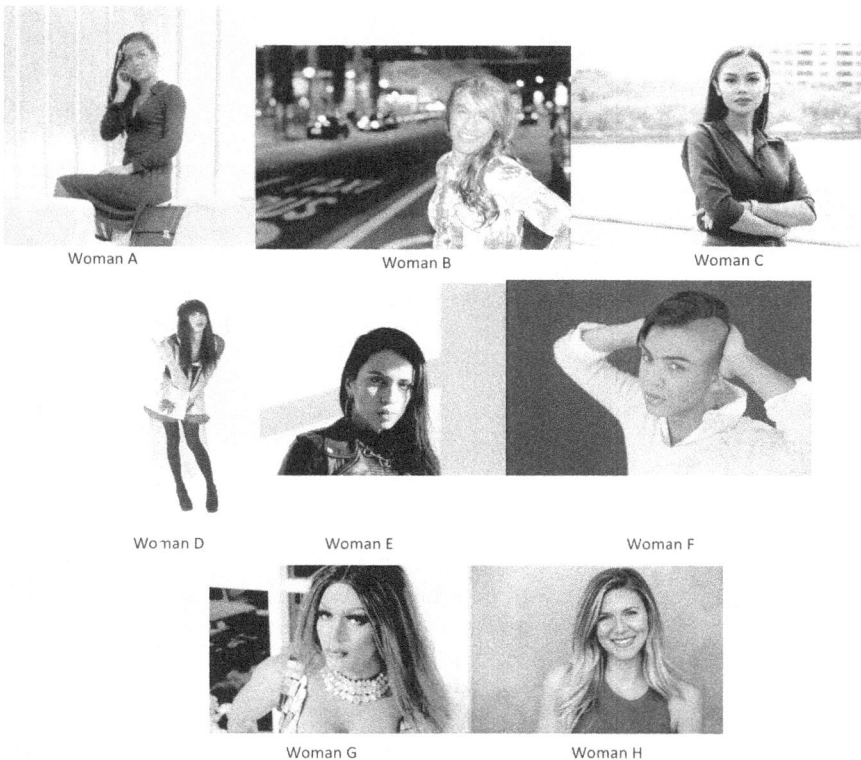

Figure 1.1 Each of These Pictures Are Also Available in Color at https://rowman.com/ webdocs/thinking%20cis.pptx. For reference, woman A is a "cis passing," Black woman. Woman B is a "more visibly trans" Latina. Woman C is a "cis-passing," Asian American woman. Woman D is a "more visibly trans" Asian American woman. Woman E is a "cis-passing" Latina. Woman F is a "more visibly trans" Black woman. Woman G is a "more visibly trans" White woman. Woman H is a "cis-passing" White woman.

the range of photos included within this study, limiting, as well, the depth of analysis regarding colorism and fatphobia. Despite this, participant responses to these photos detailed the influence of racism and cissexism on desire.

In my focus group with four White/White-passing participants, I asked participants why they felt many participants saw certain photos as trans and others as not trans. I also asked them why photos of women who appeared more "visibly trans" to participants were rated as less desirable. I asked, "Why do you think ones that look more trans like numbers B,[12] F, and G are not rated highly but the ones that don't look trans are?" Participants responded:

Adam: They did a pretty good job there [on woman H].
alithia: Okay, what do you mean?

Adam: With the makeup and the way that trans. Not, I mean, that was just typical, you know, um look.

Amy: So what you were saying is natural hair, [Adam]? Was that what it was? That their hair, I missed . . . 'Cuz I thought, which hadn't occurred to me until that's what I thought you said, but maybe that plays a part is the hair.

Vincent: Maybe like, so . . .with woman A and C, um, they're not like. . .dressed like very feminine. Um . . . hmm . . .

Amy: But it's less flashy than the top, the Snow White [woman D].

Vincent: Not like muted, just like toned down a bit.

Rachel: Yeah, and I think despite maybe like woman B and woman G not like passing well, they are dressed in like very high femme, what like makeup, jewelry, colorful clothing, and that might like kind of turn away like some people.

Adam, a Middle Eastern, cis-het man, highlighted here the ways in which trans-ness is conceptualized as a covering up of the "natural" body. Woman 8, to whom he was referring, is a White, "cis-passing," trans woman. Nearly all participants were shocked to discover that she, like the others in the photos, is also a trans woman. Adam's statement that "they did a good job" was a reference to the assumed work of gender affirmation surgeons and hormone replacement therapy clinicians who he, and other participants, believed artificially created her present beauty.

In comparison, woman B, a more "visibly trans," Latina woman, woman D, a more "visibly trans," Asian American woman, woman F, a more "visibly trans," Black woman, and woman G, a "more visibly trans," White woman, were frequently rated as the least desirable women among the eight photos. Woman B wore a white dress with variegated, neon, abstract shapes over the white. Her dress was more tightly fitting, and she wore bright red lipstick with a long blonde wig. Woman D donned a snow white-esque dress, wore heavy makeup, and had long, black hair. Finally, woman G wore a silver dress made out of metal squares with a metallic, silver-studded choker. She had on bright pink lipstick, with heavy black eyeliner, and visibly contoured cheeks and had long brown hair with dark brown roots.

Rachel, Vincent, and Amy (three White cis-lesbian women), and Adam contrasted these four participants' aesthetic with those of women A, C, and H, each of whom had softer facial features and bone structure and were wearing more business-casual and business-professional dress. Their highlighting of difference in aesthetic was not to simply compare the different styles of dress within the photos of women. Instead, what they pointed to was the connection between a more muted, professional aesthetic, "natural" looking makeup and hair, and the "passability" of transgender women.

"Passing," as a term, has varying historical meanings. C. Riley Snorton notes, "Passing is conventionally understood as the practice of moving from an oppressed group to a dominant group, that is, from Black to White, female to male, transgender to cisgender."[13] In this way, passing is something one acquires—it is an "achievement" that allows one to experience the world with fewer gendered/racialized barriers. Simultaneously, this conceptualization of "passing" elucidates the connections in the focus group discourse around "passing," the "natural" body, and trans-ness as a sort of artificial "covering up" of the body. "Passing" becomes, here, a process in which the transgender subject becomes interpreted as a cisgender subject through various means, including surgery, aesthetic, and makeup. Regarding the women in the photos that focus group participants discussed, those who appeared "hyper"-feminine were more readily recognized as transgender, while those who donned "natural" makeup that appeared to match their skin tone and clothing in muted, earth tone colors were misrecognized as cisgender.

The role of makeup, "passing," and the "natural" body was evidenced later in the focus group as Adam discussed woman G, a White, "more visibly" trans woman and why he believed she was transgender. Adam explained: "She is very masculine and um . . . I don't know like if you . . . block the hair, it could be a man, you know, if she wipe off her makeup, you know?" Woman G's hair—often referred to as a wig by participants—and her heavy makeup were interpreted by Adam as a potential covering up of her "innate male-ness." While "passing" as cisgender is discursively conceptualized as an artificial "covering up" of the "natural" body in Adam's discourse above (e.g., the doctor "did a pretty good job here"; "if you block the hair, it could be a man"), Snorton[14] notes that "social understandings of race [and gender] always contain some form of 'misrecognition of biology.'" In my participants' discourse, trans stylizations of the body were interpreted as artificial alterations to that which is already misrecognized as natural. Simultaneously, Adam's response elucidates what Marquis Bey terms traniflesh, or "flesh that throws shade on gender."[15] Adam was uncertain of whether woman G was a (cisgender) woman or not. He was left with no definitive answer from the picture, and prior to the focus group, I did not tell participants that each of the photos were of transgender women. Her hair, makeup, and clothing mixed with her more muscular arms, broad shoulders, and strong jaw rendered her unintelligible to Adam.

Participants' discourse around "natural" makeup and the "natural" body went beyond the trans body, however, with participants desiring a "natural" look on all women. Cookie, a twenty-seven-year-old, cis-homoflexible, Black woman, told me:

I prefer no makeup. I prefer like natural like period um, makeup is cool; nails are cool, it's not necessary. Like, I can appreciate, I think it's a time and a place, but like, if I'm wearing a white shirt like I don't always want like makeup on my shirt if we hug, or you know what I'm saying? Like, it's just yeah, or you, we're trying to go somewhere, like spending two hours in the bathroom to put on makeup. Like I don't have time for that.

Makeup, for Cookie, was excess physically and temporally. Her "prefer-ence" for a natural look, though, was not an individualized desire for a par-ticular look. Instead, this pull to the natural is shaped by social and cultural norms of gender. Peiss' historical analysis of US beauty culture highlights that "the ideal of pure, natural beauty" has existed since at least the nineteenth century. Peiss notes, though, that this beauty ideal has "disguised the way women's appearances were in fact dictated by middle-class cultural require-ments."[16] This ideal faded away in the late nineteenth and early twentieth centuries, replaced by large-scale marketing of makeup. However, during the 1960s, 1970s, and 1980s, a return to the "natural" arose among White, cisgen-der, feminist activists.[17] Thus, participants' "preference" for a "natural" look can be located within a particular constellation of sociocultural forces that shape what is (in)appropriate and (un)desirable vis-à-vis feminine aesthetics.

Mack, a cis-het, Black man, went further than Cookie. Whereas Cookie felt there is a time and place for makeup, Mack held a complete distaste for it. Mack explained to me:

I like their [women's] natural skin color. I don't like the makeup. I hate the . . . I hate the 50 shades of brown. You even seen that like girls, they have different, especially when they have dark skin, it's like, "Yo, your skin is already beauti-ful," and they cake it up, they try to get lighter, and they cake their face up with lighter colors of brown, and I'm like that's a major turn off. Period. Like . . . makeup is like a no for me.

Makeup, for Mack and other participants, became an unnecessary decora-tion of the face that concealed what "should" otherwise be shown. Makeup is conceptualized as a disguise rather than a form of self-expression. Musser, writing about Brown jouissance and surface-becoming discusses Anne Anlin Cheng's work on modernist aesthetic, noting, "Cheng writes that the prob-lem of the modern surface is 'distinguishing decoration as surplus from what is 'proper' to the 'thing.'"[18] Makeup, for Mack and other participants, was viewed as improper to the "thing" that is desirable womanhood. Makeup was viewed as covering up the "natural" beauty of a woman and disguising what is "truly" underneath—be that a different skin color or a "different" gender.

Race, Class, and Hair

Participants' discourse around makeup and a "natural" look not only hinged on misogyny and cissexism, but classism and socioeconomic status, as well. Much as nails bear racialized and classed aesthetics,[19] so too does makeup.

Bettie exemplifies this in her analysis of gender-race-class among White, middle-class girls (or, in her work, the "preps") and working-class, Chicana girls (or, "las chicas") in a California high school.[20] She highlights that "las chicas" tended to wear makeup in an obvious manner that did not attempt to appear as a "natural face," and often spent class time applying eyeliner, foundation, mascara, and so forth. In contrast, the "preps," or middle-class White girls, attempted to reapply powder in secret, hidden moments; they wore makeup in a way so as to appear that they were not wearing any—otherwise known as a "natural" look. Bettie notes that part of having a natural look is hiding the work one does to bear "natural" beauty within social logics of desire. Further, a "natural" look does not elide the consumption of beauty products. Amid the rise in desire for a "natural" look came a simultaneous increase in the marketing, selling, and purchasing of self-care and organic products.[21] Thus, the desire for a "natural" look among my participants, vis-à-vis makeup and aesthetic, was shaped not by individual preference but by racialized, gendered, and classed logics of desire.

This was elucidated, as well, in participants' discourse on hair. Within this discourse, participants conceptualized of "natural" hair as more "real" than "synthetic" hair. Oyedemi notes,

> The ideology of beauty that has dominated much of cultural history sees feminine beauty in Western perspectives, with dominant idea of beautiful hair constructed as long, soft and silky, typical of the Eurocentric texture of hair, and Indian/Asian hair for its close proximity to the dominant ideology.[22]

While cis-LBQ women participants overwhelmingly agreed with the dominant understanding of hair, participants, themselves (both men and women), largely desired "natural" hair and did not desire weaves, wigs, or relaxed hair.

This was evident in my interview with Spiderman, a forty-five-year-old, cis-het, Black man. During the part of the interview in which participants were asked to rate photos of women, Spiderman stated that he felt woman H, a White, "cis-passing" woman, and woman D, an Asian American, "more visibly trans" woman, were two of the most desirable women in the photos. When I asked him why, he responded:

> I don't know. Uh . . . for me, what I take away, I'm not, I'm not big on . . . I'm not big on women that take the afro out of their hair. You know what I'm saying? I'm not, I'm prejudice when it comes to women taking their permanent hair, getting it straight like that, it makes me more attracted to White women. When a Black woman makes their hair straight, it makes me more attracted to a White woman. There's a hair, original straight hair, it makes me like damn, she's more, it makes Black women more attractive to the culture of White women, so it automatically make me more attracted, because I'm a man. If

she had a afro, that'd be different, I'da been like "Okay, this is my sister right here." Yeah.

Spiderman elucidated Musser's analysis of discourse surrounding Black hair. Musser notes,

> Conversations around Black hair work to produce an ideology of Black female difference. . . . This texture, or feeling, of Black female difference is located in a set of overlapping imaginaries—that unstraightened hair offers political resistance and the insistence that Black naturalness is a source of power.[23]

Spiderman emphasized that his desire for Black women is situated upon the styling of their hair, with straightened hair eliding the distinction between Blackness and non-Blackness. Straightened hair became a synecdoche for whiteness, and, thus, shifted Spiderman's attraction away from the constructed "artificiality" of a Black woman's straightened hair and toward the constructed "originality" of a White woman and her hair.

Mack, too, desired a woman with "natural" hair. However, Mack recognized the difficulty of maintaining "natural" hair and explained that he was okay with his current partner getting weave or relaxing her hair if it made it easier to get ready in the morning. However, with both "natural" hair and weave/relaxed hair, the quality of the hair and how it appeared mattered. Mack explained:

> I'm a more natural guy. . . . but also, I'm older now and the life that I've been through, I understand that weave is way easier for a bitch. . . . But crazy weaves, like you Black, you got red, if you can pull that shit off, you bad as hell. I like a professional haircut. If it's natural, I fuck with the perms. I fuck with all that, you feel me? You wanna support your natural side but keep it above, all y'all natural bitches ain't here. You know, it's not for you, go ahead and put some, what you need, some $50 weave? Here, go ahead, go get you somethin' girl, you know what I'm sayin'?

Figure 1.2   On the Left, Woman H. On the Right, Woman D.

Mack's response elucidated the connections of race, gender, and class in participants' attraction to women. Quality wigs and weave signify a sort of feminine social capital. This feminine social capital signifies what kind of woman the bearer of the hair is, and it also signifies what kind of man Mack is by association. Mack bragging about his ability to give his partner the money to pay for a quality weave was a way of displaying his masculinity. By providing for her, he positioned himself as dominant to her and embodied a hegemonic masculinity and ensured his partner embodied a hegemonic femininity that was complementary but different from his masculinity.

Hair maintenance and weave/wigs are not cheap expenditures, though. A *Huffpost* article based on interviews with various Black women who wear their hair natural asked them how much they spent on hair products per year, and the amounts ranged from one hundred dollars to well over one thousand.[24] In 2018, companies selling products targeted at Black women's hair earned over two billion dollars,[25] highlighting not only the profitability of such companies but the high cost of hair maintenance and styling for Black women. Income, then, as well as the influence of White conceptualizations of professionalism shaped the appearance of Black women's hair for Mack and other participants.

Politics and ideas of Black consciousness also surrounded cis-het, Black men's responses regarding Black women's hair. Ky, a twenty-four-year-old, cis-het, Black man, explained to me that he preferred "natural" hair on Black women. When I asked him why, he told me:

I mean, it's just, aw jeez. It's just, it's, it's like a kind of a weirdo reason, it's uh. Gosh, how do you say it? I'm trying to think of a mainstream way of saying this. It's kind of like a Black conscious, conscious thing. So it's like that type of hair [straight] is like copying, you know, White. That's not your natural roots. I'm not like one of those haters about it. It looks great. I see why. I even like it. And I don't know if I'd completely write off a girl if she does buy in at that level. Like that's just culturally where we are in America. So I'm not like one of those who super have a problem with it. I just prefer you know . . .

Ky highlighted the tension between a socialized attraction to straightened hair and his desire for a woman who has worked to uninternalize whiteness and White norms. Musser notes that "straightened hair is read as a symptom of submission [and] unstraightened hair is viewed as an active rebuke against [White] norms."[26] Black women's hair becomes emblematic of their political orientations and how Black women do their hair signified, for many of my participants, their difference from or similarity to White women, with straightened, Black women's hair being viewed as a copy of a White "original." Black women, though, end up in a double bind with this view of their hair. The politicization of Black women's hair shaped participants' desire for "natural" Black hair, yet many participants, like Ky, highlighted a larger societal pressure for Black women to straighten their hair. Black women become pulled in two directions, with their agency to determine which style they prefer elided.

I asked Sabrina, a twenty-five-year-old, cis-lesbian, Black woman, whether how Black women do their hair shapes their desirability. She responded:

> Yep, um, natural hair is not desirable to a lot of people. Um, so I've been wearing my hair like this [natural] since I started working at [business]. Um, and I recently for my birthday, [date], I went and got 20 inches of hair [laughs]. So I walked in a whole new person, and everybody just saw me differently. Like people actually came up to me and started introducing themselves like they, I haven't been here for eight months. So, um, the fact that my natural hair did not find that, that was not a desirable to that person with natural hair, but I was with this long, straight, more stereo—more acceptable—hairstyle made me more attractive to that person, and to me, that frustrates me.

Sabrina highlighted that, despite most participants preferring "natural," unadulterated hair, there remain societal consequences for Black women with said hair. Desire for Sabrina referred not only to sexual or romantic desire but to desire as an orienting force. Ahmed notes on the phenomenology of orientation, "Bodies tend toward some objects more than others, given their tendencies. These tendencies are not originary; they are effects of the repetition of "tending toward."[27] Bodies orient themselves toward objects in part through the historical conceptualization of such objects. Sabrina's coworkers oriented themselves toward long, straight hair and away from natural, Black hair due the legacy and continuation of white supremacy and misogynoir.

Hair, whether "natural" or "unnatural," is not merely protein filaments growing out of follicles within the skin. Hair is also the images, words, and ideas that come to encompass how it is conceptualized and understood in a given society at a given time. Participants' desire for "natural" hair was shaped by race, class, and gender, and the desire for "real" hair or "real-looking" hair rather than a "synthetic-looking" wig was also shaped by race, class, and gender. Participant discourse around what is natural and what is not shaped their desire for particular types of hair, styles of hair, and clothing/makeup aesthetics. However, their desire for "natural" hair on a woman's head was in tension with their desire for hairless women's faces and bodies, even if that required hair removal or other alterations to the body. In the next section I highlight how a hairless body was viewed as "natural" even if that is not how a woman's body would look without any alteration. Thus, ideas of what is natural and what is unnatural are less about biology and more so about social and cultural views of the body.

"IT SHOULD NOT BE LIKE A WEREWOLF": CIS-HET MEN AND CIS-LBQ WOMEN'S DISCOURSE SURROUNDING BODY HAIR

In my interviews with participants, I asked them what they desired in a woman. No participant noted body hair as shaping their desire without further probing. However, upon my asking whether body hair shaped their desire for a woman, many participants shared that it did. When discussing their lack of desire for body hair, participants conflated hair with animality, masculinity, and filth. While these conflations were not overtly classed, raced, and gendered (with the exception of masculinity), the conceptualization of body hair as such is linked to White, cis-heteropatriarchal understandings of the body.[28]

Understandings of body hair have changed across time within the United States, but, in each period, these changes occurred based on prevailing conceptualizations of race, gender, class, and ability. Early European colonizers of what is now the United States were obsessed with "the Indian's 'beardless countenance.'"[29] Seeing less visible hair on some Indigenous men's faces and potential depilatory practices of removing facial hair among some Indigenous men, White colonizers viewed this as evidence of Indigenous peoples' "anachronistic" evolutionary state. However, later in the 1800s, "'body hair became disgusting' to middle-class American women, [with] its removal [viewed as] a way to 'separate oneself from cruder people, lower class and immigrant[s].'"[30] These ideas continue into the present, along with the medicalization and pathologizing of "too much" hair on women's bodies (i.e., hirsutism). In what follows, I elucidate the connection of these ideas to my participants' conceptualizations of body hair.

In my interview with Henry, a twenty-six-year-old, cis-het, Black man, I asked him whether body hair matters in terms of his attractions to women. Henry shared:

Uh yeah, I met a girl and she didn't shave her armpits, and I was like oh, no, like that's not, like I don't even, I guess because I don't have much armpit hair, and she was, I was like, "You're, I mean, the bear out here. Like you're doing it." And I think it made a difference only because like just, look, like what was ingrained into me. I don't think I want to come home to a hairy pit all the time, you know?

Henry not only conflated body hair with animality but also worked to differentiate between men's and women's bodies. As I discuss further below, the linking of body hair to animality is produced, in part, through concepts of sexual dimorphism. What I want to highlight here, though, is the conceptualization of human body hair as excess—as improper to the "thing" that is womanhood, yet simultaneously "proper" to the "thing" that is manhood.

Henry's linkage of women's body hair with animality and conceptualization of it as "improper" to womanhood builds upon White, cis-heteropatriarchal understandings of body hair. Herzig's work on hair removal includes discussion of the influence of Darwin's *The Descent of Man*[31] on gendered and racialized understandings of hair and the body. They note, "When nature was functioning properly, experts after *Descent* presumed, men had body hair, and women did not."[32]

Sheila also linked body hair to animality. In speaking with her about what she desires in a woman, I asked her if she cares whether a woman shaves her armpits, legs, and other parts of her body. She responded, "Shave your armpits. Your legs. I don't know . . . I can't say because I'm not, it's not even a complete hairless, but it should not be like . . . werewolf." Sheila looked straight at me, speaking in a calm, matter-of-fact manner. She relied upon a taken-for-granted assumption that it is only "natural" that a woman would shave her armpits and legs. Her linkage of women's body hair to seeming like a werewolf was meant not only to compare women's body hair to animality but to excessively hairy animality. Again, women's body hair is viewed as "unnatural," as something akin to the beastly, intermediate nature of the werewolf—which is both human and not, both animal and not. Further, while Sheila did not detail this, it is important to analyze the connection between women's body and the werewolf and the stories of werewolves. Stories of werewolves are, often, not simply stories of individuals who are both human and wolf but of individuals cursed with the fate of lycanthropy. While one could argue that Sheila was not attempting or did not mean to link body hair to ideas and myths of curses, it is important to home in on the meaning in the words individuals use. It is in Sheila's choice of words that women's body hair becomes conceptualized as excess, unnatural, and undesirable to oneself and those around them.

Hair, Hygiene, and Sex

Participants' conflation of women's body hair with ideas of excess and unnaturality was also core to concepts of sexual dimorphism, as I mentioned briefly when discussing my interview with Henry. In each interview, I asked participants whether they can tell if someone is trans or not. When I asked Musiteli, a twenty-four-year-old, cis-het, Black man, he responded that he could sometimes but that it depends. I asked, "What are the sorts of features that would be like, 'Okay, maybe she's trans'?" Musiteli responded:

> Um I remember one situation at my last job I was training a new coworker, I didn't know she was trans at the time. I just thought she was a guy, because she dressed, she dressed up like a guy um and had, had, had like a full on like beard, so I was, I was just assuming, just saying, "Hey bro," and so it's like, here let

me help you out and then she, because it was just like the facial features and the hair was just uh and then the fact that they were dressed up like a man in jeans and just a regular shirt I guess isn't strictly masculine, because you know women wear shirts and jeans.

While Musiteli noted that part of the reason he misrecognized his coworker as a man was because of her clothing, the woman's facial hair and structure largely shaped, in his reflection on this moment, his misrecognition of her. Body hair and facial hair, for most participants, were interpreted within social ideas of biological sexual dimorphism.

Indeed, Ferriman and Gallwey[33] assessed the density of terminal hairs on cisgender women's faces and bodies and constructed the Ferriman-Gallwey scale of hirsutism, which prevails in use today. More than the slight presence of hairs on the chest, arms, belly, face, back/buttocks, genitals, and legs comes to signal mild hirsutism, with hirsutism pathologized as "the presence of excess body or facial terminal . . . hair growth in females in a male-like pattern [and] affects 5-15% of [cisgender] women."[34] The presence of facial hair and body hair on women is deemed unnatural, in need of treatment, and masculinizing. Thus, in 2023, the hair removal industry is projected to reap revenues over 10.19 billion dollars.[35]

When I asked focus group participants again about body hair and their desires for women, Adam responded:

That's what makes the woman different, her body, I don't mind uh having hair in certain specific parts on her body um . . . in general I . . . like woman to be clean. Just in certain areas. But like I said, down in the genital, like it's okay for me.

Hair, for Adam, Musiteli, and other participants, served as the visual representation of the differentiation between "men" and "women." Further, Adam referred to a woman being hairless not only as "proper" but "cleanly," as well. Often, when I asked participants specifically about genital hair, the response was that they did not prefer hair due to cleanliness, hygiene, and other such myths surrounding body hair. The idea that hairlessness is cleanly is reflected in colloquial discourse (e.g., "clean shaven").

Ryan, an Indian American, cis-het man, explained to me his distaste for a "bush" or a large amount of hair genitally:

I just think like it's better to sometimes, maybe, fully shave it, like coordinate with your partner if you're going to do that, because then it could help but like, yeah, if like two people both have bushes then like you don't know what's going on. And, also, it's just like, cleaner. Like in terms of like keeping it clean. It's easier when you have less hair in those areas.

When I asked Liz, a cis-lesbian, Latina woman, whether she cares if a woman shaves her armpits and genitals or not, she similarly responded, "Yes (laughs). Yes definitely. It's just . . . um . . . how should I call it? Hygiene. Hygiene." In Ryan, Liz, and Adam's discourse, pubic hair is conceptualized as unclean, non-hygienic, and obtrusive. Such ideas, again, are not mere individual preference but are instead shaped by cultural and generational understandings of hair. Herzig highlights that "the normalization of smooth skin in dominant U.S. culture is not even a century old," with such ideas arising during the same years as the Cold War with individuals in the United States describing "visible body hair on women as evidence of a filth, 'foreign' lack of hygiene."[36] Porn and the framing of sexually explicit material have also shaped cultural understandings of pubic hair. While pubic hair removal for women went out of vogue after the nineteenth century, it became popular once again in the 1980s, in part, due to pornographic depictions largely including hairless vulvas,[37] and more recently, hairless bodies for men, as well. Cultural discourse surrounding pubic and body hair is, thus, shaped by racialized, gendered, and xenophobic understandings of the body and hair. The fact that these ideas are shared by immigrant participants/participants of color does not deny the racialized and xenophobic roots of such discourse, so much as it highlights the internalization of racism and xenophobia by immigrants and/or people of color, as an adaptive response to the racism of society.[38]

As participants conceptualized hair as animal-like, masculine, and/or filthy, they also conceptualized of it as excess or surplus to the human (woman's) body. Pubic hair shaped their idea of what it means to do womanhood and to be a woman. As such, participant discourse not only was shaped by racist, sexist, and xenophobic conceptualizations of hair that have proliferated in the United States but also cissexist concepts of manhood and womanhood as opposite, different, and biologically based. That which is "improper" to manhood/womanhood within White schemas of a gender binary are unnatural, unclean, and undesirable.

I focused, in this section, on participant discourse surrounding body hair, facial hair, and pubic hair to elucidate the ways in which gender and sex remain attached to ideas of the natural/unnatural and the biological within cultural discourse. My focus, thus, is not meant to critique or deny individuals' ability to choose what sexually and/or romantically arouses them in a partner. Instead, my analysis here explicates how individual preferences are not, or not only, individual desires that are either innate or uniquely chosen. Instead, individual preferences are shaped, consciously, or not, by racialized and gendered ideas of desire, and this cannot be separated from what cis-het men and cis-LBQ women participants desired in a woman.

TRANS BODIES AS UNNATURAL

In the previous two sections, I focused on how race, class, and gender shaped participants' desires for women and their ideas of what is or is not "natural." While I have focused largely on how participants made sense of particular parts of the body, I now turn to analyzing how participants made sense of individuals as "natural" or "unnatural." In particular, I focus in this section on how participants made sense of trans-ness as "unnatural" and as "excess." In fleshing out participant discourse, I connect their responses to works on the sociology of the body, Queer/Trans Studies, queer/trans of color critique, analyzing "what gets to count as a . . . normal, healthy, functioning body"[39] and what counts as a "naturally" undesirable body? Often, when participants spoke of trans bodies, they stated that such bodies are unnatural, excess, and undesirable while simultaneously highlighting that it only "naturally" makes sense that they would not be attracted to such bodies.

Sociobiological Justifications

Participants often explained their lack of desire for trans women as "natural" due to psychological or evolutionary reasons. After showing participants the eight photos of different women, I asked them to select the woman they found most desirable of the eight. Once they had selected the photo and explained their decision. I asked, "So, sticking with her for a second, if you were to meet her, and then she told you she's transgender, would that change how desirable she is to you?" When I asked Adam this question, he responded:

> Yes, it's, do you know why? It's, it's because psychology. You know when you think about how will you be attracted to them? Imagining that person that you see, you know, like I'm imagining that lady being with me in the bed. Will she be a woman of my kids in the future?

Adam, rather than stating that he simply did not want to be with a trans woman relied upon a sociobiological explanation to naturalize and universalize his lack of attraction to them. In doing so, he displaced his non-desire for trans women off himself and upon "nature." As such, it becomes "only natural" that a cis-het man would not want a trans woman. After all, it is supposedly engrained in him to want biological children with a partner who is capable of providing the egg that would be fertilized by his sperm.

Religious Justifications

In addition to using sociobiological justification to state that it was "only natural" to desire cis women and not trans women, other participants utilized

religious justification. When I asked Iceberg, a cis-het, Black man, if finding out a woman was trans would change how desirable she was to him, he
responded:

Iceberg: Uh . . . you're talking about, she transed into this [points to image of the
   woman he found most desirable out of the eight photos]?
alithia: Uh-huh.
Iceberg: No, if she told me, oh no, I couldn't do that. I couldn't do that. Because
   man made, man made for a woman. You know, everybody have they whatever,
   but like I said now, I got to believe in the word a little bit. I don't have nothing
   against it.

Here, Iceberg's reference to "the word" was meant to signify the *Bible* and
its descriptions in *Genesis* that "woman" was made from the rib of "man" so
that "man" shall not be alone. Thus, the two are believed to be the celestial
helpmates of one another. Iceberg did not view trans women as women; thus,
his reference that man is made for woman did not ignore that trans women are
women so much as it highlighted his interpretation of trans women as men.

Trans-ness as Artificial

The reliance upon the "natural," though, extended beyond participants relying
upon "science" to justify their attractions. Others, instead, felt a lack of attraction to trans women because of their conceptualization of trans women's
bodies as artifice. When I asked Sheila the same question I asked Adam and
Iceberg above, she responded:

Sheila: Um . . . I know, I know I wouldn't date her, being as she's transgender.
alithia: How come?
Sheila: 'Cuz I don't like that mix. Um it's a little awkward to me. Um . . . because
   I know like, you don't have boobs, I'm sorry. And then if you did, because I'm
   an overthinker, my mind is always gonna be like "these are not your boobs!"
   Um . . . yeah. But I mean it's like I would still wanna get to know her.

Sheila assumed trans women could only have breasts if they had undergone breast augmentation. In reality, many trans women are able to develop
breasts through hormone replacement therapy. However, what I want to
focus on here is Sheila's statement that "these are not your boobs." Sheila
conceptualized a trans woman's breasts as separate from her "real" body.
The "real" body, for Sheila and many participants like her, was that which
is unadulterated and unmodified. The body, in reality, is always altered and
modified by its environment on a molecular level, yet that adulteration is not

necessarily visible to the eye in the same way that a breast augmentation or other cosmetic alteration is. Trans women's bodies, thus, became, to Sheila, a mix of the "natural" and the "artificial," and that cyborgian enmeshment was unattractive.

Participants' conceptualization of "naturality" as it applied to women shaped which women they viewed as natural women and which they did not. Many participants, in responding to my question about whether finding out a woman is trans would change how desirable she is to them utilized the language of desiring a "natural woman." Mack, for example, responded to this question by saying, "It would. It would. I mean I'm not even goin, I don't judge nobody, you know what I mean? But um . . . yeah I really, that's just not my preference. Um I just like natural women." Ryan similarly responded, "Um yes that would. Uh I would like to like be in a relationship with a natural woman." For both Mack and Ryan, cis women were "natural" women and trans women were men who appeared as women. In this way, they relied upon a Cartesian dichotomy of the body and the self, with the trans woman's self being woman but her body being that of a man. While they both highlight their desire for a "natural" woman as a preference, it is important to question how much of their preference for cis women is an innate predisposition and how much of their preference is shaped by a society and culture in which over 75 percent of US adults have been found to not be attracted to trans men, women, and/or nonbinary people.[40]

CONCLUSION

Cis-ness, as a political, discursive, and social manifestation, perpetuates an idea of what is "natural" in conceptualizing what it means to be a "proper" and desirable man, woman, and person. Participants' desires for "natural" women existed in tension with desires for things (e.g., well-styled and well-maintained "natural" hair, "natural" makeup, hairless bodies, faces, and/or genitals, thin bodies, "thick" bodies) that require work to appear "natural." Further, their desire for a woman in her "natural" element did not necessarily extend to a desire for disabled women or trans women, both of whom were undesirable due to the seemingly "unnatural" makeup of their bodies.

In the development of norms of desirability, all women are policed and regulated. Debates on social media, in the news, and even in academia abound regarding trans women's place in feminist movements. Consistently, advancements in protections for trans women and girls are framed as infringements on cis women and girls. Throughout this chapter, though, I have shown how trans women and cis women both are held to rigid norms of what a body should look like. These norms are informed by White, middle- and upper-class, able-bodied, patriarchal conceptualizations of womanhood and women's bodies, and these norms harm trans women and cis women pushing both to contort their bodies to meet unattainable goals lest they be deemed undesirable.

Musser[41] also highlights that, culturally, individuals wish to be able to see "objectively" all there is to know of a person on their surface. Weaves, wigs, makeup, and queer/trans aesthetics, perhaps, hide parts of the body, yet it is important to ask whether these items cover the body or become extensions of the body. Further, trans-ness comes to be seen as a mystery or a factor that elicits questions upon being seen. Trans-ness blurs others' ability to discern what genitals and secondary sex characteristics lie beneath one's clothes. Trans-ness, thus, destabilizes neat, fixed, and tidy notions of attraction and desire, but the obfuscation of being able to "objectively" know whether one is or is not attracted to an individual simply based on appearance was largely unattractive to participants as discussed in this chapter.

As Bey notes, Black-ness and trans-ness "reference the process by which gender is unmoored and unmade as an otherwise way to become a subject in excess of gender."[42]Black-ness, trans-ness, fat-ness, and disabled-ness all exceed that which was a desirable body for cis-het men and cis-LBQ women participants I interviewed. In detailing this to me, they sought to base their answers in sociobiology, religion, and "commonsense," all of which are fixed in racialized, gendered, and ableist logics that have become so institutionalized as to be taken for granted as universal, "objective" truths. Participants were not attracted to that which obfuscates the ability to see all there is to know about a person when looking at them, yet cis-ness, itself, relies upon an obfuscation of the reality that that which appears "natural" and that which appears "unnatural" are both socially constructed and agreed-upon notions. In the next chapter, I delve further into the ways cis-het men and cis-LBQ women participants discussed attraction to trans women by fleshing out their responses to the eight different photos of women I asked them to rate.

NOTES

1. 1987, "Doing Gender, Doing Heteronormativity."
2. 1978 [1992], *The Straight Mind*.
3. 1978 [1992], *The Straight Mind*, 32.
4. 1978[1992], *The Straight Mind*, 193.
5. 1997, *The Invention of Women*.
6. 1997, *The Invention of Women*.
7. Byrd and Tharps, 2014, "When Black Hair is Against the Rules." Oyedemi, 2016, "Beauty as Violence."
8. Fahs, 2011, "Dreaded 'Otherness.'

9. Joseph-Salisbury and Connelly, 2018, "If Your Hair is Relaxed, White People Are Relaxed." Lyon, 2020, "Pajón Power."

10. Bettie, 2002, *Women Without Class.* Oyedemi, 2016, "Beauty as Violence." Sims, Pirtle, and Johnson-Arnold, 2020, "Doing Hair, Doing Race."

11. Kang, 2010, *The Managed Hand.*

12. See Chapter Two for the photos.

13. 2009, "'A New Hope'."

14. 2009, "'A New Hope'."

15. 2019, "Black Fugitivity Un/Gendered," 56.

16. 1998, *Hope in a Jar*, 30.

17. Brooks, 2020, "The Pigments of Patriarchy," 127.

18. Cheng, 2010, *Second Skin,* cited from Musser, 2018, "Surface-Becoming."

19. Kang, 2010, *The Managed Hand.*

20. 2002, *Women Without Class.*

21. Peiss, 1998, *Hope in a Jar.*

22. 2016, "Beauty as Violence," 542.

23. 2016, "Surface-Becoming," 2.

24. Lambert, 2020, "How Much It Costs to Maintain Natural Black Hair."

25. Holmes, 2019, "The Industry That Black Women Built."

26. 2016, "Black Hair and Textures of Defensiveness," 4.

27. 2006, *Queer Phenomenology,* 53.

28. Herzig, 2015, *Plucked.*

29. Herzig, 2015, *Plucked,* 25.

30. Stearns, 1999, *Battleground of Desire.* Herzig, 2015, *Plucked.*

31. 1871.

32. Herzig, 2015, *Plucked,* 67.

33. 1961, "Clinical Assessment of Body Hair."

34. Yildiz, Bolour, Woods, Moore, and Azziz, 2010, "Visually Scoring Hirsutism."

35. FACT.MR, 2023, "Hair Removal Wax Market."

36. Herzig, 2015, *Plucked,* 12.

37. Fahs, 2011, "Dreaded 'Otherness'."

38. Pyke and Dang, 2003, "'FOB' and 'Whitewashed'."

39. Moore and Kosut, 2015, *The Body Reader*, 5.

40. Bame, 2017, "21% of Americans."

41. 2016, "Surface-Becoming."

42. 2019, "Black Fugitivity Un/Gendered," 55.

Chapter 2

"That's a Guy"

Viewing Trans Women's Photos

An online forum user anonymously asks, "How can you know if someone is transgender? Is [sic] there specific traits to look for?" Answers abound, ranging from those arguing that the only way to determine if someone is trans is to hear them explicitly tell you they are to those arguing that innate differences exist in skeletal frame, muscle composition, jaw, hair, hands, and more. This user was not the only to pose the question, though. Ten related questions are linked on the right-hand side of the forum similarly asking, "How can you tell if a woman you meet was actually born a man," "How can I know if someone is a man or a woman," and "How can you tell if a transgender person is passing or not?" Even more critical to this chapter is a user who asks, "Am I attractive for a trans woman?" What does it mean for a trans woman, or any woman, to feel uncertain of her beauty, to question whether she is beautiful *for* a trans woman, as though other trans women are unattractive or, at least, less attractive than cis women? How do certain bodies get interpreted as transgender and others as cisgender, and what does that have to do with beauty? These are the questions I take up in this chapter.

During interviews, I would give participants eight photos of women (see figure *2.1* and table *2.1*). I would ask them to rate these women on a scale of one to ten as to how desirable they find them to be with a one being entirely undesirable and a ten being entirely desirable. I would then ask participants to elaborate on their ratings and to select which women they found most desirable out of the eight. Using the woman they found most desirable, I transitioned to explicit questions about trans women. I asked, "If you met this woman and then found out she was trans, would that change how desirable she is?" Continuing from here, we spoke at length about dating, having sex, or forming relationships with trans women and what it would mean to date a trans woman, along with further questions.

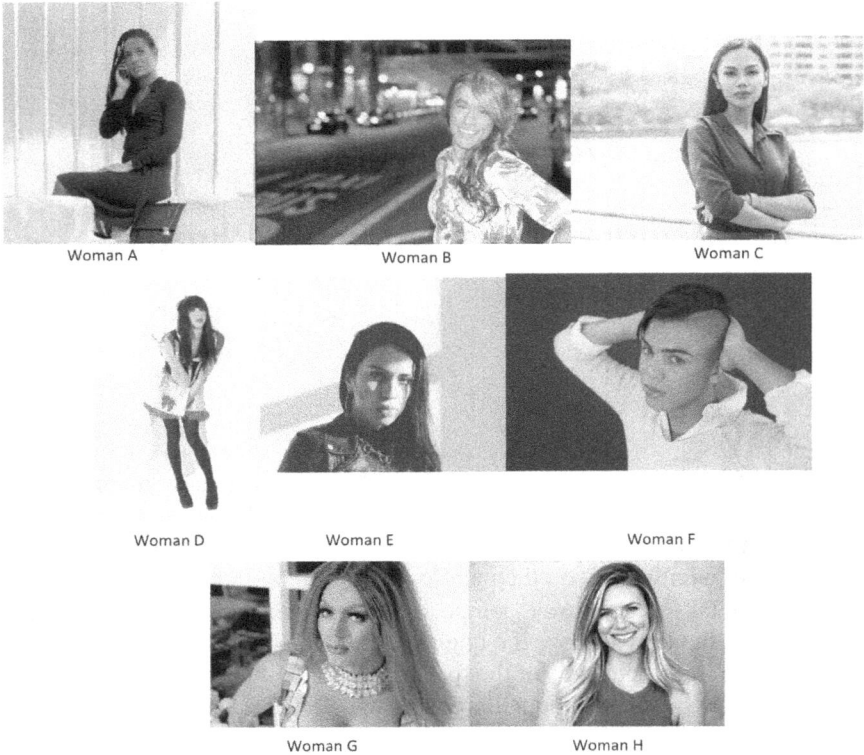

Figure 2.1 For Reference, Woman A Is a "cis passing," Black Woman. Woman B is a "more visibly trans" Latina. Woman C is a "cis-passing," Asian American woman. Woman D is a "more visibly trans" Asian American woman. Woman E is a "cis-passing" Latina. Woman F is a "more visibly trans" Black woman. Woman G is a "more visibly trans" White woman. Woman H is a "cis-passing" White woman.

While psychology studies have used photo ranking methods to analyze cisgender people's desire, or lack thereof, for trans women, most previous studies have utilized predominantly White samples, White vignettes/photos, and/or not engaged in a racial analysis of their data.[1] In this chapter, I focus on data I collected utilizing photo elicitation and photo ranking. I highlight how each of the women were rated, and I elucidate how race-gender-sexual orientation, education, and class shaped the rankings of women. While doing so, I discuss participants' discourse, looking at the words they said and what meaning was embedded within them to illuminate the cis-ness of Eurocentric beauty standards.

The photos of women I utilized in interviews do not represent all trans women. No single photo or collection of photos could represent all trans women or even sub-communities of trans women. In collecting photos, I aimed to find photos of trans women rather than use photos of models who could be cisgender or transgender. At the end of interviews, several participants asked which women were "really" trans. I explained that they all were, and repeatedly, they were shocked by, in particular, woman A (a "cis-passing" Black woman[2]) and woman H (a "cis-passing" White woman). I felt it important that, when participants found out all photos were of trans women, that they learned to see some diversity of what "trans" looks like. In the process of finding photos of trans women, I sought out photos of women who were not celebrities, activists, or well-known figures. I wanted participants to see photos of random women and any discussion of trans-ness regarding the women to arise naturally from the participants. For example, I could have utilized a photo of producer, director, writer, activist, and actress, Janet Mock, as a representation of a "cis-passing," Black and/or Asian American/Pacific Islander woman. However, numerous participants, lesbian, bisexual, and/or queer (LBQ) women in particular, may have known that she is trans.

Throughout, I utilize the term "more visibly trans" to describe those women who did not necessarily "pass" as cisgender, both to myself and to participants. In describing these women as "more visibly trans," I am simply comparing them to those who were "cis-passing" and not to other trans women outside of these photos. I use the phrasing "more visibly trans," because, in reality, there is no particular look that is "visibly" trans nor "visibly" cisgender. Instead, in doing gender, individuals are often recognized and/or misrecognized[3] as a particular gender/sex. Women described throughout as "more visibly trans" were recognized as trans, while those described as "cis-passing" were misrecognized as cisgender. As I highlighted in chapter 1 and as I detail below, "passing" is not necessarily about whether one is truly cisgender or transgender, nor is it about whether one is "really" a woman. Instead, a woman's "passability" says more about the individual(s) looking at her than it does about her, as "passing" relies upon the interpellation of an individual by another and shifts according to racial, gendered, cultural, and social schemas.[4] Still, it is necessary to highlight the differentiation in terms of how various women were interpreted by myself and my participants in order to make sense of participant discourse within a cisnormative society.

Further, photos of random trans women that are available for public use are not aplenty. The photos used were of slender women with lighter complexions due to the limitation of options. Even if there were an abundance of photos of trans women available for public use, the photos selected or crafted for any study would not be representative. The data I write about in this chapter are but a glimpse of how cis-het men and cis-LBQ women desire (or do not desire), view, respond to, and make meaning of trans women vis-à-vis these particular photos, but this does not make these data insignificant. Roland

Barthes, in his reflections on and theorizations of photography, noted, "It seems that in Latin 'photograph' would be said 'imago lucis opera expressa'; which is to say: image revealed, 'extracted,' 'mounted,' 'expressed' (like the juice of a lemon) by the action of light."[5] Images—as well as data—reveal and express moments in time of particular people and allow the viewer/researcher to extract meaning from—or analyze—what is presented. In what follows, I discuss the rankings of the photos I used in the interviews and analyze participant discourse surrounding each of the women.

"I'M GONNA GIVE IT AN EIGHT": RATING WOMEN

While cis-het men participants rated woman A, on average, more highly than other photos, they repeatedly selected woman H as the most desirable woman of the eight. Woman A's photo was of a "cis-passing," Black woman, while woman H was of a "cis-passing," White woman. Seven of fifteen cis-het men participants selected woman H as the most desirable, another three selected woman C (a "cis-passing" Asian American woman) as the most desirable, three chose woman A, and one selected woman G (a "more visibly trans" White woman). The participant who selected woman G was the only cis-het man to select a "more visibly trans" woman as the most desirable. This participant, though, was solely attracted to trans women. One additional participant refused to pick any woman as the most desirable. He found them all undesirable, as he felt all of them were trans women. I write more about this participant in chapter 4.

In comparison, seven out of seventeen of cis-LBQ women selected woman A as the most desirable photo. An additional two selected woman C, two others selected woman F, two selected woman E (a "cis-passing" Latina), two chose woman H, one chose woman B (a "visibly trans" Latina), and one chose woman G. The participant who chose woman G was extremely shy and had a difficult time rating the photos and selected a random woman. She did not find woman G more desirable than other photos. She was attracted to women "who are more on the femme side," thus the predominance of feminine women did not make it difficult for her to rate them. She simply did not want to rank photos of women. Rachel, a low-income, cis-lesbian, White woman with a college degree, was one of the two women who chose woman F. She as well explained, "She just looks really cool, and I don't know, I like her style . . . I like her sweater, shirt combo and her lipstick." Rachel was particularly immersed in queer and trans settings and felt a deep kinship to spaces that celebrated gender identities and expressions of all kinds.

Across cis-het men and cis-LBQ women, photos of "cis-passing" women were rated more highly than those that were "more visibly trans," excepting for woman F (see table *2.1*). Woman F is a " more visibly trans," Black woman. She has a short haircut with the side shaved. She wears no makeup other than lip gloss and wears a shirt that could be either a men's or women's style sweatshirt. While this was unappealing to most cis-het men participants, many cis-LBQ participants interpreted her to be a stud or butch,[6] and rated her, on average, much higher (2.7 and 6.6, respectively). Cis-LBQ women ranked "more visibly trans" women higher than cis-het men participants, but they still ranked them as less desirable than "cis-passing" women. The one exception was woman D, who was the highest ranked "more visibly trans" woman by cis-het men (4.5) but lowest ranked "more visibly trans" woman by cis-LBQ women (3.7). While many participants sought to describe "more visibly trans" women as still beautiful, they simultaneously did not view them as the kind of woman they saw themselves with. Further below, I elucidate how participants utilized "polite" but coded language to disregard "visibly trans" women without sounding overtly cissexist.

Education and Income

While I was not able to adequately assess how participants ranked photos by race due to my smaller samples of Whites, Asian American participants, and Latinx participants, I did assess how education and income shaped participants' rankings. There were not drastic differences in participant ranking of photos between those with some college and those with a bachelor's degree or higher. However, differences arose between those with a high school diploma or less and those with some college or a bachelor's degree. Those with a high school degree or less rated "more visibly trans" higher than those with some college or higher (see table *2.2*). Those with a high school diploma or less still rated "more visibly trans" women lower than "cis-passing" ones, but they found them more desirable than those with higher levels of education did. Participants with a high school diploma or less rated woman B a 5.1, woman D a 7.2, woman F a 5.0, and woman G a 5.3 (compared to 4.1, 3.7, 4.6, and 3.9, respectively, for those with higher levels of education). While those with a high school diploma or less were not less cissexist in their discussion of the photos and trans women than those with higher levels of education, they did rank "more visibly trans" women as more desirable than "cis-passing" trans women.

Liz, a cis-lesbian Latina, earned a low income;[7] however, she lived with her wife from whom she was separated, but continued to contribute to her livelihood. Liz also was close to finishing her bachelor's degree at the time

Table 2.1   Average Photo Rankings by Sub-Sample

Sub-Sample	Woman A	Woman B	Woman C	Woman D	Woman E	Woman F	Woman G	Woman H
Cis–Het Men	7.3	3.2	6.9	4.5	5.0	2.7	2.9	6.5
Cis–Les/Bi Women	6.9	4.8	7.7	3.7	7.6	6.6	4.9	5.3

Figure 2.2 Woman B.

we spoke. When I asked Liz to rate the photo of woman B, a "more visibly trans" Latina, she described the photo in this way:

Liz: Uh . . . this is a wig [on woman B]? [pause] um (laughs) [pause] I don't know. It's going to be a [pause] 5 [for woman B]. . . . Because is [pause] she has, I mean she's a woman. I know she's a woman, because if she's dressed up like that and she is, you know, she's posing like that for the picture, she looks like a woman. So is, she should be considered a woman, but uh in terms of how attracted I am, I'm not because [pause] I see the masculine um [pause; gestures at face]
Alithia: Facial structure?
Liz: Yes, facial structure, so I'm not attracted and I also see that it's obviously a wig. So yeah, but I'm gonna give it a 5, because it's, I always appreciate and I always uh admire that, you know, they feel like a woman and regardless of what they are, I, I really, I call it bravery. And I love that, but the question is how attracted I am right? Yeah, so I'm gonna give it a 5.

Liz's response highlights a disapproval of the wig's visibility as synthetic hair, rather than real human hair. Such a statement points to her desire for a natural look in a woman. Liz's lack of attraction to a woman due to her wearing a synthetic wig, though, as detailed in chapter 1, is attached to classed and racialized notions of hair and "real" hair. Human hair wigs that use hair grown and harvested from people (mostly women often in the Global South) cost hundreds of dollars, with some even costing up to two-thousand dollars.[8] Transgender women, though, do not always have the financial resources available to afford higher quality wigs that also require higher upkeep than a synthetic wig. Liz additionally highlighted earlier in the interview a desire for a White woman, in particular. While cisgender, White women wear wigs, wigs remain more associated with Black and/or trans women than they do others. Earlier in the interview, Liz explained to me that education mattered to her in terms of her attractions to women. She preferred "women who have some kind of education . . . They don't necessarily need to have a bachelor's degree . . . but at least the intention of pursuing one." Liz's lack of attraction to this woman was not simply out of dislike for a particular hairstyle or a particular wig. Instead, Liz's description of woman B was shaped by raced and classed femininities and notions of desire. Woman B's wig and aesthetic, in many ways, exemplified what Schippers terms "pariah femininities," or the embodiment of those characteristics and behaviors that "are simultaneously stigmatized and feminized."[9] Woman B was hyperfeminine but did not embody hegemonic femininity.

In comparison to Liz, Amanda was a cis-bi, Black woman who lived in poverty, did not have stable housing, and had not completed high school. Amanda was the only cis woman participant to intentionally choose a "more visibly trans" participant. Amanda desired a woman who looks like she parties and goes out to clubs and bars often. She did not find woman B to be more beautiful than the others, but she liked the way woman B dressed. Amanda chose woman B "only because it looks like I'll have more fun with that person, and then just by the background, it looks like they have that street life like that." Amanda, then, both chose "visibly trans" women not because of their physical features but more so based off dress in comparison to others who found these women unappealing because of their physical features and clothing. Amanda herself wore clothing like woman B and had brightly colored box braids, and she desired a woman that was a "hustler . . . because you know how to get money." Amanda's attraction to woman B because she "looks like [she has] that street life" highlighted her affiliation for pariah femininities. Amanda did not desire a woman who embodied hegemonic femininities nor White, middle-class femininity. "More visibly trans" women like woman B displayed a pariah femininity that, for Amanda, was desirable not because of how it looked but for what it represented.

In comparison to Amanda, Cookie, a middle-income, cis-homoflexible, Master's degree-holding, Black woman desired a woman who was, in her words, "equally yoked" vis-à-vis education and income. She was currently going through a separation with her wife, and Cookie had been financially supporting them both while her wife was in law school. Cookie found woman A to be the most desirable of the eight photos. I asked Cookie to explain why, and she responded:

> I mean, she's cute. I can't say she's necessarily chocolate, but I could tell she's, you know, she's of, of the descent. Um I will say she looks professional which I find attractive. Something about, um I don't know something about like a, a,

Table 2.2 Average Photo Rankings by Education

Sub-Sample	Woman A	Woman B	Woman C	Woman D	Woman E	Woman F	Woman G	Woman H
High School Diploma or Less	7.8	5.1	7.0	7.2	5.7	5.0	5.3	6.1
Some College, Vocational School, or Bachelor's Degree	7.3	4.1	7.5	3.7	6.3	4.6	3.9	5.6

Figure 2.3   Woman A.

a woman in power that I like. So like leadership type swag like, you know, you know how to dress well you know how to handle your business, whatever, like I love that. Um, so yeah, she would be the highest.

Prior to this moment in the interview, Cookie had explained to me that she was most attracted to other dark-skinned, Black women. Woman A had a lighter complexion, but Cookie still desired her because she was of African descent. For Cookie and other Black, cis-LBQ women, race mattered vis-à-vis desirability; in that, they particularly desired other Black women. Further, Cookie, like Amanda did not necessarily find this woman to be the most desirable of the eight based on her physical looks. Instead, she desired this woman, as well, for what she represented. Cookie desired a woman who embodied a middle-class, respectable femininity different from the "street look" or pariah femininity embodied by "more visibly trans" women.

Mignon Moore notes the disdain for transgressive, Black lesbian women who embody a racialized and non-middle-class masculinity.[10] Similarly, many of my participants did not find the hyperfemininity of the "more visibly trans" women to be attractive, in part, due to how they dressed. Woman B's dress and cheap wig and woman G's dress, cheap wig, and caked on makeup were often the first things participants mentioned upon seeing these two photos. The differences between Amanda, Liz, and Cookie were emblematic

Figure 2.4   On the Left, Woman B. On the Right, Woman G.

of differences between numerous participants of differing social classes. The embodiment of pariah femininities rather than a respectable, professional femininity by photos of "more visibly trans" women was less desirable to middle-class participants and/or participants with a college education. Further, their expression of said femininity also correlated with participants perceiving them to be trans.

This was particularly exemplified in my interview with Mack a middle-income, cis-het, Black man who was in the process of finishing his bachelor's degree. Mack described woman B in this way:

Mack: Um, her face is too bold for me. A one [for woman B]. Her face is too bold.
Alithia: Too bold, what do you mean?
Mack: Um like strong, manly picture. But [clears throat] I think it probably be a man, but [pause] that's who she wanna be you know? But that's not my type. Yeah, so probably be a one. Yeah, her weave is all fucked up too see? Her weave is fucked up son. You know what I'm sayin? And he didn't even do his eyebrows right. He looks like, he's confused, not confused about being transgender, but he's not doin' it right? You know like he's, he's not, he doesn't take care of his hair. You know what I'm sayin'? And then them eyebrows are fuckin' hideous. If you're gonna do it son, get your eyebrows done. The red makeup, like it looks you just did it just to do it. Like I don't get it. This is a cheap, very cheap, yeah it's, that would be, if it was still my type, that's still not my type. It's cheap. That's ratchet. Too ratchet son. Ratchet, ratchet, ratchet.

Woman B's more "visibly trans" appearance rendered her "masculine" and "manly" for Mack, Liz, and other participants. Mack, too, criticized the woman for not passing as cisgender. Her "failure" to do so rendered her "performance" as woman a poor performance. If she is "going to decide" to be a woman, then she must be the ideal of middle-class, White womanhood. Her wig/weave must be high quality and well groomed, her eyebrows must be thin and arched, and her makeup must be more "natural." Mack's perception of this woman as trans was, in large part, shaped by classed understandings of femininities. Her aesthetic represented a lower class look that rendered her Other than woman. Cis-het men and cis-LBQ women's discourse regarding photos of trans women explicated the role class plays in terms of "passability." Income, education, and class not only shape the opportunities trans women have to pass (i.e., through attaining hormone replacement therapy, gender affirmation surgery, or other gender-affirming needs) but also shaped, for my participants, the ways in which women's bodies were viewed, with professionally dressed women wearing minimal makeup viewed as more desirable than other women. Indeed, middle-income participants rated photos A, C, and H most highly, all of which are women who appear more professional, in business clothing, and/or with a muted aesthetic.

"That's a Question Mark": Race, Passing, and the Discourse of Desire

In the previous section, I focused on the numeric ranking of photos by education and income, and I discussed the ways in which class shaped notions of "passability" and "proper" femininity. Now, I flesh out the ways in which "passability" and race shaped participant attraction to the photos I provided during interviews. I include word clouds that capture the most frequent words used by participants when discussing each photo (see figures *2.5–2.12*).

Figure 2.5   Woman A.

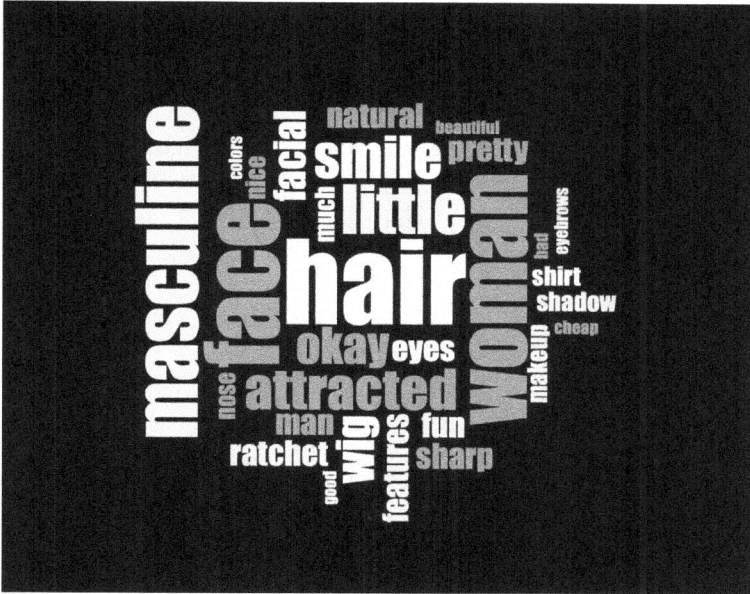

Figure 2.6   Woman B.

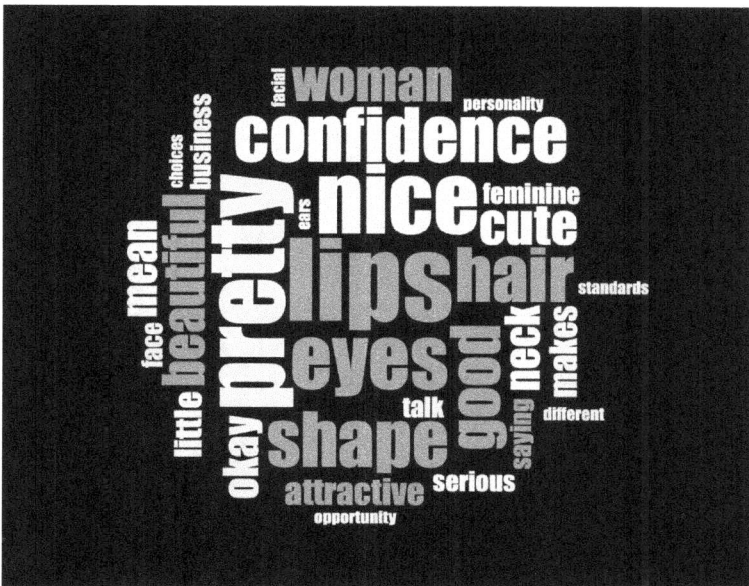

Figure 2.7   Woman C.

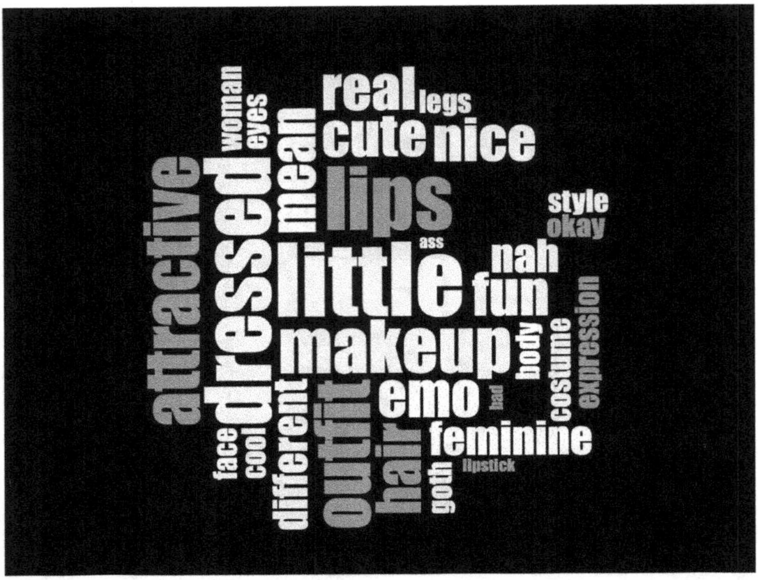

Figure 2.8   Woman D.

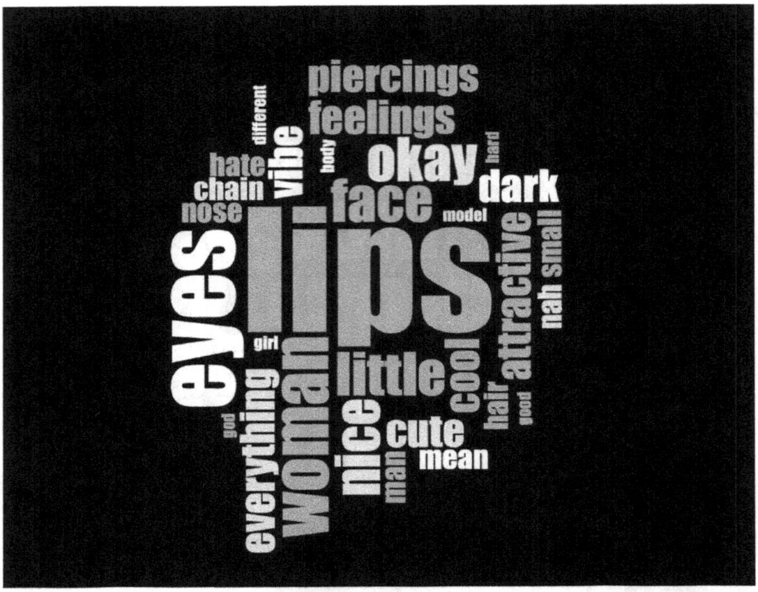

Figure 2.9   Woman E.

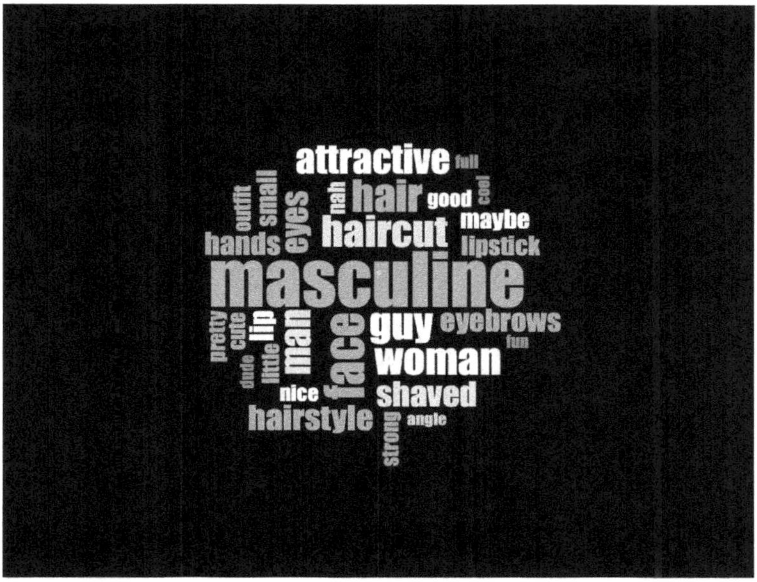

Figure 2.10   Woman F.

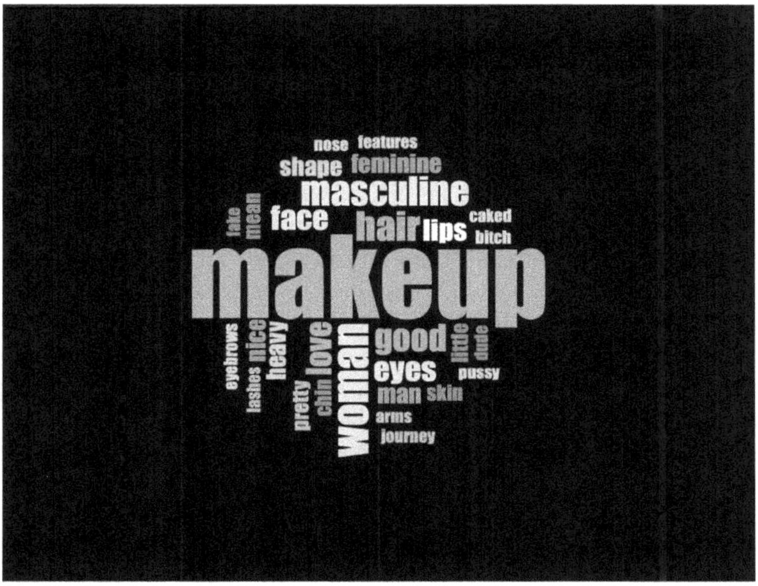

Figure 2.11   Woman G.

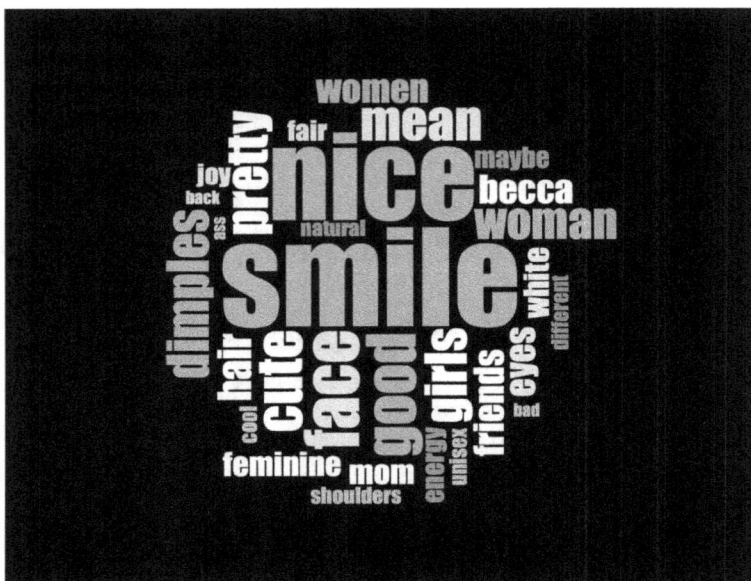

Figure 2.12   Woman H.

I use the word clouds to aid in elucidating how participants conceptualized hyperfemininity as masculine and the different ways Blackness, whiteness, and mixed-ness/racial ambiguity were viewed and referenced by participants.

As I described in the previous section, participants, on average, did not find more "visibly trans" women as desirable as they did "cis passing" women. This finding was not surprising. What did surprise me was how participants often conceptualized woman B and woman G as masculine. These two women both wore dresses in bright and flashy styles, wore long hair with makeup, and visible cleavage. Despite their hyperfeminine appearance, participants repeatedly felt a lack of desire to these two women for "strong" and/ or "masculine" features. Among the most common words used to describe woman B were "masculine," "woman," "man," "ratchet," and "sharp" in regard to her facial features—in particular her jaw bone. While some participants did still refer to her as a woman, just as many referred to her as a man, because they did not feel she was "really" a woman. The word "ratchet," here, comes from African American Vernacular English (AAVE). Black YouTube performer Philip Hudson explains, "Ratchet is basically a lack of home training—being out in public and acting like you don't have any sense. Putting a weave in the microwave just to curl it, that's ratchet."[11] As I show momentarily, woman B repeatedly was referred to as ratchet regarding her wig and her clothing. She was simultaneously described as both over the top and not "doing well enough" at "trying" to be a woman. Woman G, as well, was repeatedly referred to as "masculine." While some participants did note her femininity, they did so to highlight that she was "too" feminine, as if her femininity were an over-the-top performance or an ill curated performance. Her "too caked on" makeup, wig, and strong arms were invoked to refer to her as a "man" by numerous participants.

For example, when I asked Adam, a low-income, cis-het, Middle Eastern man who was in the process of finishing his bachelor's degree, about woman G, he described the photo as such:

alithia: Okay, what about [woman G]?
Adam: Uhh, you mean this man? [pause] No. No. . . . I think it's fake. Everything is fake. . . . I'm being generous giving her a one.
alithia: Okay [both laugh]. Is it because everything is fake or?
Adam: Yes and it's masculine, it's like [pause] it's like having [pause] why [pause] woman has, woman should not have, good shape, you know, it's okay like you know . . . being in good shape and but not masculine. Because she's a woman. Masculine is mostly for men. If she playing a sport, understandable. Like, she is doing a challenging thing but [pause] yes. Uh that's why I don't like her, to me, is like a guy.

Adam's description of masculinity as something for men is in contradiction with the reality of studs, butches, masculine straight women, and intersex women who have physical traits often deemed "masculine." For Adam, a strong figure with muscular arms and shoulders corresponds to a man's body. Adam, much like other men, conceptualized women as individuals meant to complement a man. Norms of hegemonic masculinities and femininities, in which hegemonic masculinities are those masculinities that are different, "opposite," and complementary to hegemonic femininities, shaped participants' responses to these photos.[12] A man "is supposed" to have muscles, a large body, a strong figure, a broad jaw. A woman "is supposed" to be dainty, small, and narrow. The woman must be able to fit into the physical and metaphorical crevices of a man. She is nurturing while he is protecting. She is weak while he is strong. She is soft while he is rough. A woman's masculinity rids her, for Adam, of her womanhood. She becomes not only no longer woman but no longer desirable. Further, despite woman H wearing an enormous amount of makeup, a flashy, camisole-cut dress, long blonde hair, and bright lipstick, she remains conceptualized as masculine.

While sociologists and scholars of women's, gender, and sexuality studies distinguish between gender expression, gender identity, and sex assigned at birth, that simply is not the case for most cis-het men participants I interviewed. Cis-LBQ women accepted that women can be masculine or feminine, as many of them either were studs/butches, dated studs/butches, or felt they were neither masculine nor feminine. Even they, though, conceptualized more "visibly trans" women's bodies as masculine. Others, such as Kylee who, herself, was a stud, desired masculine features on "cis-passing" women but not on more "visibly trans" women. Hyperfemininity, instead of deeming a body feminine, remains separated from the "visibly trans" woman's "masculine" body. Any semblance of an assignment of male at birth relegates her body to the realm of masculinity for participants like Adam. While participants conceptualized masculinity and femininity more flexibly for other cis people and photos of "cis passing" women, masculinity and femininity were conceptualized as rigid categories that did not overlap. "Masculine" features of a body overpowered, in a sense, the hyperfemininity of dress that trans women in these photos may indeed have been utilizing to pass. Paechter notes that the differences between hegemonic femininities and masculinities are actually not that great in extent. Instead, the difference is in the mobilization of power.[13] Similarly, cis and "cis-passing" women are able to mobilize and utilize power through hegemonic femininities and hyper-femininities, while "visibly trans" women are unable to do so.

These notions of what is a feminine body and what is a masculine body are not only sexist and cissexist, but they are also dyadist; that is, they are endemic to the oppression of intersex people. Intersex people assigned female at birth with what is medically termed congenital adrenal hyperplasia (CAH) may develop clitorises that are larger in size—and may indeed even resemble a penis—"or labia that look like a scrotum," as well as "dense body hair, a receding hairline, deep voice, prominent muscles," and other "masculine" traits. If they are "untreated" before going through puberty, intersex people assigned male at birth with CAH may, on average, be much shorter as adults than others.[14] Cis women with polycystic ovary syndrome (PCOS) may develop facial and body hair in "a male pattern."[15] What is masculine and what is feminine when the human body does not naturally fit into dyadic categories of sex and gender?

Indeed, even participants felt confused about bodies as they discussed them. Spiderman, a cis-het, Black man high school graduate living below/near poverty, felt that woman G was a man, and I asked him to explain why. He responded:

Spiderman: I can tell by the um [pause] the, the, the, the chin. And right here, the chin and the shape, and right here [points to the chin dimple].
alithia: What about women who have the dimple? So women can't have a dimple?
Spiderman: I've never ever seen a woman like that.
alithia: No? My mom as a dimple.
Spiderman: Really? Oh! I've never seen that.

The physical features participants discussed were often contradictory, arbitrary, or entirely nonsensical, such as Spiderman's here. I did not bring attention to it for fear of outing myself, but I too have a chin dimple. During the interview, though, Spiderman did not question my chin dimple. On the contrary, he commented on his physical attraction to me and suggested we date after the interview. A chin dimple on woman G who is "more visibly trans" made her a man. However, a chin dimple on a "cis-passing" woman, such as myself in that moment, is not even recognized as there. Cis women and "cis-passing" women's bodies are given greater latitude to do masculinities and/or to have "masculine" features, while more "visibly trans" women are punished for these qualities even when doing hyperfemininity.

Kylee, a cis-lesbian, Black woman living below/near poverty who was in the process of finishing her bachelor's degree, for example, found "masculine" facial features appealing on "cis-passing" women but not on those who were more "visibly trans." Kylee found woman A, a "cis-passing," Black woman, to be very desirable. When I asked her to explain why, she told me:

Kylee: Um she has a nice nose, nice jawline. She has nice bone structure, yeah.
alithia: What about her bone structure and her nose is nice to you?
Kylee: Um [pause] it's just like sharp. I like sharp features yeah. Um, symmetrical I guess. I like her hair too. It's long. Yeah.

Shortly after, though, Kylee explained that she did not find woman B very desirable. She rated her a four on a scale of one to ten, and I asked Kylee to explain her reasoning. Kylee explained:

Kylee: Um . . . maybe uh too sharp. Too sharp yeah.
alithia: Of facial features?
Kylee: Yeah sharper facial features.

Figure 2.13   On the Left, Woman A. On the Right, Woman G.

I was unable to get Kylee to explain further. She, in general, was not a particularly talkative participant but was even more reticent when discussing the photos. However, in these small exchanges during the interview, Kylee highlighted a desire for sharp features with woman A before, and, soon after, Kylee did not find a woman desirable because of her sharp facial features. Both woman A and woman B have flatter, broader jaws, often attributed to individuals assigned male at birth. Woman B's face, though, is longer, with a longer jaw, longer forehead, and a more prominent nose than woman A. Woman B is also more "visibly trans" because of these features. "Masculine" facial features made woman A a ten out of ten for Kylee, but on a "visibly trans" woman, those features functioned to make her less desirable.

It is important, as well, to highlight the raced desire for a smaller jaw in a woman. While, in the United States and other parts of the West, a more narrow, v-shaped, soft jaw is characterized as a desirable, "feminine" jaw, such a jaw is more likely to adorn the faces of White women. Indeed, "during slavery . . . Black women with darker-skin hues, kinky hair, *and broader facial features* tended to be field slaves" rather than enslaved within the household, around enslaved masters, their families, and their guests.[16] The desire for a narrow jaw reflects cissexist and racist desires for particular women. One common facial "feminization" procedure for trans women is a mandible and chin contour, which involves the shaving down of jaw and chin bone, smoothing out the area, and creating a narrow, soft jaw. Richie notes, "Attempts at medical feminization [for cis and trans women] are constitutive of a White, youthful, exaggerated ideal."[17] Whiteness and cissexism function in tandem in the conceptualization of a desirable, "feminine" face.

This same process occurred across participants. "Masculine" features repeatedly were praised on "cis-passing" women and disparaged on "visibly trans" women. Peaches, a cis-bi/queer, mixed Black woman with a bachelor's degree and living below/near poverty, found woman C, a "cis-passing," Asian American woman to be "really cute." Peaches rated her an eight out

Figure 2.14   On the Left, Woman C. On the Right, Woman G.

of ten, and explained, "She gives me like um [pause] I like, she has a smaller neck, I like her neck too, and I like that like her shoulder blades are out and like really prominent." In comparison, Jake, a low-income, cis-het, Black man, found woman G to be entirely undesirable. He referred to her as a "dude . . . pretending to be a woman." I asked Jake repeatedly to explain to me why he found her unattractive and believed her to be a man. Each time, he would tell me, "You can just tell." Finally, I asked, "Let's say I'm an alien coming from outer space. I don't understand human genders. Explain it to me." At this point, Jake was able to shift out of his belief that it is merely "common sense" that everyone can tell who is a woman and who is a man and the qualities that make up each category. Jake said:

> Okay, look at this, you see this arm right here? That shit is too muscular. Now you got women who work out, alright? But that shit is too muscular, and let me tell you why. It's because, if you look right here [points to shoulders], like bruh you can see this shit.

On "cis-passing" women, participants, like Peaches, found more prominent features like strong shoulder blades to be attractive. At the same time, participants also found muscular arms, prominent shoulders, and other "large" bodily features to be unattractive on more "visibly trans" women. On "cis-passing" women, such features result in them being viewed as more attractive than they otherwise would be seen to be. On more "visibly trans" women, these features come to distinguish them from "real" women and to be used as "evidence" that they are not cisgender.

Standardizing the Body

While it could be argued that these characterizations of bodies as desirable or undesirable are merely relegated to the level of preference or individual taste, these characterizations come to form part of a larger structure cissexism within the United States. These same sorts of contradictory, arbitrary, and nonsensical ways of conceptualizing, gendering, and sexing bodies proliferate on blogs across the web "warning" cis-het men about what to look for in a woman to spot a "tranny." One blogger encourages cis-het men to ask girls to do an "elbow" test, for example. Amante explains that when a cisgender woman stretches out her arms and her elbows are facing the floor, the arm will bend and arc at a 195 degree angle, while a cisgender man's elbow will not entirely unbend, only unbending to a 158 degree angle.[18] Others, like Pattaya Nightlife, explain to cis-het men traveling to Thailand how to take care not to take a "ladyboy" home. Much as participants conceptualized hyperfemininity as masculine, this tourist blog explains that excess marks a person as Khatoey and not a "woman." They explain, "Ladyboys do not just exaggerate their femininity; they exaggerate everything! Every word and action is excessively flamboyant." This exaggeration marks a woman as not only "unnaturally" feminine but "unnaturally" a woman. While these characterizations may seem strange, wild, or confusing to some, they come to form the logic of others.

What influenced my participants' notions of a desirable woman also influenced the Department of Housing and Urban Development's proposed regulation under 24 CFR Part 5 to allow homeless shelters to refuse service to transgender people. In these regulations, HUD offered ways to know if a woman is transgender or not. To identify who is trans and who is cis, HUD offered "reasonable considerations," which "may include, but are not limited to a combination of factors such as height, the presence (but not the absence) of facial hair, the presence of an Adam's apple, and other physical characteristics which, when considered together, are indicative of a person's biological sex."[19] Who, for the Trump administration, counted as a woman and who did not? Must cisgender women with facial hair also sleep on the streets if homeless? Must cisgender women with higher levels of testosterone resulting in more prominent Adam's apples be excluded from women's shelters? Ideas of who is desirable, what constitutes a woman, and what constitutes a desirable woman are part of the same discourse used to qualify some for rights and others for marginalization.

Standards applied as to what counts as a "real" woman versus a "tranny," as well, are not only cis-centric but also Eurocentric. Amante's blog, for example, directs readers to look at a woman's hands and feet to determine if she is a woman or a "tranny." Amante, too, warns of a "man" nose, or in other words, a large nose on a woman, while others warn of large foreheads, for example. The depiction of certain noses as not womanly or less than womanly also proliferates within anti-Semitic and anti-Black discourse. The desire for small, narrow noses is a Eurocentric desire. Scientific attempts to root race in the body have also aimed to analyze differences in hand size and nose size between Whites and Black people, finding Black people's hands to be "larger" than Whites, and White noses to be longer and more narrow than Black women's.[20] What comes to qualify a woman as a woman is not merely gendered but raced.[21] Cis-centricity and Eurocentricity are bound together in what constitutes a woman and what constitutes a desirable woman.

Further, those who fit cis-Eurocentric standards of beauty and are White come to shape the ideal of womanhood. Hegemonic femininities that shaped participants' discourse above regarding the photos of women used during interviews are not only cissexist but also anti-Black.[22] Participants repeatedly described woman A and woman H in varying, racialized ways. Among the most common words stated by participants about the two were Black and White, respectively, which is not surprising, given that woman A is Black and woman

H is White. It is surprising, though, that this is the case given other women's races were not as invoked as these two. The two, as "cis-passing," Black and White women were also ranked among the most desirable women, with cis-het men on average rating woman H as the most desirable and cis-LBQ women rating woman A as the most desirable. Participants across race-gender, though, differed in how they responded to the races of these two women.

Racing Desire

Musiteli, a cis-het, low-income, Black man attending a technical school, was particularly attracted to Black women. However, he desired light-skinned women more than dark-skinned women. He acknowledged during the interview how colorism influenced his attractions, but he did not have any sense of urgency or desire to undo this influence. Regarding woman A, Musiteli told me that he would rate her a nine. When I asked him to explain why, he responded:

> Um I guess the symmetry in the face um, jawline um . . . has like attractive, I don't know how to describe it, it's like um [pause] I guess it's well-defined. Um, um I like her hair, I like her hair, that's uh, that's really attractive, Black so she gets a, she gets a bonus in my head automatically [both laugh]. Or she could not be, but the shading of the background throws it off. But if she is, she gets one, an extra point, but if she's not, she gets an 8, which is still good.

While non-Black participants did not often desire Black women over White women or other women of color, Black cis-LBQ women and some Black cis-het men participants, like Musiteli, specifically became more

Figure 2.15   On the Left, Woman A. On the Right, Woman H.

attracted to a woman if she were Black. Musiteli could see himself talking to, getting to know, and dating. Black participants were more likely than others to prefer monoracial partnerships.

In comparison to Cookie and Musiteli, Ryan, a cis-het, Asian/Indian American man living below/near poverty, was uncertain regarding woman A specifically because of her Blackness. Talking to me about woman A, Ryan stated:

Ryan: She seems to have a fit body but uh just her hairstyle is like not really speaking to me personally.
alithia: How come?
Ryan: Um I don't know, I've never dated who, who's Black and I've never like had any experiences with like somebody with that kind of hair, like I've never even yeah, like yeah my friend's Black, I've like touched his hair before but like never in like any other situation, so I'm just not familiar with it really and same with just dating a Black person in general. I'm not against it but I just have no experience with it so that's why I'm just like kind of like on the fence, but she seems attractive yeah.

Rather than explicitly saying he is or is not attracted to Black women, Ryan tried to center the conversation on his uncertainty with and lack of proximity to Blackness. Ryan did not make similar comments about other women, though. Woman A's hair, though, is in long braids, draped to one side. From the picture, one cannot decipher woman A's hair texture. His discourse, here, was also choppier than in other parts of the interview. When I asked him why he did not like woman A's hair, his thoughts became scattered. Hair, in essence, became an easier object to fix his attention on in saying that he is unsure if he could find a Black woman attractive or develop a relationship with a Black woman. Hair is something that is styled in numerous ways, is easily changed with weave/extensions, wigs, and hats. It is something that people have preferences in and speak openly of their preferences in hair. For example, it would not be uncommon to hear a straight man say he would not want his girlfriend to shave her head bald. To say that one does not want to date a Black woman or is unsure if they want to becomes more explicitly racist. The four non-Black, cis-het men I interviewed all chose women who were not Black as the most desirable of those photographed. Two of eleven of Black, cis-het men and nine out of seventeen of cis-LBQ women (six of whom were Black women) found woman A or woman F to be the most desirable.

Two cis-het, Black men and one cis-het, White man found woman C (a "cis-passing," Asian American woman) to be the most desirable, with no cis-het man finding either Latina photo to be the most desirable. Two cis-LBQ,

Figure 2.16   Top Row (Left to Right): Woman B and Woman C. Bottom Row (Left to Right): Woman E and Woman F.

Black women, found woman C to be the most desirable, two found woman E (a "cis-passing," Latina) to be the most desirable, and one selected woman B (a more "visibly trans" Latina).

Those who chose these women were more likely to fetishize "foreign," racially ambiguous, and/or mixed-race women. Gee, a low-income, cis-het, Black man, for example, found "exotic and foreign women" to be the most desirable women, with a particular desire for Dominican, Colombian, "Hispanic," and immigrant Black women. Vincent, as well, a middle-income, cis-lesbian, White woman, was particularly attracted to "ethnically ambiguous" women. When I asked Vincent whether race shapes her attraction to women, she explained:

Vincent: They're normally either pretty uh ethnically ambiguous or uh Hispanic.
alithia: What do you think maybe attracts you more to ethnically ambiguous and Hispanic women than other women?
Vincent: Um I mean they tend to have like black [colored] hair, curlier hair, stuff like that. Uh I'm just gonna sound super weird but it's the eyebrows. You know? Like it's a certain shape in em. . . . Like thicker? More, like not unibrow thick but like. . . [trails off and digresses]
alithia: Do you have any hesitancy dating other women?

Vincent: I have never really been attracted to like the blond haired, blue eyed, kind of White women. I think I, yeah, I dated a couple Black women. But that's not like. . . when I think of my type I don't normally think of a Black woman.

Vincent and other White, cis-LBQ women repeatedly attempted to distance themselves from whiteness throughout interviews. Vincent's lack of desire is not for *a* "blond haired, blue eyed," White woman but, instead, for what she represents. Vincent is not attracted to that *kind of White woman.*

Vincent and other cis-LBQ, White women repeatedly attempted to distance themselves from whiteness. In this process, White womanhood was conceptualized as bland, heterosexual, ignorant, and unexciting. Vincent's desire ignores the fact that Latina and/or ethnically ambiguous women may in fact be Black and/or multiracial. Still, the "ethnically ambiguous" woman is far enough away from, yet similar enough to, whiteness in comparison to the "obviously" Black woman. In interviews with multiracial and multiethnic individuals, Waring highlights how "racial ambiguity, gender and sexuality intersect to generate intimate opportunities that . . . are unavailable to non-racially ambiguous women."[23] Waring's participants even pointed to the gendered-racialized work White women and Black women do to appear ambiguous by tanning and/or straightening their hair, respectively. Stepanova and Strube's research, as well, found "mixed-race faces [to be] perceived as more attractive than single-race faces."[24] The women Vincent is attracted to have dark, curly (but not tightly coiled) hair, thick eyebrows, and, although she does not say it, light skin. Gee, for example, desired "exotic and foreign women," because they were a mystery, a "question mark" in his words, that he could learn and grow from.

Ryan, too, desired particularly racialized women. Toward the end of interviews, I asked all participants whether everyone is entitled to their own preferences and/or whether individuals should problematize their preferences. Ryan felt that everyone should be able to desire whatever qualities they desire in a woman without critique. He felt that individuals' preferences would change on their own if they were meant to. To explicate this, he told me:

I've had phases before like where I like, liked certain like, I can just talk about it, I had a phase where I really liked Asian girls in like, it was like for one year in high school, and like and my friends would all make fun of me for that, 'cause like it was like a really apparent thing. Like Oriental Asian girls, like not like Asian or Middle Eastern, like none of that, it was just like Oriental Asian girls. . . . Chinese, Korean, Japanese, it was just that, but it only lasted for like a year.

Ryan believed his preference was merely a fleeting occurrence that happened out of nowhere. Yet his desire for East Asian women reflects a colorist, Indian hierarchy of desire in which "the lighter you are, the higher on the hierarchy you stand."[25] Ryan continued to have a lack of desire for Black women at the time of our interview. Southeast Asian women are more likely than East Asian women to also have darker skin, and it is here that the connection between a lack of desire for Blackness and a preference for "Oriental" Asian-ness connect. The White woman and the East Asian woman both form the ideal of Western, hegemonic femininities.

Mack, too, fetishized Asian women, as well as Latina women. Mack's fetish, though, was for particular Asian women, much like Ryan's. Mack had told me he prefers to date Black women and that he would not date a White woman. I asked him whether he had any hesitancy dating Indigenous, Latina, and/or Asian American women, to which he responded:

> I love em. I love em. Latinas, Asians, Indian. I don't like the hairy Indians though. I don't like hair, nah you should've asked hair on the arms, do that count? Yes, like oooh, I'm sorry! I understand that it comes naturally, it's just something, I don't want a hairy girl or facial hair . . . Um [pause] Indians, I don't really like Indians as much as I like everybody else. Cuz the smell on Indians like . . . the other side a Guyanese, so my girl's Black Guyanese, the other side of Guyanese is like y'all n****s stink. Like y'all smell like curry all the time, son.

Both Mack and Ryan desired Asian women, and in Mack's case Latinas, who hold greater proximity to whiteness. Mack's fiancée at the time of the interview was Afro-Guyanese, and while he preferred Black women at this time in his life, he had previously preferred Latinas and Asian American women. As highlighted in chapter 1, Mack's aversion to hairy women is both cissexist and racist. The desire for hairless, smooth-skinned women arose in the United States through Darwinian logic that posited women were supposedly less hairy than men because of men's natural selection of "superior," hairless women as mates historically, which "bred out" the possibility of hairy women.[26] Odor, too, is not mere individual preference. Odor historically and contemporarily figures into typologies of race. The racialized disgust with particular smells can be traced, for example, to the 1700s, with novels and works of nonfiction characterizing Black people as having "bestial or fetid smell."[27]

Woman H, a "cis-passing," White woman, for example, was repeatedly referred to as "rice," "mom," "Becca/Becky," and other similar words. Becca/Becky, here, was a reference by participants to a particular representation of White women who are racially ignorant, prone to harming Black people by

Figure 2.17   Woman H.

calling the police, for example, and hypersensitive to being critiqued or called out for their racism. Non-Black participants and Black cis-het men participants repeatedly viewed woman H as someone who "looks like their mom" or a woman who could be a soccer mom in a suburban neighborhood. Viewing someone as a mom is not, generally, a particularly sexy conceptualization in US society. Despite this, seven cis-het men participants found woman H to be the most desirable. Five of these seven were Black men, one was Middle Eastern and White-passing, and one was Indian/Asian American. Only two cis-LBQ women selected woman H as the most desirable. One was Black, and the other was a Brown, Latina woman who desired White and/or light-skinned Brown women only. Interestingly, no White participant selected woman H as the most desirable. Black, cis-LBQ women, in contrast, were more likely to express a discomfort with dating White women or a lack of desire for White women. Cookie, for example, found woman H to be the least attractive of the photos presented. When I asked her why, she explained:

Cookie: The challenge I foresee with her is, you know, like the cultural thing, the racial cultural thing, um [sigh] it's, I don't know it's hard. Because like I said, I mean I could be friends with someone all day. But my thing is like when I'm dating or when I'm, cuz I also don't do a lot of dating like it's all about connection to me and building [pause] it's I don't have like flings or like late night stands or whatever. So it's like, you're in my life if I've shared things with you, you know, we're building something, whether it's a friendship or whatever of some sort.

alithia: And her whiteness might make that hard?

Cookie: I mean, we could, like I said we could have, like my best friend is a White guy, his, well I don't know if I could say his name, my best friend is a White guy and like, we've been friends since seventh grade. And I love him to death. I mean, he's a guy. So it's a little different, you know, but it's like, as far as intimacy and telling you my deepest, darkest secrets and fears and, you know, going to your family's house and expecting to be looked at the same as if you brought some White guy or White girl there, it's gonna be completely different. And that's scary. And it's kind of uncomfortable. Because I've gotten so much, you know, kind of hatred or looks or whatever, because of my Blackness, because of my hair, because of my you know, orientation or whatever.

Cookie, here, highlighted the amount of vulnerability present within a relationship. As a Black woman, she remained vulnerable everywhere in society (e.g., at work, at school, when driving, and even when at the movies). She sought a relationship where she did not have to face anti-Black violence, and she could not trust a White woman to wholly embrace and love her Blackness. Cookie also pointed to what Steinbugler terms "race-work," or the effort that individuals in interracial relationships engage in to negotiate differences in racialized lived experiences and racialized power dynamics.[28] Whiteness, for Cookie, presented an unknown that was not enticing as the unknown of "ethnic ambiguity" or "exotic women" was for Vincent and Gee. The unknown of whiteness did not, for Cookie, present opportunities to learn, grow, and share in cultural enrichment. Instead, the unknown of whiteness presented opportunities to be harmed and let down.

In comparison, Mack focused on what woman H would bring to the relationship sexually, physically, and potentially in ways that would benefit Mack. Flipping the pages of the photos to woman H, Mack exclaimed:

Becca! (both laugh). Becca, damn, actually, it depends on her personality, but . . . off first looks, I'm not hollerin' at Becca (laugh). I'm not gonna lie, but nah. Becca don't got no ass or none of that. Yeah, Becca don't, Becca don't have no ass. I'm not hollerin' at her, her lip is skinny. Her top lip is very skinny. Becca look like she, we could smoke though. You know, we'd be cool. She cool. We'd smoke gas. She look like she'd give me some money though. Let's start a day-care together, Rebecca. Looks like she's got a daycare too. She's a soccer mom. She's totally down for that. I can see that in Rebecca.

Woman H is not particularly exciting. Mack's comments on her lips and butt point to a lack of sexual enticement. Woman 8's whiteness made her approachable, trustworthy (with children), and safe, allowing Mack to want to be her friend. Cookie and other Black women found a lack of ability to trust White women or a discomfort in being with them. In contrast, cis-het,

Black men like Mack found White women to be bland, unappealing, and not particularly noteworthy. Cookie did not find White women to be noteworthy, but she did not easily dismiss them either. For Mack, woman H is a joke. For Cookie, woman H is a worry. While stereotypical "Becky's" might call the police on Black men and in this way present trouble, Mack and the majority of cis-het, Black men I interviewed lived in racially segregated areas and mostly interacted with Black people, meaning that there was a lesser chance of interacting with White women and thus having to worry about them. In contrast, Cookie and other women like her worked in multiracial environments that did not provide the same distance.

Whiteness as Bland

White participants, too, found woman H to be bland and unappealing. Randall, a low-income, cis-het, White man, felt that woman H was too familiar to be desirable. Ranking woman H, Randall stated:

> Um, I think superficially you know, eight or nine [for woman H] but um . . . it also looks so generic and bland. Like I've seen that person 100 times on these, these apps [laughs]. Yeah, I mean, again, again nice smile, but it's just so plain. You know, I went to church with this girl I think growing up so.

For Randall and other White participants, woman H presented an already known, already had experience. There was nothing different between her and other White women on Tinder, OkCupid, or any other dating/hook-up app they were on. This same comment was not made about the other women, though. There are also many Black women, Asian American women, and Latina women who utilize these apps for intimacy, yet for Whites, it is White women like woman H who present a "generic," over-supplied product. This became apparent in their photo rankings and selections of the most desirable woman in the eight photos, as well. Both cis-het, White men participants chose a woman of color as the most desirable. One selected woman C (a "cis-passing," Asian American woman), and the other selected woman A (a "cis-passing," Black woman). Two cis-LBQ White woman chose woman A, as well. Another chose woman C, and a final woman chose woman G (a "visibly trans" White woman). As I stated earlier, no White person chose a White person as the most desirable of the photos.

During our interview, Vincent explained her response to woman H:

> I wouldn't date her. . . . I just feel like . . . I don't know... hmmm...knowing nothing about her, I'm gonna say something about her. Um I just feel like she'd have like a really limited perspective . . . on everything . . . Yeah. Kind of realized throughout this interview I'm kind of trying to distance myself from

whiteness and being White. Like, I am White and I...have moments where I will like be ignorant or say something ignorant, but like . . . I don't know. It's not like . . . she's not any more White than me. And it doesn't even work like that. So I don't really know.

Vincent, Randall, and other White participants were not somehow less White vis-à-vis personality, less violently White, or less physically White. However, when presented with a "cis-passing," White woman, they found her undesirable. In lacking desire for White women because of the women's whiteness, White participants did not merely reject these women and prefer and pursue women of color. Instead, their romantic choices and pursuit of women of color coincided with an unacknowledged, perchance subconscious, distancing of themselves from "those racist Whites." In doing so, they allowed themselves to cease doing the work that Whites must actively engage in to challenge racism. Vincent, though, was only one of two White participants to begin to realize this during the interview.

In addition to a viewing of whiteness as bland and unappealing, White cis-LBQ women participants also conceptualized whiteness as heterosexual, and a White-passing, cis-het man participant viewed woman H as more feminine than the other photos. This can be seen in the following exchange between Amy (a low-income, White, cis-lesbian Latina), Vincent, Rachel (a low-income, cis-lesbian, White woman), and Adam:

Amy: Can you have straight energy in a picture? [All women laugh.]

Vincent: I wouldn't say that but yeah [laughs].

Amy: 'Cause that's yeah, I couldn't remember everyone in these but then I was like oh yeah, the straight chick [all women laugh.]

Vincent: Mmm heterosexual. Yeah gotcha.

Rachel: This is also present in some of like the other photos, but she's like apparently happy and like warm; whereas, some of the other photos come off as more like serious or intimidating.

Adam: Yeah, that's true, and I totally agree with her, and she has that traditional look and um that smile. Makeup and long hair, I believe other women are kind of like more masculine and um . . . yeah. To me, as a man, I think she's attractive more than other pictures?

Repeatedly in interviews, White, cis-LBQ women referred to woman H as appearing heterosexual. Focus group participants were also shocked when I told them woman H is transgender. What is conceptualized here as traditionally feminine, warmth, kindness, and heterosexuality are intimately connected to woman H's "cis-passing" whiteness. Woman B, for example, is seen smiling, staring at whomever is taking her photo. Yet, Adam and Rachel conceptualize woman H as the only photo that is not intimidating, masculine, and/or closed off to others. Women A and C are also feminine, but their confidence is found intimidating. These views of Black women and Asian American women as intimidating, cold, and/or masculine are informed by controlling images[29] of Black women as the "Matriarch" and Asian American women as the "Dragon Lady."[30]

Cis-ness and whiteness here worked in tandem to produce a particular version of womanhood. Woman G, too, was White. However, she wore flashy, hyperfeminine, exaggerated clothing and makeup. She was more "visibly trans" and did not fit ideals of White, hegemonic femininities. Woman H, though, as a "cis-passing," White woman became the warm, kind, nurturing counterpart to the intimidating, cold, and masculine trans women/women of color. Anti-Blackness, whiteness, and cissexism are intertwined in these conceptualizations of woman H by White/White-passing participants and Black men participants. In this section, I have detailed how cissexism, whiteness, and anti-Blackness functioned jointly in participants' conceptualizations of a desirable woman. White supremacy, colonization, and anti-Blackness birthed cissexism and binarism. As such, they continued into the present, hand-in-hand, in the discourse of my participants.

"It's Not My Type of Woman": Gender-Blind Language

In his analysis of colorblind racism, Eduardo Bonilla-Silva conceptualized "abstract liberalism" as the use of "ideas associated with political liberalism (e.g., 'equal opportunity,' the idea that force should not be used to achieve social policy) and economic liberalism (e.g., choice, individualism) in an abstract manner to explain racial matters."[31] An example would be Whites stating that they simply prefer to date other Whites and should not be forced to date individuals of color—but *"they are not racist."* A similar form of discourse operated in my interviews with cis-het men and cis-LBQ women. Repeatedly, individuals utilized a language of preference and individual choice in tandem with coded language that I explicate below to highlight a lack of attraction to trans women without explicitly saying they are not attracted to trans women. Doing so allowed them to shift any culpability off of themselves, as they believed individuals should be free to date whomever they desire. However, they simultaneously did not want to appear transphobic.

I analyzed participant discourse, in part, through an attention to their speech patterns and body language. I categorized participant discourse as coded language when their responses relied heavily on tautological reasoning, were highly repetitive with participants having difficulty explaining what they meant, were more incoherent due to an increase in usage of speech fillers (e.g., um, uh), and/or coincided with more reticent or nervous body language.

When relevant, I highlight how their body language and responses jointly shaped my analysis in this section.

Henry, a cis-het, Black man living near/below poverty, for example, did not find woman B to be particularly attractive. When I asked Henry why, he responded:

> It's not my type of woman, but um, um just what I'm naturally attracted to. Just never been naturally attracted to um . . . Just because it's not that she's ugly, like she's definitely not ugly (laughs). But it's just I guess it's not my type, and I guess 'cause it's like I said. It's not my type.

Henry attempted repeatedly to say woman B is just not his type of woman without ever admitting that a trans woman is not his type of woman. With each photo of "more visibly trans" women, he repeated, "It's not my type." While he otherwise sat with his legs open wide, his arms relaxed on the chair arms, and a smile across his face, during these moments, his body shrank in, legs slightly closing and hands coming together, as he stopped smiling and his eyes bounced around the room rather than maintaining the eye contact we otherwise had throughout the interview. I asked Henry, as I did all participants, if the woman he found most desirable told him she was trans, would it change how desirable she was to him? He responded, "Uh yeah, only because I'm not into trans women." With each woman who was more "visibly trans," he rambled as he did above to say, "It's not my type of woman." He did not want to appear judgmental; thus, he did not refer to a woman's trans-ness until explicitly asked, assuming that by not referring to it, he was not perpetuating cissexism.

Figure 2.18   Woman B.

At the end of the interview, I asked Henry if there was anything else he would like to share, to which he replied:

> My dad is one of those people that shuns, "Oh, look at that boy-girl, look at that this-that," and I grew up with that, and I got to Atlanta and it was like "Pssh, like look around you, there are plenty of trans people," and like they're, it showed me that they can you know, people can work together and still accomplish and do whatever, it doesn't take away from the fact that they're less than people. They just made a choice to do that. . . . Like literally some of the coolest people I've ever met were trans, so no, seriously, like my, my cousin, her best friend is trans, and I was like, she's like dope! Like if you ever met her, she's really, I mean she's a business woman, but she's really dope, I was like this is, this is cool.

Henry made an appeal here to individual rights, equality, and the ability for all to have access to opportunities to survive and thrive. I did not ask any participants, though, about workplace discrimination, work opportunities, or the like. Instead, his comment here, as the ending comment after telling me he would not date trans women, was meant to signal to me that he was not cissexist. Trans women can exist around him. He can spend time with them, even find them "cool," but he simply cannot date them.

Friend-zoned

Other participants less explicitly used coded language to signify a lack of attraction to a trans woman. Cookie, for example, spoke to me of woman B, saying:

> Um . . . I swear I know her [woman B]. But nah she was cool. That was my boo if that's her. It might not be but it very, very well might be um it's so funny. . . . I would say like 4, that would be my, that would be my homie. We would have a lot of fun. Beautiful smile.

Without context, such a comment would not seem noteworthy. Cookie found the woman undesirable but still beautiful, with the potential to be the best of friends. However, shortly after, Cookie spoke to me of woman G. Cookie told me, "I, I've dated a trans woman, and it was great. Like, I love her, and I still talk to her to this day. Um . . . But I haven't . . . I've never experienced anything other than pussy." In both cases, Cookie was unsure of whether she could date a trans woman. She attempted, though, in woman B to say this by saying that they could be friends. Cis-LBQ women repeatedly made similar rhetorical maneuvers, explaining that "more visibly trans" women were beautiful but unattractive to them and that they could not be lovers, but they could be friends. In these cases, trans women are covertly relegated to the realm of friendship and out of the realm of desire. They are not someone who can be desired, but someone with whom it is enjoyable to spend time.

Hyperfemininity

Others, like Janelle, a middle-income, cis-queer, Black woman, cited dress, makeup, and aesthetics as a particular reason that they found a woman less attractive. As Janelle flipped to woman G, she remarked:

> Okay this, this woman is gonna get a 1 [woman G]. As in like, would I go up to her and be attracted to her and whatever. But like if I saw her, I'd be like go off sis, but like I'm not attracted to her. I just . . . like . . . a woman who is more natural. And I'm seeing a lot of like flashiness and it's too much.

Janelle celebrated and embraced woman G's attire but was overwhelmed by woman G's hyperfemininity. Often, participants like Janelle desired a natural look rather than one that was "flashier" or "exaggerated." As Amber Jamila Musser notes, there exists a cultural desire in which individuals wish to be able to see "objectively" what, who, how, and all there is to know of a person on their surface.[32] Makeup, flashy, hyperfeminine, and/or exaggerated clothing, jewelry, weave/extensions, and wigs, rather than being seen as an extension of a person, become seen as a covering up of what is "natural." Black, Latinx, and/or trans aesthetics, though, exist amid excess, surplus, and plurality.[35] A focus on dress, hyper femininity, and makeup, additionally, ignores the reality in which trans women live. Trans women must appear

Figure 2.19   Woman G.

resolutely feminine to others lest they are questioned or denigrated for their gender, as seen in Mack's comments earlier in this chapter. Makeup addition-ally allows a woman to contour her face, allowing her to portray a face that is societally seen as more "feminine." While participants like Janelle desired a "natural face," they also conceptualized women's faces, such as woman F who wears little to no makeup, as masculine. Trans women are caught in a double bind. On both ends of this bind, cis participants discussed facial structure or aesthetic as the reason for a lack of attraction rather than explic-itly saying they did not desire trans women, yet the facial structure and the aesthetic are a part of trans-ness.

Coded language, as in the case of Henry, Cookie, and Janelle, allowed participants to present gender-blind arguments as to why they were unat-tracted to "visibly trans" women. Rather than overtly stating that they thought these women were "dudes" or "ugly" or other such remarks as others made in the previous sections, they invoked language of preference, friendship, and individual choice. Rather than making their comments less egregious or unproblematic, though, this discursive maneuver merely allows cissexism to remain harder to find and more difficult to root out.

CONCLUSION

Race, gender, class, and education shaped participants' ranking of photos of women regarding how desirable they perceived each woman to be. Each of these factors mattered in terms of how, in particular, "more visibly trans" women and/or Black women were ranked. Those with a lower level of edu-cational attainment and lower incomes rated "more visibly trans" women and/ or Black more highly than others. It is important, of course, to recognize that across these categories, "visibly trans" women and/or Black women were still ranked lower than others. For example, even though those with only a high school diploma or less rated "visibly trans" women more highly than those with a college education, they still rated "visibly trans" women lower than they did "cis-passing" women. The differences, here, were by gradation.

Further, classed and raced norms of femininities shaped the ways in which "more visibly trans" women's bodies were interpreted, with White, "cis-pass-ing," and/or professionally dressed women being viewed as more desirable by participants. Photos of "visibly trans" women were viewed as masculine even when appearing in hyperfeminine attire. While cis women and "cis-passing" women are able to have the same physical features (such as a chin dimple) or dress in hyperfeminine attire and still be viewed as feminine, women like woman G who wore hyperfeminine clothing but did not "pass" as cisgender were conceptualized as masculine.

To end, I want to highlight the gendered differences in how cis-LBQ women and cis-het men responded to and ranked the photos before turning to why "preferences" and desire matter. Throughout the interviews, cis-LBQ women, across race, had a harder time ranking and discussing photos of women than cis-het men did. Two cis-LBQ women participants would rank a woman or respond to a photo and immediately follow their response with an apology. An additional six cis-LBQ women explicitly told me that they had a difficult time doing the ranking. Two women who had the most difficult time rating women and repeatedly signaled discomfort with ranking women were both White; one was middle-income and the other lived off parental income that fell in the highest income tax brackets. In comparison, only one cis-het man had a difficult time ranking. This participant's difficulty, though, lay in his desire to know more about their personalities, who they were, and for greater context. Cis-LBQ women, in contrast, found it hard to rank not because they needed more context. Instead, they simply did not want to attribute numbers to other women. Women, more than men, are expected within US society to remain polite and to be kind, nice, and compassionate toward others. In addition, cis-LBQ women participants were women ranking other women. Women often experience being gazed upon, objectified, and ranked by others, and women who were uncomfortable ranking other women may have intimately known this. Part of this difference in gender, though, was also about race. "Politeness" and keeping quiet are often constitutive of White womanhood, and the desire to not speak about others, to appear reticent to speak, is a performative act.[34] Some women I interviewed found it too difficult to say anything other than a number, wishing simply to move on to the next woman and end that part of the interview as quickly as possible. At these times, I focused on their body language, wrote field notes regarding their body language after the interview, and included these data in my analyses above.

Desire, much like politeness, is imbricated in racial-gender-sexual power dynamics. I have explicated this through photo rankings and an analysis of participant discourse regarding the photos of women included in the interview. I sought to problematize, in this chapter, the sentiment of most participants that "preferences" should be left to individuals, as people "cannot choose who they desire." Desire, rather than being simply about who individuals wish to fuck, marry, or date, is shaped by and shapes the "matrix of domination."[35]

Eurocentric-ciscentric standards of beauty shape life chances. Light-skinned, Black people are able to gain prominence in fields in which dark-skinned, Black people are otherwise absent. Women, like woman H, who is "cis-passing" and White, are viewed as kind and motherly. They are both desired by men and less likely to be viewed as a threat by men. Desire and attractiveness influence employment opportunities, income, loan approvals,[36] social networks,[37] and even health.[38] The anti-Black, cissexist discourse of participants I interviewed, while focusing on who they find attractive, simultaneously shaped their responses in the subsequent three chapters regarding the murders of Black trans women. These two issues are not separate issues. Instead, the same set of symbols circulate in the discourse of participants regarding both. "Thinking cis," or understanding the world through a cisgendered epistemology, perpetuates and is perpetuated by anti-Black, cissexist violence and hierarchies of desirability, as I show in the next chapter.

NOTES

1. Gerhardstein and Anderson, 2010, "There's More Than Meets the Eye." Broussard and Warner, 2018, "Gender Nonconformity." Mao, Haupert, and Smith, 2018, "How Gender Identity and Transgender Status Affect Perceptions of Attractiveness."

2. Throughout, I place "passing," "passability," "cis-passing," and "visibly trans" in quotation marks because there are no characteristics that make one person look "more" trans than another. While trans women are singled out for larger hands, taller height, squarer jaws, facial and body hair, and even lower-set eyebrows, cis women also have these features. There are cis women with hairy faces and cis women who are six feet tall with large hands and broad shoulders. The focus of these features on trans women is a function of transmisogyny and transmisogynoir, as trans women's bodies are policed and deemed a man for any "masculine" features.

3. Pfeffer, 2016, *Queering Families.*

4. Connell, 2009, "Accountable Conduct."

5. 1980, *Camera Lucida*, 81.

6. Stud and butch both refer to masculine-expressing women. Stud was, as would be expected, used by Black participants, while butch was used by White participants.

7. A low income is categorized as between $20,000 and $44,999 by the Pew Research Center.

8. 2019, "How Much Do Human Hair Wigs Cost?"

9. 2007, "Recovering the Feminine Other," 96.

10. 2006, "Lipsticks or Timberlands?"

11. Ortved, 2013, "Ratchet: The Rap Insult That Became a Compliment."

12. Connell, 1995, *Masculinities.* Schippers, 2007, "Recovering the Feminine Other."

13. 2018, "Rethinking the Possibilities for Hegemonic Femininity."

14. ISNA, 2020, "Congenital Adrenal Hyperplasia."

15. Bode, Seehusen, and Baird, 2012, "Hirsutism in Women."

16. Patton, 2006, "Hey Girl, Am I More Than My Hair?" 26 (my emphasis added).

17. 2018, "A Queer Feminist Bioethics."

18. "12 Ways to Spot a Transsexual."

19. 2020, 20".

20. Garn, 1990, "Sex Differences and Ethnic/Racial Differences." Ohki, Naito, and Cole, 1991, "Dimensions and Resistances of the Human Nose."

21. It is important to note that these embodied differences are not "evidence" of race as biological. The presence of differences in how individuals' bodies manifest does not mean race is natural or preordained. Rather, differences in embodiment became racially categorized and then imbued with racialized meaning.

22. Collins, 2005, *Black Sexual Politics*.

23. 2013, "They See Me as Exotic," 308.

24. 2017, "Attractiveness as a Function of Skin Tone."

25. Kho, Thanapal, and Dierkes-Thrun, 2015, "Chinese Privilege."

26. Herzig, 2015, *Plucked*.

27. Tullet, 2016, "Grease and Sweat."

28. 2012: *Beyond Loving*.

29. Collins, 1990, *Black Feminist Thought*.

30. Lee, 2018, "East Asian 'China Doll' or 'Dragon Lady'?"

31. 2014, *Racism without Racists*, 76.

32. 2018, "Surface-Becoming."

33. Rodríguez, 2014, *Sexual Futures*. Ellison, 2017, "The Labor of Werqing It." Musser, 2018, "Surface-Becoming."

34. Ross, 2013, "The Politics of Politeness."

35. Collins, 1990, *Black Feminist Thought*.

36. Hamermesh, 2011, *Beauty Pays*.

37. O'Connor and Gladstone, 2018, "Beauty and Social Capital."

38. Weeden and Sabini, 2005, "Physical Attractiveness and Health."

Chapter 3

Cisgender Women Thinking Cis

In the previous two chapters, I have focused on the discursive and cultural contours of cis-ness as regards desire. In this chapter, I discuss and explicate what exactly it means to "think cis." In particular, I home in on how cis-lesbian, bisexual, and queer (LBQ) women "think cis" to elucidate the diverse ways cissexism manifested among cis-LBQ women participants. The term "thinking cis" builds on Ingraham's previous work within queer sociology on "thinking straight." Ingraham defined "thinking straight" as:

> [It is] that way of thinking that conceals the operation of heterosexuality in structuring gender and closes off any critical analysis of heterosexuality as an organizing institution. The effect of this depiction of reality is that heterosexuality circulates as taken for granted, naturally occurring, and unquestioned, while gender is understood as socially constructed and central to the organization of everyday life.[1]

For Ingraham, thinking straight functioned as the ideological base for the structural, cultural, and interpersonal means through which heteronormativity (i.e., the taken-for-granted process of heterosexuality being assumed as the norm) and heterosexism (i.e., the systemic and institutional oppression of lesbian, gay, bisexual, queer, and other non-heterosexual individuals) are perpetuated.

While Ingraham argued that gender "is understood as socially constructed," I would argue otherwise—that gender remains popularly connected to sex, with sex largely understood as biological and fixed. As a corrective, I define thinking cis as that way of thinking that conceals the operation of patriarchy in structuring (cis)gender and closes off critical analysis of cis-ness, resulting in cis-ness and heterosexuality being understood as naturally occurring. In this way, I define cis-ness as a political, discursive, and social

lens through which the world is interpreted. Thinking cis is a way of thinking within this lens. Cissexism refers to the ways in which such thinking
structures everyday life, institutional operations, and the life opportunities
of non-cisgender individuals. Transphobia refers to the interpersonal act of
anti-trans discrimination.

Thinking cis is a way of making sense of the world that both results in the
perpetuation of cissexism and functions to justify and naturalize cissexism. It
is the reduction of human bodies to a "naturally" occurring sex binary of male
and female that supposedly correlate with a "naturally" occurring gender
binary of man and woman. It is the belief that trans identity and community
and nonbinary gender identities are a new facet of human society and the co-
belief that the gender binary has been core to humanity since the evolution
of the species or the "divine creation" of man and woman. To think cis is not
only to believe that trans women are not really women and trans men are not
really men but that gender operates as a binary the world over, as well as that
gender exists the world over.

Thinking cis is not only a cissexist and sexist manifestation but a racist and
colonialist one, as well. To think cis is to believe that men and women are
fundamentally different: they behave, look, and act differently. It is to believe
that men are meant to be the dominant "head" of the species, with White men
superior to all and White women their helpmate. Thinking cis proliferates
white supremacist ideas that White men and White women must join together
in heterosexual matrimony to reproduce the White, cisgender, heterosexual,
and able-bodied nuclear family and protect it at all costs from those who
"infringe" on their White picket fence (e.g., immigrants, Black, Indigenous,
and other People of Color, queer/trans people, and disabled people).

One example of thinking cis is trans exclusionary radical feminist (TERF)
thought. In an interview with *The Trans Advocate*, cisgender, feminist blogger, TigTog, explains why she and others began using the word TERF to
describe a particular version of feminism. TigTog states, "We wanted a way
to distinguish TERFs from other radfems with whom we engaged who were
trans*-positive/neutral."[2] Radical feminism, different from liberal feminism,
does not seek to reform a patriarchal system. It aims, instead, to get at the
root causes of patriarchal oppression.[3] Radical feminism, different from liberal feminism and other feminist theoretical strains and activist organizing,
focuses in on the social construction of the gender and sex binaries and ori-
ents itself around a (a racially and gender reductionist[4]) women's liberation
by women as a "sex class" rather than a group of people "born" and iden-
tifying as female. Most importantly to my analysis, radical feminists argue
that the sex and gender binary function as a "set of arrangements by which
a society transforms biological sexuality into products of human activity."[5]
Thus, radical feminism shares with a critical trans politic the understanding of

the sex/gender binary as a sociocultural construction fabricated for purposes of domination. Despite this fundamental overlap between the two forms of thought, trans exclusionary radical feminism argues that "'sex' is immutable" and pro-trans legislation provides "men" "unfettered access to women-only spaces."[6]

In my interviews with cis-LBQ women, several brought up their disappointment with trans exclusionary radical feminism. Indeed, it served as the reference point of what constitutes a transphobic, cis woman. In this chapter, though, I argue that TERFs are only one version of how transphobia manifests among cis women. I distinguish between TERFs and what I conceptualize as the "Conditionally Accepting Cis-ter" and the "Casual Transphobe." I then discuss what I conceptualize as "Critical Cis-ness," or an active and sustained pushback against cissexism (i.e., the systemic and institutional oppression of trans, nonbinary, and gender-nonconforming individuals).

DIFFERENT WAYS OF THINKING CIS

Cis-ness is a way of making static, stable, and controllable an otherwise dynamic, fungible, and disorderly world. Human life is not static, stable, or orderly vis-à-vis the social, biological, historical, and/or psychological. The study of epigenetics examines how environmental factors can alter the phenotypic expression of genes.[7] Epigenetics details how factors like air pollution, the food we eat, or how much we sleep can activate or inactivate specific genes within our DNA to cause them to express differently. Just as these factors may shape or alter genetic expression, biologists and psychologists have explicated how environmental factors may shape neural networks and influence our gendered development as individuals.[8] History scholars elucidate the varying shapes "gender" takes across time and place, including ways in which many societies historically did not have a concept of gender prior to colonization, had different systems of gender, or had different conceptions of what constituted a man and a woman.[9] Despite countless evidence detailing the fictitious nature of the gender/sex binary[10] and the harm of the White, gender/sex binary and cissexism,[11] cis-ness remains a predominant ontology vis-à-vis seeing, categorizing, and reacting to myriad bodies.

In an essay on "sex and gender issues," author J. K. Rowling declaratively stated and explicated why she believes trans-ness poses a potential threat to cisgender women. She wrote:

As many women have said before me, "woman" is not a costume. "Woman" is not an idea in a man's head. "Woman" is not a pink brain, a liking for Jimmy Choos or any of the other sexist ideas now somehow touted as progressive. Moreover, the "inclusive" language that calls female people "menstruators" and "people with vulvas" strikes many women as dehumanising and demeaning. I understand why trans activists consider this language to be appropriate and kind, but for those of us who've had degrading slurs spat at us by violent men, it's not neutral, it's hostile and alienating.

Statements like Rowling's are not new. Divisions within feminist and/or lesbian spaces have repeatedly engaged with and debated the "transgender question." Lesbian feminist, Charlotte Croson, in her essay regarding the Michigan Womyn's Music Festivals' trans exclusionary politics wrote, "We as feminists owe it to ourselves . . . to deconstruct and oppose . . . trans politics. In a feminist analysis, they are, to put it simply, on the wrong side. In opposition to feminism."[12] A study surveying cisgender, lesbian, gay, bisexual, and heterosexual participants about their reactions to a transgender character in an early 2000's soap opera found cisgender lesbian participants to repeatedly deny the validity of a trans woman's womanhood and the possibility that a trans woman, and any woman who dates her, could be a lesbian.[13]

While individuals like Rowling and Croson who espouse feminist ideas that intentionally exclude trans women view trans women as "men" masquerading as women and regard gender-inclusive language as a detriment to society are the predominant image of cissexism, such forms of overt cissexism are only one manifestation of cis-ness. Even more insidious than overt forms of cissexism are the "brief and commonplace, daily verbal, behavioral, or environmental indignities, whether intentional or unintentional, that communicate hostile, derogatory, or negative" slights against trans, nonbinary, and/or gender-nonconforming people.[14] These include the sensationalized inquiry of what genitals a trans person has, the fetishization of trans people as "the best of both worlds," and the belief that one can tell who is transgender and who is cisgender. Such occurrences are not identical to the language espoused by Rowling above. However, these actions are so recurrent and commonplace that they often go unquestioned and come to form the basis of a cissexist discourse utilized by TERFs and other overtly cissexist individuals.

CATEGORIZING THINKING CIS

Trans Exclusionary Radical Feminists (TERFs), who also often refer themselves as gender-critical feminists, are overtly cissexist not only in their exclusion of trans women from feminist movements and organizations but also in how they conceptualize and (dis)regard trans women. TERFs recurrently regard trans women as male due to their conceptualization of sex as "biological," immutable, and dyadic.[15] Further, they conceptualize trans women as men[16] or "simulacra" of women[17] and foster a notion that trans women pose a threat to women and women's movements and spaces.[18]

TERFs often highlight a hyperbolic fear that allowing trans women into women's restrooms, for example, will open the door to men in dresses entering women's restrooms to sexually assault (cis) women. Due to these beliefs, TERFs and "gender-critical" feminists often misgender trans women, referring to trans women with he/him pronouns and with male adjectives and descriptions.[19] As TERFs and gender-critical feminists do not believe trans women are, indeed, women, many do not believe trans women can be lesbian.[20] Much akin to many of my participants, TERFs argue, as well, that a lack of "disclosure" of one's trans identity "constitute[s] cases of rape by deception."[21] Each of these beliefs and behaviors constitute only a portion of what constitutes trans-exclusionary radical feminism and/or gender-critical feminism. However, I introduce them here to provide a concise description of TERF/gender-critical feminism and to differentiate this position from other ways in which my participants engaged in "thinking cis."

None of my participants engaged in a wholly TERF discourse. Instead, many engaged in trans-inclusive and trans-exclusive discourse at different times in the interview. Thinking cis, rather than a binary of TERF-ism and Pro-Trans Feminism, is much more a spectrum of fluid categories that participants moved in and out of depending on what was being asked (e.g., whether trans women are women and/or female, whether a cis woman-trans woman relationship is a lesbian relationship, how they would respond to having sex with a woman they did not know to be trans). Adjacent to TERFs are those participants I conceptualized as "Conditionally Accepting Cis-ters" (see table 3.1). Conditionally Accepting Cis-ters are women who seek to appear trans inclusive while still pulling from a repertoire of anti-trans rhetoric. While TERFs disregard the reality that trans women are women and female, Conditionally Accepting Cis-ters conceptualize trans women as women and female *if* they have had surgery.

In analyzing interview and focus group data, I began to see distinct patterns in how cis women discussed trans women's bodies. While some were TERF-adjacent, others spoke overtly of support for trans women but continued to mirror a discourse like those who were TERF-adjacent. These women viewed trans women as women and believed trans women have a right to women's and lesbian spaces, but they also often misgendered photos of "more visibly trans" women and perpetuated the idea that trans women not outing themselves was dishonest. Finally, other cis women participants were highly critical of cis people, cis-ness, and the gender binary in comparison to these two other groups. In seeing these patterns, I analyzed participant discourse for those characteristics that were most shared across interviews and were either similar to or different from characteristics common among TERFs.

Table 3.1 Ways of Thinking Cis

TERFs	"Conditionally Accepting Cis-ters"	"Casual Transphobes"	"Critically Cis"

• Conceptualize trans women as:
  • Male
  • Men
  • Dangerous
  • Mentally ill due to their trans-ness
• Belief that sex is immutable and biological
• Belief that trans women cannot be lesbian and that cis women attracted to trans women cannot be lesbian
• Belief that trans women are deceptive and dishonest if they do not "out" themselves
• Misgender trans women and other trans/nonbinary people
	• Conceptualize trans women as:
	  • Female & women *if they have had surgery*
	  • Fundamentally different from cis women
	• Conceptualize desire as individual
	• Belief that "preferences" for cis women and not trans women are not transphobic
	• Belief that trans women are deceptive and dishonest if they do not "out" themselves
	• Misgender trans women and other trans/nonbinary people
		• Conceptualize trans women as:
		  • Female
		  • Women
		• Belief that you cannot tell who is trans & who is cis but that you can ask
		• Conceptualize desire as individual
		• Belief that "preferences" for cis women and not trans women are not transphobic
		• Belief that trans women are dishonest *but not deceptive* if they do not "out" themselves
		• Referring to trans women with they/them pronouns in place of she/her
			• Conceptualize trans women as:
			  • Female
			  • Women
			• Belief that you cannot tell who is trans & who is cis
			• Refusal to ask people about their genitals & bodies
			• Desire to protect trans people from cis people
			• Reflexivity vis-à-vis:
			  • Their own gender
			  • Their desires
			• Belief that trans women can choose whether to "out" themselves or not at their discretion
			• Referring to trans women as she/her

From there, I placed participants into the categories that most fit—or which represented most of their discourse about trans women. These categories, though, are not fixed. Instead, they are porous, as I detail later. In this chapter, I explicate three conceptual categories of "thinking cis." These include Conditionally Accepting Cis-ters, and "Casual Transphobes." I also flesh out an additional category I termed "Critically Cis," which included participants who discursively positioned cis-ness as an assault on trans people.

The "Conditionally Accepting Cis-ter"

I categorized three participants as Conditionally Accepting Cis-ters. Each of the three expressed their gender in ways that mirrored the desires of many early radical feminists to embody "any potpourri of masculine and feminine characteristics . . . that strikes their fancy."[22] These participants' gender expression and how they engage in "thinking cis" were both adjacent to TERF and other anti-trans feminist cis women. Jessica had short hair and did not wear any makeup. She wore pants and a loose top. Liz described herself:

> I consider myself in the middle [of masculinity and femininity] . . . . I don't really like a lot of makeup. I don't do a lot of makeup. Um, I'm gonna say, I can't do makeup at all sometimes. Um but I don't really like also wearing, you know, boy's clothes. Mostly, I mean, sometimes I like feeling comfortable, but no. Like someone that I see, they just look, like they wear guys' clothes, and I don't like that. I just like something in the middle, yeah.

Sheila was also not explicitly feminine or masculine. She wore her hair natural and shaved close to the scalp. She did not wear any makeup other than a touch of bright pink lipstick. She wore a dark blue, puffy "women's" jacket with jeans and a grey sweater. Her nails were long but were neither painted nor manicured. She described herself, "I'm the kind of person who can get dressed in thirty minutes and be out." She embraced a masculine aesthetic approach with a desire for "comfort" over "style," while also having minor, "feminine" touches like lipstick. Indeed, each of these women bore a similar gender expression.

I asked participants questions regarding whether they would still desire a woman if they later found out she was trans and how dating a trans woman would potentially shape or reshape their gendered and sexual understandings of self and their social and familial lives. I also asked participants whether they regarded trans women to be women and/or female and trans men to be men and/or male. I intentionally asked both woman/female and man/male to assess whether participants saw the two words differently and whether they saw gender and sex as separate concepts. When I asked Jessica, this question, she first responded simply, "Yes. For me, I think that it's the genitalia, so

Table 3.2 "Conditionally Accepting Cis-ters"

Participant Name	Race/Ethnicity	Sexual Orientation	Education	Income	Religion
Jessica	Black	Lesbian	High School Diploma	Middle Income[1]	Christian
Liz	Non-White Latina	Lesbian	Bachelor's Degree	Low	SBNR[2]
Sheila	Black	Bisexual	Some College	Low	Christian

[1] Below/Near Poverty (Less than $20,000); Low Income ($20–44,999); Middle Income ($45–139,999); Upper Middle Income ($140–149,999); High Income ($150–199,999); Highest Tax Brackets ($200,000+)
[2] Spiritual But Not Religious

like if you're completely changed over then I feel like you're a man, you're a male. But if you're a man walkin' around with a vagina, then I feel like, I don't know, you're still a woman." For Conditionally Accepting Cis-ters, like Jessica, trans women were only women and/or female and trans men were only men and/or male if they had undergone gender affirmation surgery.

While trans people are often criticized by TERFs and other trans exclusionary feminists for "reifying" gender/sex essentialism by altering their bodies to fit with their own gendered/sexed perceptions of their bodies, Conditionally Accepting Cis-ters and TERFs alike view gender as inherently tied to the body. The difference between the two is regarding the (im)mutability of gender/sex. For TERFs, gender and sex are immutable. A trans woman is permanently a man/male simply because she was born with a penis and potentially (if endosex[23]) higher levels of testosterone and XY chromosomes. For Conditionally Accepting Cis-ters, a trans woman is a woman/female and a trans man is a man/male if they have undergone surgery. Gender/sex were mutable for participants I categorized as Conditionally Accepting Cis-ters. However, its mutability, for them, did not disconnect gender/sex from one's genitalia. The belief that gender/sex are mutable, then, does not inherently negate gender/sex essentialism.

Additionally, such a demand for individuals to alter their genitalia to be appropriately recognized as a man or a woman ignores the cost of gender surgeries. Gender affirmation surgery (GAS)—sometimes referred to as gender confirmation surgery, gender reassignment surgery, or sex reassignment surgery—is an expensive procedure. GAS (as I'll refer to it) can cost anywhere "from $7,000 to $50,000, although average male-to-female surgery costs only $23,000 over two years."[24] For trans men and trans people assigned female at birth, there are three surgical options vis-à-vis genitalia: (1) Metoidioplasty, or the extension of "clitoral" tissue into a small penis; (2) Phalloplasty, or the creation of a penis from skin and tissue grafts from elsewhere on the body and the extension of the urethra; (3) Scrotoplasty, or the creation of a scrotum with prosthetic testicles from "labial" tissue, which can be done alone or in combination with either other surgery. Metoidioplasty, though, costs between $6,000 and $30,000 on average and phalloplasty costs between $20,000 and $150,000 on average.[25] Without universal and/or affordable health care, such a demand is not only problematic from a feminist and critical trans standpoint but also financially unreasonable.

Further, the reliance upon the body by both TERFs and Conditionally Accepting Cis-ters relies upon a White, Western view of sex, gender identity, and gender expression. A focus on the genitalia one was born with and the genitalia one has at present is core to what Oyěwùmí terms "body-reasoning," or "a biological interpretation of the social world."[26] Disentangling sex and gender from the body is a nearly impossible endeavor for many individuals socialized within a Western understanding of sex and gender. For example, articles, reddit questions, and online forums abound with individuals seeking to understand what it means to be nonbinary, what nonbinary identities "look like," how to use they/them, zie/zer, and other pronouns, and how to *definitively know* whether an individual is a man, a woman, both, or neither. In comparison, Yorùbá peoples, prior to colonization did not organize society according to sex or gender and did not "privilege the physical world over the metaphysical."[27] To conceptualize the body as the definitive marker of an individual's identity is to perpetuate a White, cissexist notion of the self and to disregard the varied and differential ways in which the self—and selves together—can be interpreted. A system of gender/sex built on "body-reasoning" is but one present form of what could and should be.

Trans Women as Fundamentally Different

In addition to womanhood and manhood hinging on genitalia for Conditionally Accepting Cis-ters, these participants also viewed trans women as fundamentally different from cis women. For Conditionally Accepting Cis-ters, even if a trans woman had elected to medically transition, her body and her womanhood were not equal to cis womanhood and cis women's bodies. Instead, trans womanhood and trans women's bodies were a curious amalgamation of "male" and "female" physicality. When I asked Sheila whether the words female and woman meant the same thing, she responded:

> Female? No. I feel like female's a gender term. Female and woman . . . granted they're the same thing but I feel like in my mind, they're different. A female is because you . . have female genitalia. A woman is . . . a state of mind. A way of life. A becoming.

While Jessica did not differentiate between sex and gender, Sheila felt that trans women can indeed be women, but they can only be female if they have had bottom surgery. Gender, for Sheila, was tied to a "part of the psychic self."[28] Sheila conceptualized gender as something one feels and sex as something one has. However, Sheila felt that, even if a trans woman had undergone GAS, her body would not be a "real" female body. She explained:

> I don't like that mix. Um it's a little awkward to me. Um . . . because I know like, you don't have boobs, I'm sorry. And then if you did, because I'm an overthinker, my mind is always gonna be like "these are not your boobs!" Um . . . yeah. But I mean it's like I would still wanna get to know her. . . . I would wanna see it [the trans woman's vulva], like [breaths in] I gotta see it. We gotta talk about this. We gotta have this conversation.

Sheila assumed that trans women cannot physically develop breasts through hormone replacement therapy even though many trans women can. Regardless, Sheila's characterization of a trans woman's boobs as "not her own" is not a statement that the trans woman's boobs are not a "real" part of her body. Rather, trans women's genitals and secondary sex characteristics were conceptualized as something separate from "real" or "natural" materiality. While Haraway[29] celebrated the cyborg as a being heralding the blurring of boundaries, identities, and the fictive separation of artifice and the natural, Conditionally Accepting Cis-ters, like Sheila, found trans women's bodies to be an undesirable amalgamation of what is deemed proper to the body and that which is not and of that which is deemed female and that which is male. Repeatedly when viewing photos of trans women, Sheila would laugh while characterizing various "visibly trans" photos as men. As a bisexual, cis woman, Sheila desired feminine women and masculine men.

Deceptive and Dishonest

In addition to conceptualizing trans women and trans men as only female and male, respectively, if they have undergone GAS and trans women as fundamentally different from cis women, Conditionally Accepting Cis-ters also conceptualized trans women as deceptive and dishonest if they do not tell intimate partners that they are trans. Take for example Liz's response to my question, "If you met a woman and she had a vagina and you had sex, then she told you afterwards that she's trans, how would you feel or react?":

> I would be upset. Yeah, because why wouldn't she be honest with me before? Like I said, it's something no one should be hiding. Um . . . I always, I talk with my friends that are gay, I have a lot of guy friends that are gay, and a lot of them are . . . they stay in the closet for a long time and some of them, they were like just out to their family so easily, and I, I see the ones that were out to their family

Figure 3.1 Photos of "More Visibly Trans" Women. Top Row, Left to Right: Woman B, Woman D, Woman F. Bottom Row: Woman G.

like, hey this is who I am, it's up to you if you're gonna accept me and love me who I am, I call that bravery. If you are a man and you feel like a woman, you wanna be a woman, or, or other way around, it's just like, just be brave and face it. Don't hide it. Yeah, so I would be upset, definitely.

Liz highlighted what other Conditionally Accepting Cis-ters also explained, which is a greater embrace of trans women who unapologetically "out" themselves with each new person they meet despite the potential risk inherent in doing so. It was more important to these participants that they know a woman is trans than it was to acknowledge the physical and emotional risks that one makes herself vulnerable to in "outing" herself. While Liz and other participants explained that women who "outed" themselves were brave because they chose to express who they are no matter whether they would be accepted or not, they minimized the emotional and physical violence to which one is often subjected when telling others they are trans. As Black trans women and other trans people are ushered into "coming out" and are increasingly made visible in media, they are also subjected to greater "surveillance, institutionalized exclusion, and violence."[30] The conceptualization of those who "out" themselves as brave and those who do not as "weak" constructs a false binary of invisibility and visibility, safety and harm, resistance and acquiescence.

Meadow,[31] for example, highlights the complex negotiations that parents of transgender and gender-nonconforming kids make regarding whether others know their child is trans. Parents in their study often feel pressure to usher their children into a stealth lifestyle, in which they do not tell others they are trans, to protect them from the violence they may otherwise be subjected to by making themselves visible Others. Additionally, "coming out" is not a universal phenomenon. Rather, it is a Western, White conceptualization of sexuality that ignores the numerous and differential ways gender and sexuality manifest across space and time.[32]

Much like Liz, Sheila felt that trans women should "out" themselves to others. Rather than creating a false dichotomy of brave women and weak women, though, Sheila called for the physical chastisement of women who do not tell cisgender people they are trans. For example, when I asked Sheila her feelings and reaction to the murders of trans women, she explained:

> I feel like a homophobic people are people who um . . . struggle with homo-sexuality like, it's something that um . . . they deal with that they're not dealing with, so when they counter it um encounter it um, I wanna say, unknowingly, it's a shock to the system. And instead of handling it like an adult, they act out. I have a tantrum because you quote-unquote tricked me. You knew. Granted, you should've said something. You shoulda got beat up, but . . . not kill. Because I feel like you should disclose that information.

Sheila did not explicitly describe trans women as deceptive and dishonest if they do not "out" themselves. However, her call for the physical assault of women who do not tell men they are with that they are trans highlights the assumed intensity of wrongdoing. To call for the physical assault of a woman who does not "out" herself while simultaneously describing a woman telling a man she is trans as a "shock to his system" is to conceptualize trans-ness and the safeguarding of one's trans identity as an assault against the man. The trans woman being assaulted for not "outing" herself would function both as a punishment as well as a warning to other trans women. Further, this conceptualization of women as dishonest and deceptive if they do not "out" themselves as trans elucidates Conditionally Accepting Cis-ters conceptualization of trans women as fundamentally different from cis women. If one recognizes a trans woman as, indeed, a woman, then she is keeping nothing from a potential partner if she does not "out" herself. However, to argue that a woman is specious for not "outing" herself is to conceptualize her womanhood as a disguise or sham. For Conditionally Accepting Cis-ters, a trans woman's transition is what ultimately defines her womanhood, marks her womanhood as fundamentally different from cis womanhood, and requires different expectations of her than of cis women (e.g., "outing" oneself as trans).

The "Casual Transphobe"

While TERFs and Conditionally Accepting Cis-ters were overtly transphobic, "Casual Transphobes" were not. Participants I categorized as Casual

Transphobes may overtly appear to be trans inclusive and trans friendly, and, indeed, they may even identify as such. However, the language they use and their beliefs regarding gender/sex remain imbricated in cissexism. As racism and white supremacy have increasingly become more covert and reified through coded and discrete language,[33] cissexism has as well—in large part due to the coproduction of cissexism and white supremacy. While participants coded as Casual Transphobes recognized trans women as women and female and did not openly conceptualize of trans womanhood as fundamentally different from cis womanhood, they perpetuated transmisogyny in other ways, including a comfort in asking people who "appear to be trans"[34] if they are trans, referring to trans women only with they/them pronouns, and viewing trans women as dishonest if they do not "out" themselves to potential partners. Additionally, one trait that both Casual Transphobes and Conditionally Accepting Cis-ters shared is the conceptualization of desire as individual. Both groups of participants hold a neoliberal conceptualization of desire, which holds that (1) individuals are entitled to "preferences" vis-à-vis race, body size, disability, and trans-ness, among other characteristics; (2) who one desires is biological, psychological, and/or otherwise ingrained; (3) who one desires is not reflective of power dynamics in the larger society; and (4) who one desires does not shape or reify power dynamics in the larger society.

While Casual Transphobe-coded participants categorized trans women as women and female, their responses were more complicated than a mere yes or no. Amanda most exemplified this in her response after I asked her whether a trans woman is a woman and/or female. Amanda replied:

> Um if they get the surgery, then yes I would. But a lot of people don't have to go through getting the surgery done, if they, you know, because they already have little things, but hey, it takes a lot for them to get their body the way that they want to, so of course I would just go along and go with the flow, whatever.

Amanda's response, while ultimately signifying a recognition of trans women as women and female, in comparison to those in the previous section and those in the forthcoming section was not a mere disavowal of trans women's womanhood nor a complete recognition of it. Instead, Amanda's response explicated what is core to those participants I categorized as Casual Transphobes; that is, a rambling answer due to a lack of forethought. Throughout the interview, Amanda repeatedly noted a lack of thinking about these questions prior to that day. For example, at the end of the interview, I asked Amanda if there were anything she wanted to share that I had not otherwise asked. She responded, "That was a good one. I just can't get over that one. I don't see myself tryin' it, but hey, that was a good question. I've never had that question before." Here, Amanda did not mean a single question I asked. Instead, she meant the entirety of the interview. She had never thought about whether she would date a trans woman, whether trans women

Table 3.3 Casual Transphobes

Participant Name	Race/Ethnicity	Sexual Orientation	Education	Income[1]	Religion
Alyshah	Black	Lesbian	Some College	Poverty[1]	SBNR[2]
Amanda	Black	Bi	Less Than High School	Poverty	Christian
Amy	White Latina	Lesbian	Some College	Low	N/A
Kylee	Black	Lesbian	Some College	Poverty	N/A
LaLa	Black	Bisexual	Some College	Low	Christian
Renee	Black	Lesbian	Bachelor's	Low	SBNR
Sabrina	Black	Lesbian	Bachelor's	Middle Income	SBNR

[1] Below/Near Poverty (Less than $20,000); Low Income ($20–44,999); Middle Income ($45–139,999); Upper Middle Income ($140–149,999); High Income ($150–199,999); Highest Tax Brackets ($200,000+)
[2] Spiritual But Not Religious

are women and/or female, why cis-het men murder Black trans women, and other questions throughout. There was neither an overt hatred, fear, or intolerance of trans women by these participants, nor an overt celebration, acceptance, and/or love for trans women. Such lack of attention to trans women and cissexism resulted in responses akin to Amanda's above.

A lack of forethought also resulted in microaggressive responses that did not signify an intent to harm trans women. Alyshah felt that trans women are women and female. However, when I asked her if others would see a trans woman differently for being with her as a cis woman, she responded, "Probably or maybe . . . . Because I'm the actual female, probably." While Alyshah recognized trans women as women, her responses at other points like this reified a differentiation of trans females and cis female.

Are You Trans?

Such microaggressive responses were evident in another factor regarding my categorization of Casual Transphobes. Casual Transphobes, in comparison to TERFs and Conditionally Accepting Cis-ters, acknowledged that one cannot tell who is trans and who is cis. However, Casual Transphobes responded that one should feel comfortable asking individuals if they are trans if it appears that they may be. Such a concept may seem contradictory. If one cannot tell who is trans, then how would one ascertain that it is okay to ask certain people if they are trans and not everyone? For example, during the focus group with White/White-passing participants, I asked the group which photos of trans women in the photo elicitation portion of the interview they thought were transgender. Each of the cis-women participants stated a discomfort with doing so. Amy, for example, explained:

> Yeah it's definitely uncomfortable and even if I had to guess, I don't have an exact guess, 'cause there's a couple that I don't know. I mean I've seen very . . . that's, that, there's all body types within that, so it makes me uncomfortable to begin with but even moreso when I'm like, there's no way I could know that. I can tell you which one isn't [laughs].

Amy, like other participants I categorized as Casual Transphobes did not feel that they as cisgender women should contribute to the gendering and sexing of bodies. However, during our interview, Amy's responses differed. The two other cis-lesbian women in the focus group had shared a response like Amy's prior to Amy speaking. This signifies a potential desirability bias during the focus group. In comparison, during our interview, Amy selected woman A, a "cis-passing," Black woman as the most desirable of each of the photos of women. I asked Amy whether people would view her differently if she were with this woman and this woman were trans. Amy responded:

Figure 3.2   On the left, Woman A. On the Right, Woman B.

Amy: Um . . . I think they're gonna view her . . . this just occurred to me, I think
   . . . so we're using [woman A]. I think they're gonna view her differently than
   . . . if she looked more like the one whose eyes I loved [woman B].

alithia: What would you say are the differences between how people would view
   woman A and woman B?

Amy: They would probably say that [woman B] looks a little more masculine. See
   but it's the hair that throws me every time um and that may just be me um . . .
   I also am not crazy about their shirt I just realized where [woman A] is like, I
   like black [the color]. [Laughs] that could also be what it is too, I don't know,
   um . . . but for like someone else looking, I don't think me, I don't think me
   standing next to either one of those is gonna make a difference. It's not me, it's
   what, it's where people are and what they do when they look at you.

Amy's response, like Amanda's earlier, was a rambling one. Her answer
was not necessarily preconfigured, unlike those I categorized as Conditionally Accepting Cis-ters or "Critically Cis." Thus, along the way, her response
was variously essentialist and constructionist. In many ways, Casual Transphobes highlighted how difficult it is in US and Western discourse to move
beyond the body in describing individuals. At various points in the interview,
Amy attempted to stray away from "body-reasoning," but her discourse continually referred back to the body before shifting to an undefinable "energy"
that signified to her whether someone was a man or woman and gay or
straight.

Amanda, too, despite her recognition of trans women as women and female
and belief that you cannot tell who is trans and who is cis, felt comfortable

asking individuals who "appear" to be trans if they are. For example, Amanda noted:

> You just really have to ask questions . . . . I would just be right upfront with it, because of the simple fact that it goes a long way. Hey, I know you're cool and all but you (whispers) one of those little trannies right?

At this moment in the interview, Amanda was smiling, kind, and calm. She did not use the slur "trannies" as an attempt to injure others or engage in microaggressive behavior. Amanda was living in a homeless shelter, did not have a high school education, was unemployed, and had previous interactions with the criminal legal system. Her use of the word "tranny" may have been more about not having had the chance to learn yet that the term is a slur. However, the fact that Amanda and others in this category felt comfortable asking individuals whether they are trans reifies the mis-categorization of certain attributes, characteristics, and behaviors as fundamentally female and/ or male. In reality, if one feels the need to ask anyone if they are trans while also believing that one cannot tell who is trans, then they should be asking every single individual if they are trans or not. Otherwise, a contradiction arises between what they are saying and what they are doing. There was a desire among Casual Transphobes to not be transphobic, yet their actions did not align with this desire.

The Requirement to Come Out

This gap between belief and action was evident in interviews with participants in this category when discussing whether trans women must "out" themselves. Casual Transphobes did not feel that trans women were deceiving anyone by not "outing" themselves as they recognize and validate trans women as women. However, they continued to perpetuate the idea that trans women not "outing" themselves was somehow dishonest. The desire to not be transphobic had not yet fully translated into understanding the disconnect in this sentiment. In my interview with LaLa, I asked:

Alithia: If you met [a woman] at like a bar or somewhere and y'all went back to your place or her place and you hooked up and she had a vagina, y'all had sex, and then the next day she told you she was trans, how would you react or how would you feel?

Lala: I don't know. It, it wouldn't . . . matter. Cuz I mean the deed was already done so. Um . . . yeah. It wouldn't matter

Alithia: Okay, would you be upset at all or no?

Lala: I would be upset that I wasn't informed first, but it wouldn't. . .it wouldn't matter. Like cuz it's . . . I feel like, like. . .if, if you went through like a major change like that, that's something that you should inform someone who you potentially might have sex with or potentially see. Because then it's like, it's kind of like lying I guess, but not. I don't know. I don't know how to explain it. But yeah I would wanna know first if . . . it might not change my mind, it might change my mind. I don't know. Depends on how I'm feeling that day type.

LaLa's desire to know "if you went through a major change like that" reflected that of other participants in this category. Cis-LBQ women in this category felt that, if one did not disclose that they are trans and have undergone GAS, then they are keeping secret major life events that may affect intimate partners. There was not the same sentiment of being "deceived" as there was for TERFs and Conditionally Accepting Cis-ters, but the responses stated here pulled from the prior categories' discursive repertoire. Further, the pressure on trans women to "out" themselves in order to not be "dishonest" places a double bind on trans women. The demand to "come out" assumes there is something fraudulent, nefarious, or—again—deceitful about the individual's womanhood. It additionally places the trans woman in a vulnerable situation in which she may be subject to greater violence.[35] This is evident vis-à-vis media visibility and anti-trans violence. Scholars have highlighted what is termed the "paradox of visibility," in which, as visibility of and education about trans-ness increases, so too has violence against trans women.[36]

While it could be argued that individuals have the right to desire to know information that is salient or important to an intimate partner's identity, it is important to question which information about another's body is deemed need-to-know and which is deemed okay to find out later. For example, do cis women who undergo labiaplasty to have smaller labia more akin to those disproportionately represented in porn need to share that information with intimate partners? Alternatively, do individuals generally ask cis women partners if they have undergone labiaplasty during the formation of a relationship? I did not ask participants about their thoughts regarding cis women and plastic surgery, although future research should attend to cis people's perceptions vis-à-vis cosmetic surgery and the similarities/differences with those perceptions and those of GAS. It still bears questioning, though, how different bodily alterations are viewed by cis women partners.

Misgendering Trans Women

Casual Transphobe participants' emphasis on "coming out" as trans was connected to the other microaggressive behaviors and beliefs they portrayed, such as how Amy and Amanda discussed trans women's bodies above. "Casual

Transphobe" participants also often misgendered trans women when discussing photos of women that appeared "more visibly trans." When approaching the photo elicitation segment of interviews, I would explain to participants:

> For the next several questions, I have some photos I want us to focus on of eight different women. For each woman, you will rate her one to ten, with one being that you find her completely undesirable and ten being that you find her completely desirable. You can, of course, choose a number anywhere on that scale, and then just explain.

At this point, I would place the photos in front of the participant, and ask, "Alright, what do you think of woman A?" At the bottom of each photo, I also had captions stating "Woman _," with the blank being filled with a number between one and eight, so the participants and I could easily reference which photo we were discussing. Despite numerous statements describing the photos as being of eight women and referring to them with she/her pronouns, "Casual Transphobe" participants would refer to photos of "cis-passing" women with she/her pronouns and photos of "more visibly trans" women with they/them pronouns. While they/them pronouns are gender-free, meaning they can be used to refer to any person of any (a)gender, a dissonance arose when participants would use different pronouns of a set of photos of all women. I did not give them photos of people and allow them to assume the genders of people in the photos. I did not give them photos of two or more genders of people. I, instead, overtly gave participants photos of women, and I made it clear that they were photos of women. Saguy et al. highlight how using gender-free pronouns for everyone would decrease misgendering and decrease gender inequality.[37] In comparison, the use of they/them pronouns for "more visibly trans" women who are not "clearly" interpreted as "women" or "men" singles such individuals out and signals a lack of validation for their womanhood.

The photo of woman A is of a "cis-passing," Black woman. The photo of woman F is of a "more visibly trans," Black woman. In response to woman A, Amanda said, "So I would say, I would give her a three . . . she just look like she stressed out . . . so that's why I would give her a three." In comparison, in reference to woman F, Amanda stated, "Okay, um . . . this is a different look. Um but they're attractive." Amanda's use of gendered pronouns for "passing" women and gender-free pronouns for "non-passing" women signifies a disconnect between how she is interpreting these women. Amanda was not alone in this. In response to woman A, Amy stated:

> She's a ten. Uh, because she . . . 'cause she's gorgeous. I mean, she's got like . . . the uh general standard of beauty, you know what I mean? Like her face, her skin. Um . . . I love her hair. She's, you know, the standard thin, fit, all of that.

Figure 3.3   On the left, Woman A. On the Right, Woman F.

In comparison, woman B is a photo of a "more visibly trans," Latina woman. In reference to woman B, Amy responded, "Pretty. Uh, I probably would not be attracted to them myself . . . But I do think that she's very pretty." Amy first used they/them pronouns before switching to she/her pronouns after a pause in her explanation.

Kylee did the same. Kylee found woman A to be the most desirable woman among the eight photos. I asked Kylee, "We're gonna stick with [woman A] for a bit, and, remember there is not right or wrong answer, but if you met her, and you're into her, and you found out that she is transgender, would it change how desirable she is to you?" Kylee responded:

> It would depend on um, if they're . . . if they're . . . if she was going to get the operation. Because like sexually, you know, that's a big part of a relationship, you know, so that would be something.

It would be easy to write Kylee, Amy, and Amanda's use of they/them pronouns off as accidents or slips in speech if they were one offs, but they were not. Instead, the use of gender-free pronouns for women who are "gender-nonconforming" or who are "more visibly trans" signals a misinterpretation of these women as not properly woman or not recognizably woman. The use of they/them pronouns in place of he/him pronouns shows an intent to not misgender, but the use of they/them pronouns for individuals known to the participants as women is a lack of recognition of the womanhood of women known to be trans. To misgender someone is to refer to them with incorrect gender pronouns, adjectives, and signifiers. To refer to women who "appear" to be cis women and women who "appear" to be trans women with different pronouns is not a matter of impoliteness. Instead, it is an often unintentional, discursive Othering of individuals who do not fit cisnormative standards of womanhood.

Individualizing Desire and Preferences

In addition to not problematizing the use of they/them pronouns for "more visibly trans" women, the conceptualization of not "coming out" as dishonest, and the belief that you can or should ask people if they are trans, Casual Transphobe participants also conceptualized desire as individuated and preferences as natural and/or inevitable. This conceptualization is shared by both casual transphobes and Conditionally Accepting Cis-ters, though most striking among this group of participants due to their intent to not harm or hurt others and simultaneous lack of problematizing the many ways in which their actions and/or beliefs do cause harm.

As I approached the end of interviews, I asked each participant, "How do you feel overall about which bodies are deemed beautiful, attractive, and desirable in society? Do you feel individuals are entitled to like who they like or should their preferences be problematized?" Alyshah responded:

> I think . . . preferences aren't bad. Preferences aren't bad at all. It's okay to have a preference, but it's also okay to be open. It's all about how you go about doing it. And like I said, some people, their preferences, it's like, okay, well, these are my preferences, they gotta be your preferences too. Um that's the problem with that. People are saying that you should do this and not do this. And you should do that and not that. It's kind of like you're pushing your beliefs on me.

Alyshah mirrored Althusser's note that one can never escape ideology by arguing that one can never escape preferences (i.e., to be open to anything is to prefer anything and anyone).[38] That sentiment is largely unquestionable. However, Alyshah also felt that individuals should not be pressured to problematize their preferences. Scholars note the problem of particular preferences, such as racial preferences for Whites or light-skinned people of color, with such preferences conceptualized as sexual racism and colorism.[39] Such analyses also extend to the idealization of thin bodies and enabled bodies,[40] and I argue here that these analyses must also extend to the idealization of cis bodies. As discussed in Chapter Two, the conceptualization of certain faces as "feminine" (e.g., faces with narrow, v-shaped jaws, small, narrow noses, small foreheads, high eyebrows, and no facial hair) is both cissexist and racist. It is a cisnormative, Eurocentric standard of women's faces. Participants' preferences for such faces was, unquestionably, an individual preference, yet their individual preferences cannot be separated from the social forces that shaped said preferences.

Participants categorized as Casual Transphobes, though, felt that preferences are shaped by each individual and not by the social. My first few cis-
lesbian woman interview participants mentioned witnessing transphobia in
lesbian spaces online or in person, so I began to ask participants about this. I
asked Sabrina, "Have you, in lesbian spaces or online in lesbian groups, heard
people say anything in particular about lesbian women dating trans women or
trans women being in lesbian spaces?" Sabrina responded:

> Um . . . I might have seen one or two comments. Um but they haven't been
> negative. No. Like I've just seen people say that they would date a transgender
> woman. And then some people said they wouldn't, just a preference thing. Mhm.

Much as Sabrina nonchalantly noted that some people are open to trans
women and some are not, Amanda felt similarly about individuals' attractions vis-à-vis race. I asked Amanda, "Do you think in terms of who is seen
as desirable that race shapes who is seen as attractive?" Amanda stated, "In
society probably not. But when we have a man and we ask a man that question, he probably has his set kind of race he prefers. So I couldn't answer that
one." Amanda and Sabrina's acceptance of individual racialized and gendered
preferences was core to Casual Transphobes' lack of forethought regarding
issues of cissexism and desire, race, and gender. Casual Transphobes aimed
to be open to all individuals, including those who hold racialized/gendered
preferences. Their openness to all individuals, though, stopped there. They did
not seek to interrogate cis-ness and whiteness further than to make space for
all individuals to desire what they wish sexually and romantically and for all
individuals to actualize their gender and sexuality in ways that they desired.
The emphasis on the individual apart from the social is influenced by neoliberal logics of individual responsibility, self-actualization, and maximization of
one's interest apart from any social concern, understanding, or accountability.[41]

Casual Transphobes were not overtly cissexist in the ways that TERFs and
Conditionally Accepting Cis-ters were. Instead, Casual Transphobes perpetuated cis-ness through microaggressions. These microaggressions included
misgendering "visibly trans" women by referring to them with they/them pronouns instead of she/her pronouns and asking individuals who "appear" to be
trans if they are trans. These microaggressive behaviors appeared to be trans-
inclusive to participants, but the normalization of these behaviors reified cis
logic of gender/sex binaries. If the gender binary is taken to be true, then there
are men and there are women. If one cannot tell if one is a man or a woman,
then they must ask if they are to know how to refer to them and treat them.
In reality, there is no way to tell if anyone is a man or a woman unless they
declare that they are. Manhood and womanhood have no essential physical
characteristics, social attributes, or individual behaviors. To ask individuals

who "appear" trans if they are, is an attempt to make sense of where an individual fits within the binary. To use they/them pronouns for women who "appear" trans is to point out they do not appear to fit within the binary. Finally, an unquestioned acceptance of individual, racialized and gendered preferences allows cis and White hierarchies of desire to go unquestioned. That Casual Transphobes engaged in microaggressive (i.e., unintentional harm caused by one's language or behavior) rather than overtly oppressive behavior, though, signifies the potential for change through education. In the next section, I attend to participants I categorized as "Critically Cis," who did interrogate cis-ness/whiteness on each of these bases.

"Critically Cis"

While TERFs and Conditionally Accepting Cis-ters overtly perpetuate(d) cis-ness and Casual Transphobes unintentionally perpetuate cis-ness, this final set of participants, categorized as "Critically Cis," went the farthest in actually interrogating cis-ness and whiteness. In doing so, they worked to actively challenged cis logics and cis privilege. They did this by conceptualizing trans women as female and women, refusing to ask people about their genitals and bodies, and referring to trans women with she/her pronouns. Critically Cis participants also believed that you cannot necessarily discern who is trans and cis and that trans women can choose whether to "out" themselves or not at their discretion. These participants additionally desired to protect trans people from cis people and interrogated their own genders and desires. These participants' point to the ways in which they interrogate cis-ness, and detail how Critical Cis-ness can work to counter the necropolitics of cis-ness (i.e., the production of cis-ness through violence and death).

During the focus group with White/White-passing participants, I asked participants which photos of the eight women shown to them during their interviews they assumed to be trans. While the one cis-het man participant, Adam, immediately pointed out who he assumed was trans and referred to our interview, during which he had done so as well, the cis-lesbian women participants were more hesitant to do so. Rachel and Vincent discussed their hesitance, saying:

Rachel: I mean I know that some of the women are transgender, but I feel kind of uncomfortable pointing it out?
alithia: Okay why?
Rachel: Um I don't know because communities that I'm in, I've kind of learned that it's like not appropriate to like point out if somebody is trans unless they're talking about it with you or something. Or even nonbinary. I don't know, basically as a cis person, I try not to talk too much about people's bodies.

Vincent: I mean it's kinda weird asking like what makes this person different than other women, like. . .
Rachel: Yeah because it's kinda like pointing out how they're like not passing.

Participants who engaged in what I conceptualize as Critical Cis-ness aimed not only to be inclusive but to actively learn how to better be in solidarity with trans people and to interrogate the questions individuals ask interpersonally and as a society about marginalized people. Vincent highlighted that marking someone as "cis-passing" and someone as "trans-appearing" marks one's womanhood out as somehow Other and deviant from cisgender womanhood. This not only would Other "visibly trans" trans women but also "visibly trans" cis women who have traits deemed "trans."

Janelle, too, refused to assume who is trans and who is cis. She highlighted the oddness of this bodily preoccupation. I asked Janelle, as I did all participants, "In general, can you tell if someone is trans or not?" She responded:

> In general . . . you know, I don't like, I don't like to um assume. If you tell me, I'll be like, "Okay," but like . . . if not . . . then . . . I'm not gonna assume. I know there are some trans people who are more cis passing, that's perfectly fine, but like I'm not just, I'm not, I don't try to assume. Usually I'm minding my own business; I'm not looking at someone like, "Hmmm, I wonder if they have a vagina," like no! Like I'm worried about my own vagina, like when am I getting my period [laughs]? You know? So I don't try to worry about things like that.

Here, Janelle, highlighted a need to shift away from a focus on others' bodies to her own body. The refusal to ask about other's bodies and genitals and the refusal to categorize bodies not only works against cissexism but against Western, White ontologies of gender, as well. As noted earlier, Oyěwùmí highlights the West's preoccupation with the body in how the self is understood in relation to others. Rachel and Vincent, having learned to not ask about bodies, had now internalized a discomfort in even hypothetically engaging in "body-reasoning." This discomfort has the potential to open the way to new ways of relating as people.

Protecting Trans Women

This potential new way of relating as people is evident in this group of participants' desire to protect trans women from cisgender people. In aforementioned groups of cis-women participants (i.e., TERFs, Conditionally Accepting Cis-ters, and Casual Transphobes), there was a focus on trans women "outing" themselves in order to make a cis person feel trusted, not "deceived," and not "pressured" to feel as though they must be open to desiring trans women. Participants categorized as Critically Cis sought to ensure

Table 3.4 Critically Cis

Participant Name	Race/Ethnicity	Sexual Orientation	Education	Income[1]	Religion
Alyx	Non-Latinx White	Bi	Some College	Poverty	N/A
Cookie	Black	Homoflexible	Grad Degree	Middle Income	SBNR[2]
Janelle	Black	Queer	Some College	Middle Income	Christian
Peaches	Black/Multiracial	Bi/Queer	Some College	Poverty	SBNR
Rachel	Non-Latinx White	Lesbian	Bachelor's	Low	N/A
Shantelle	Non-Latinx White	Lesbian	Some College	Highest Tax Brackets	N/A
Vincent	Non-Latinx White	Lesbian	Some College	Middle Income	N/A

[1] Below/Near Poverty (Less than $20,000); Low Income ($20–44,999); Middle Income ($45–139,999); Upper Middle Income ($140–149,999); High Income ($150–199,999); Highest Tax Brackets ($200,000+)
[2] Spiritual But Not Religious

that trans women felt that *they—trans women*—could trust cisgender people to not harm them. This was a shift from conceptualizing trans-ness as deceptive and as an assault to a conceptualizing of trans-ness as vulnerable to the harms of cisgender people.

Take, for example, Alyx. At the time of the interview, she was dating a trans individual. Alyx, as a bisexual woman, was open to people of any gender. Her current partner as a genderfluid individual assigned male at birth who primarily used he/him pronouns. When I asked Alyx, "Would you have any hesitancy introducing a trans woman partner to friends, family, or coworkers," she responded by relating her answer to how she chooses whether to introduce others in her life to her partner's trans-ness. She explained:

> Um friends no. Um family, (sighs) a little bit, and I hate to say that, but like also I know how my family can be and that's part of why my dad doesn't know that Tim's genderfluid, because he's like that. Uh and I would, it's not something that I would be the one to outwardly like say. It would be up to her to come out to them, um . . . unless she like actively wanted me to, but even then it's sort of a touchy situation as far as like my dad goes. Mom, I'd be more lenient with um but yeah.

Alyx's hesitancy regarding introducing her partner to her family did not center her feelings of the potential discomfort, embarrassment, or shame she may face as someone who dates trans people. Instead, Alyx actively reflected on how individual family members' behaviors, discourse about trans people, and the amount of empathy and willingness to learn that she perceived in them. This is a dramatic shift from Sheila, who was a Conditionally Accepting Cis-ter. Sheila had a young child, and when I asked her if she would be open to dating trans women, she responded, "I think a lot with my child too, like I got a child, like . . . that's a deep conversation." Sheila was worried about how her child would respond to and digest such information, even though studies find young, elementary school aged children are extremely capable of understanding trans-ness.[42]

Other participants who displayed Critical Cis-ness also demonstrated a concern for how their people beyond their immediate family would treat their trans partners but a willingness to follow the lead of their partners' in making decisions regarding familial, friend, and work introductions and discussions about the partner's trans identity. When I asked Janelle, "Would you be hesitant to introduce a trans woman partner to your friends or coworkers," she responded:

Janelle: Friends or coworkers, no. I mean when I like people, I have to show them off, so like, I mean, if I like her, Ima show her off, but [pause] you can still like show people off [pause] and be brave but still be scared. You know?
alithia: Would you be scared about being a woman with another woman or scared for how they'd react to her being a trans woman or?

Janelle: Her being a trans woman, because you know people [pause] like people are trained to discriminate people based [pause] I don't, they're like doing a lot of things in law that has to do with like if you like [pause] depending on your sexuality, you can be fired from a job or things like that, so like that's very scary or and also the family like just so many factors. It's just like anxiety-driven for me. So yeah, I, I, I feel like [pause] being scared or timid is [pause] justified in this sense. In this world that we live in.

Janelle was not afraid of how others would perceive her for being with a trans woman. Instead, she worried about them both living in a society that punishes individuals who deviate from cisgender, heterosexual norms of dating and relationships. Such fears of being harmed were perhaps more pronounced for her, with her and a hypothetical partner being two women vulnerable to the harms of cis-heteropatriarchy. These fears, though, were not simply about whether they would be accepted by others, but whether they would be able to survive and thrive, as LGBT people, particularly trans people, do not have workplace discrimination protections in many states across the United States.

Peaches connected such fears to race. I asked Peaches, "If you were with a woman and knew she was trans, and y'all had been together for awhile, would you be hesitant at all to introduce her to your family?" Peaches responded:

Peaches: No. That's a lie yes. Like my family are, they, they can be ignorant and like my mom especially, love her to death, but she says like a lot of insensitive things. My mom's White. She doesn't think before she talks a lot. So, if anything, I would just be like a little bit hesitant to like take her around my family, because I wouldn't want them to say anything in front of her um that could make her feel uncomfortable.
alithia: Okay would they do that whether it was a cis woman or a trans woman?
Peaches: Um I think it, they wouldn't do it as much with a cis woman, yeah.

Peaches was raised by a White, Portuguese mother and a Black father, and she noted her mother's whiteness as integral as to why she microaggressed others. Peaches was referring to gender and racial ignorance and highlighted a fear of how her mother would treat a trans woman partner. Her connection of this ignorance, cissexism, and racism is part of a larger epistemology of White ignorance that functions to protect "those who for "racial" [and gendered] reasons have needed not to know" how their understandings of the world deny the lived experiences of Black, Indigenous, and other cisgender/transgender people of color and other transgender people.[43] This White ignorance produces a misunderstanding of reality as inherently binary vis-à-vis sex and gender and an inculcated "alexithymia," or a socialized inability to feel empathy for racialized Others.[44] Thus, Peaches' mother's repetitive "[saying of] a lot of insensitive things" is not so much about a hatred of trans people/of color but the result of an actively developed ignorance.

You Don't Need to Come Out

In comparison, Peaches, and other Critically Cis women, aimed to understand the lived realities of other marginalized people. This extended to this group of participants' beliefs that trans women can "out" themselves at their own discretion without being considered dishonest or deceptive. For example, I asked Shantelle, "If you met someone, would you want them to tell you straight up, before going on dates and getting to know each other that they're trans?" Shantelle responded, "That's for them to decide because you have to be like comfortable enough with yourself to share that with other people. Just like telling someone you're gay." Shantelle had nothing more to add upon probing other than to repeat what she had already stated. For many participants who engaged in "Critical Cis-ness," there was a connection to their own lived experiences and an active interrogation of self that led to their refusal to force trans women to live according to the whims of cisgender people.

Alyx, for example, stated that she respected if someone did not want to immediately tell her they are trans. In response, I asked her, "What makes you respect that decision?" Alyx explained:

> I grew up in [a predominantly White, wealthy, conservative city in Georgia,] and it's not exactly like the most welcoming place, so like I super understand if you don't wanna like put that out there immediately. That could be dangerous for some people. Um so it's, yeah, it's someone's own personal decision.

Alyx "came out" in middle school, and her first non-cisgender, man partner was an individual who "came out" to her as a trans man in the middle of their relationship. After "coming out," she experienced overt and covert heterosexism from adults in her school, and her experiences of discrimination led her to understand why people would not want to be out as LGBTQ.

Another participant, Cookie, utilized her sociological imagination to understand why a trans woman would not want to tell her that she is trans. When I asked Cookie how she would react if she dated or slept with a woman who later "came out" to her as trans, she answered:

> I wouldn't really be mad because I understand. From her standpoint, how scary something like that might be, um, just because of how, you know, people may have responded to her in the past, or fear of how people might respond, or the fear of losing me as a friend, as a partner, whatever. So, I would be like, "Damn," but

like, it wouldn't change anything. Like we wouldn't stop talking, like I wouldn't stop talking to her because she neglected to tell me until late or wouldn't stop talking to her because it, that was the reality of the situation. Like I get it, like people go through their own stuff. People, you know, heal and grow and learn in their own ways. And I would be a bullshit ass person to just, 'cause I'm sure there's things that I probably might not tell her 'til sometime down the road. You know?

Cookie understood the reality of a cissexist world that socializes trans women to be hyper-vigilant regarding to whom and when they "out" themselves if at all. Cookie shifted the emotional labor off the trans woman regarding "outing" herself and onto cis partners to process potential feelings of disappointment on their own. Further, Cookie highlighted the time it takes for individuals to share various pieces of themselves. Rather than viewing trans women not "outing" themselves as deceptive or dishonest, she normalized it by comparing trans women's decisions to any other mundane decision when dating.

While Cookie's response was a longer, more introspective answer, most participants who engaged in Critical Cis-ness answered questions regarding trans women "outing" themselves succinctly and nonchalantly. I asked Peaches, "Do you care whether a woman tells you right away or not that she's trans?" Peaches said, "No, I think that should be someone's option when they're ready to tell you, they can tell you . . . I don't think I would be upset because if she identifies as woman, then she's a woman at the end of the day." Peaches did not have to consider her response, nor did she figure herself into the equation. Instead, she like other participants in this category centered trans women and displayed forethought regarding the lived experiences of trans women.

Interrogating Their Own Genders

Their forethought factored into an interrogation of their own genders and desires. Participants in this category did not believe that their desires and "preferences" were individual, innate, or disconnected from racialized, gendered, and sexualized notions of desire and attraction. Further, they questioned themselves regarding why they consider themselves to be women. This interrogation of the "self" highlighted the internal work they had done previously to better understand trans women and their lived realities. Additionally, this interrogation highlighted the work others had done to help them challenge internalized cissexism. I asked Rachel, for example, "If you approached a woman and she told you she was trans, how would you respond?" Rachel explained:

Rachel: Like that's okay with me.
Alithia: Okay has that always been okay with you or was it something you had to figure out or?

Rachel: Um I think like—because of the community that I kind of like went
  through my coming out process in like I've always been around like other
  women, I've always been around trans people, so it's not, it wasn't like exclusionary. I don't feel like it was something I really had to learn but it was just
  kind of like yeah.
Alithia: Okay and that's from like childhood on or college [at women's college] or?
Rachel: Not like childhood, but I guess like [pause] I came out at like the end of
  middle school, and like my first girlfriend was very like [pause] um [pause] like
  playing with her gender. Like wearing binders, and she like changed her name
  and stuff so um I guess like, I wasn't ever like um [pause] like lesbians are only
  attracted to certain types of women or something like that.

While only 16 percent of the United States has been found to report
knowing someone who is transgender,[45] Rachel's intimate connections to
trans-ness through her individual queer community provided her an entrée to
queer-ness and lesbian-ness that normalized and embraced trans-ness. This
connection to trans people and an understanding of the lived experiences of
trans people provided her with a different understanding of being cisgender
and a lesbian woman than she otherwise may have developed.

Rachel, though, also interrogated and reflected upon what it means to
be a lesbian in contemporary US society. I asked her, "If you were with a
trans woman, would it in anyway change how you see yourself?" Rachel
responded, "No," and explained:

Um I guess like I feel like—I mean like I know that I am a woman. I identify
as a woman and like, I guess like if I'm dating someone [pause] um [pause I
think like, I'm in love with the person who they are and so um like I do consider
myself to be attracted to women but like even like if I were dating a nonbinary
person, I would still identify as a lesbian, because it just makes sense to me. Like
I don't think I would be like bisexual or pansexual. Like I'm just more comfortable with the label, lesbian. I think like as um times are changing, I think like
the lesbian like identity is kind of like becoming more like malleable and can be
like applied to nonbinary people and things.

Rachel's reflection upon the meaning of being lesbian due to her individual
queer community and her proximity to trans individuals led to the development of a lesbian identity that was not only inclusive and accepting of trans
women but a lesbian identity that was not built upon a gender/sex binary.
While homosexuality and heterosexuality are often conceptualized as sexual
identities built upon a same-sex/opposite-sex paradigm, Rachel's construction of lesbian identity refutes the binary. A lesbian is not solely a woman
attracted to other women. Instead, for Rachel, a lesbian is simply one who
says she is a lesbian.

Other participants in this category worked as well to interrogate how they know themselves to be women. Shantelle had mentioned at the beginning of our interview that she was still working to figure out what it means for her to be a woman. I asked her, "What are some things that are prompted you to want to figure that out or to need to figure it out?" She responded:

> Okay, so one time I had this therapy session . . . my therapist, I don't even know what, what the reason was, but she asked me about it. And . . . she was like, "What, what's different for you between like, men and women? What do you feel like you are?" I was like [shrugs] and I've been sitting on that for like, three years, I still don't know. So, I just don't know. Yeah. 'Cause I'm like growing up in the age where people really talk about gender like a lot more than they ever have. So, it's like, I don't know, I know I'm not like nonbinary or anything. That doesn't really fit for me, but I can't really figure it out. But I like being a woman.

Shantelle continued beyond therapy to interrogate what it means to be a woman but was never able to arrive at an answer. Trans people are often expected by doctors, clinicians, and everyday strangers to explain why they know themselves to be a man, woman, or another gender. Shantelle, though, elucidates the difficulty in arriving at an answer beyond comfort or discomfort with one's assignment at birth. Her therapist's encouragement of her to begin questioning gender and her generation's proliferation of discourse vis-à-vis gender reconfigured womanhood for her as a place of comfort rather than a biological pre-destination.

Desire as Socially Shaped

Finally, participants in this category were critical of social understandings of desire, beauty, and attraction. Rather than conceptualizing of everyone as having their own innate preferences, participants who engaged in a Critical Cis-ness viewed desire as socialized and connected to power. At the end of each interview, I asked participants "How, if at all, should our understandings of who is beautiful, attractive, and desirable?" Janelle responded:

> I think—they should change. They should change. You know that store Aries, you know American Eagle and like they have this, they have like a little mini story for like lingerie. Yeah, and if you go onto their advertisement or you go onto Aries, their models are Black, White, skinny, fat, disabled, like it's honestly amazing. It needs to be like that, like I feel like all places should cater to all types of individuals and like also the range of sizes and things like that. If I go to Victoria's Secret and I can only be a small, medium, or large or XL but I'm a 2x or a 3x, Ima be like I'm less desirable, but if I go to Aries and they got a range up to like 4XL, I'm going to feel really good about myself. I'm going to

feel like whoa, I can buy things from here, it's beautiful, it makes me feel sexy. I'm gonna feel desirable. So we just have to, us as a society has, we have to stop like neglecting other [pause] types of people . . . Things like that and like the media like I said . . . The media, capitalism, needs to change, like if you really wanna make money, even though I hate capitalism, but if you're really tryna make money, you need to stop looking for, to make one demographic happy and try to make all demographics happy. Period.

Janelle connected who is seen as desirable to what is sold as being desirable within a hyper-capitalist society. This contrasts with those in previous categories who saw desire as an individual preference, potentially something innate, but inherently disconnected from social forces. Further, Janelle highlights that being desirable is not merely about being desirable to others but also a inner feeling of self-attraction. When one cannot find clothing in their size at any store or see themselves reflected in the advertisements, branding, and ownership of a business, it becomes that much more difficult to feel as though there is something beautiful and of value about oneself. Continuing to discuss this within our interview, Janelle discussed Eurocentric standards of beauty and issues of colorism. Janelle elaborated on the connection between white supremacy, colorism, capitalism, and desire:

It's like the more White you seem, that equals the better opportunities you can have. So, like that's why people are usually more attracted to like European features, because not only are people in general attracted to it, but jobs are attracted to it and things like that, work opportunities.

Such a connection to beauty and job opportunities is even more exaggerated for women and feminine individuals who are held to White standards of hair styling,[46] scrutinized for how they do their nails according to White and classist standards,[47] and policed for wearing "women's" items if they are not women or are not perceived to be women.[48] This is even more evident among trans women, for whom expectations to "pass" according to cisnormative, Eurocentric, middle-class standards of what a woman should look like drastically affects not only one's workplace opportunities but whether one will be more likely to be targeted for violence and harassment.

Alyx, too, felt that social conceptualizations of desire, beauty, and attraction should change. In explaining her answer, she noted:

Um I mean there's always like, with, with any social issue, I feel like there's um some group in a position of power that would like to stay in a position of power, and [pause] beauty standards might sort of play into that a lot. Um and that people who are deemed pretty would like to continue to be deemed pretty.

Alyx, Janelle, and other participants in this category conceptualized beauty and power as interconnected rather than separate phenomena. Race, class, and gender shape how others perceive individuals and what they have to offer at home and the workplace. For TERFs and Conditionally Accepting Cis-ters, trans women were conceptualized as offering dishonesty, deception, and difficulty. For those engaging in Critical Cis-ness, trans women were conceptualized as potential partners with cis people conceptualized as the ones offering difficulty, harm, and violence.

Participants who engaged in Critical Cis-ness worked to actively challenge the necropolitics of cis-ness. They constructed trans women as vulnerable to the harms of trans people and cis-ness as an assault. Black trans women, thus, need protection (including self-defense) from the harms of cis-ness. Cis-ness is marked as pathological, problematic, and violent. Finally, participants' discussion of desire and power as interconnected challenges those in prior categories who argued preferences were apolitical and biologically innate. Instead, participants in this category argued that power shapes who is seen as desirable and that those marked as desirable have greater access to power.

CONCLUSION

While no participant engaged in trans exclusionary radical feminism, many participants continued to perpetuate transphobia in differing ways, including Conditionally Accepting Cis-ters. While TERFs and Conditionally Accepting Cis-ters were more overt in their perpetuation of cis-ness and whiteness, Casual Transphobes were more covert in doing so. Casual Transphobes believed trans women were women and female and as such believed that there could be no deception if trans women did not "out" themselves as trans. However, Casual Transphobes still believed trans women were not wholly honest if they were not transparent about their trans-ness. Casual Transphobes also microaggressed trans women, referring to "visibly trans" women with they/them pronouns even when they knew the women to be women. Casual Transphobes often perpetuated cissexist microaggressions, not because they were anti-trans, but because they simply had not reflected upon trans-ness, cis-ness, and gender/sexuality as systems prior to being asked to do so in an interview setting.

While microaggressions are shown to cause harm and take a physical toll on one's mental health,[49] they also pose an opportunity, in this case, for education. Casual Transphobes engaged in microaggressive behavior due to a lack of forethought, discussion, and education on trans issues. The solution, then, is to provide greater education and space for conversations, workshops, and forums where all individuals can be taught how to unlearn these behaviors and language.

Casual Transphobes, as well, elucidated the porosity of these categories. The categories of TERF, Conditionally Accepting Cis-ters, Casual Transphobes, and Critically Cis are fluid and interlocking categories. Often, those now categorized as Critically Cis previously engaged in cissexist behavior and discourse before engaging in an active attention to their cis-ness. Amy, for example, also displayed Critically Cis behavior, such as some attention to her cis-ness. However, that was just one piece of her discourse, and I categorized her as a Casual Transphobe because her discourse fell much more in line with the beliefs and behaviors of this category than those of the Critically Cis category.

Finally, Critical Cis-ness is not a state of arrival. Instead Critical Cis-ness was an active attention to cis-ness that required constant reflexivity and self-awareness, meaning that individuals may not once and forever fit in this category and instead may shift back and forth across their life. Engaging in Critical Cis-ness meant that participants were actively working to reflect upon, interrogate, and challenge cis-ness, gender, and sexuality, recognizing that one makes mistakes in the process. In doing so, they challenged the necropolitics of cis-ness that conceptualizes the deaths of Black trans women as the justified reactions of cisgender people acting in self-defense to maintain themselves, their genders, and their sexualities.

NOTES

1. 2005, 4.
2. Williams, 2014, "TERF."
3. Tong, 2014, *Feminist Thought.*
4. For example, see: Kubala, 2020, "Teaching 'Bad Feminism': Mary Daly and the Legacy of '70s Lesbian-Feminism," *Feminist Formations.*
5. Rubin, 1975, "The Traffic in Women," 159.
6. Pearce, Erikainen, and Vincent, 2020, "TERF Wars."
7. Weinhold, 2006, "Epigenitics."
8. Fausto-Sterling, 2000, *Sexing the Body.*
9. Laqueur, 1990, *Sexing the Body.* Oyěwùmí, 1997, *The Invention of Women.* Lugones, 2007, "Heterosexualism and the Colonial/Modern Gender System." Patil, 2017, "Sex, Gender, and Sexuality in Colonial Modernity."

10. Laqueur, 1990, *Sexing the Body*. Oyěwùmí, 1997, *The Invention of Women*. Fausto-Sterling, 2000, *Sexing the Body*. Driskill, 2016, *AsegiStories*.

11. Schilt and Westbrook, 2009, "Doing Gender, Doing Heteronormativity." Spade, 2011, *Normal Life*. Haritaworn, Kuntsman, and Posocco, 2014, *Queer Necropolitics*. James et al., 2016, "The Report of the 2015 U.S. Transgender Survey."

12. Croson, 2001, "Sex, Lies, and Feminism." Cited from Green, 2006, "Debating Trans Inclusion in the Feminist Movement."

13. Morrison, 2010, "Transgender as Ingroup or Outgroup?"

14. Sue et al., 2007, "Racial Microaggressions in Everyday Life."

15. For example, see: Rustin, 2020, "Feminists Like Me Aren't Anti-Trans—We Just Can't Discard the Idea of 'Sex'."

16. For example, see Wark, 2015, "Germaine Greer: Transgender Women are 'Not Women'."

17. For example, see: Pateman, 1988, *The Sexual Contract*.

18. For example, see: Weinberg, 2018, "Derogatory Language in Philosophy Journal Risks Increased Hostility and Diminished Discussion."

19. For example, see: Raymond, 1979, *The Transsexual Empire*.

20. For example, see: "About Us." *Get the L Out UK*. http://www.gettheloutuk.com/.

21. Wild, 2019, "Lesbians at Ground Zero."

22. Tong, 2014, *Feminist Thought*, 28.

23. Endosex refers to individuals who are not intersex, while intersex refers to individuals whose bodies, gentialia, hormones, and/or chromosomes do not fit the medical definitions of what it means to be "male" or "female."

24. Zimmerly, 2013, "The Real Costs of SRS."

25. Clary, 2018, "Bottom Surgery."

26. 1997, 5.

27. Oyěwùmí, 1997, *The Invention of Women*, 14.

28. Meadow, 2018, *Trans Kids*.

29. 1985, "Manifesto for Cyborgs."

30. Pimentel, and Segura, 2018, "Paradoxes of Visibility," 94.

31. 2018.

32. Almaguer, 1993, "Chicano Men." Decena, 2011, *Sujetos Tacitos*. Moore, 2011, *Invisible Families*.

33. Bonilla-Silva, 2014, *Racism without Racists*.

34. I place "appears to be trans" in quotations here to highlight that trans bodies and aesthetics are not a monolith. There are cisgender women who are six feet and taller, as evidenced by the WNBA. There are cisgender women with facial, chest, buttocks, arm, shoulder, hand, and back hair. There are cisgender women with square jaws, larger chins, large gaps between their upper lip and bottom of their nose, large noses, wide noses, protruding brow bones, receding hairlines, short and/or no head hair, large hands, large feet, large clitorises that may resemble a small penis, internal testes, and deep voices, among other characteristics.

35. Bettcher, 2007, "Evil Deceivers and Make-Believers."

36. Gossett, Stanley, and Burton, 2017, *Trap Door*.

37. 2019, "We Should All Use They/Them Pronouns . . . Eventually."

38. 1972, "Ideology and Ideological State Apparatuses."

39. Caluya, 2006, "The (Gay) Scene of Racism."

40. Long, 2018, "Sexual Subjectivities within Neoliberalism."

41. Winnubst, 2012, "The Queer Thing About Neoliberal Pleasure."

42. Ryan, Patraw, and Bednar, 2012, "Discussing Princess Boys and Pregnant Men."

43. Mills, 2007, "White Ignorance," 35.

44. Feagin, 2006, *Systemic Racism.*

45. Adam and Goodman, 2015, "Number of Americans Who Report Knowing a Trans Person."

46. Greene, 2012, "A Multidimensional Analysis of What Not to Wear in the Workplace." Opie and Phillips, 2015, "Hair Penalties."

47. Kang, 2010, *Managed Hand.*

48. Bartlett, 1994, "Only Girls Wear Barrettes."

49. Ogunyemi et al., 2020, "Microaggressions in the Learning Environment." Smith et al., 2007, "Assume the Position."

Chapter 4

"They Kill Us Because They Hate What It Means to Love Us"

Desire and Symbolic Violence

A headline for *The Guardian* in June 2022 reads, "America is steeped in violence." Chris Cuomo, brother of the former governor of New York, titles a piece for *NewsNation*, "Violence is in the very fabric of America." A Pennsylvania State University blogsite asks, "Why are we so obsessed with violence in America?" The United States is no stranger to violence. Indeed, the nation was born through violence enacted on Indigenous Peoples and enslaved Black individuals, both of whom continue to experience the violence of white supremacy and colonialism today. Gun violence, often carried out by white supremacist and misogynist men, tends to also be at a higher rate in the US than other nations. Comparing the United States with sixty-three other high-income nations and territories, the United States ranks eighth for rates of gun violence.[1] However, several of the nations it falls below remain colonized territories of the United States (i.e., Puerto Rico, the Virgin Islands). There are, of course, numerous structural and systemic issues that facilitate this heightened rate of state violence. Focusing on intimate partner violence (IPV), researchers in Latin America have found that greater income inequality increases likelihood of intimate partner violence.[2] Similarly, researchers in the United States have pointed to the roles of historic trauma, cultural disruption, boarding schools, and other manifestations of structural oppression are connected to the high rates of IPV experienced by Indigenous women.[3] Inequality, a form of violence itself, is also a facilitator of violence.

Rather than extending the literature on structural causes of various forms of violence, in this chapter I utilize a symbolic interactionist framework to analyze how violence is understood, how it functions culturally and discursively, and how individuals make meaning of violence. I analyze the interconnections of heterosexism, transmisogyny, and whiteness as they relate to the perceived symbolic value of one's intimate partner(s). I first attend to participants' openness to dating trans women. Then, I elucidate participants' "desire to be sexually unmarked and normatively gendered."[4] Cis-het men and cis-lesbian, bisexual, and queer (LBQ) women participants felt that attraction to and/or relationships with trans women would shift how they were viewed and treated by others. Finally, I tease out the differences between those who were willing to accept the "consequences" of being with a trans woman and those who had a deeply felt desire to remain unmarked and untainted by intimate relations with trans women. Structural roots of violence must be mitigated and dismantled to prevent future violence, and cultural and discursive roots of violence must be, as well, for culture and discourse provide the justifications and rationalizations for such violence.

CIS-HET MEN PARTICIPANTS' OPENNESS TO DATING TRANS WOMEN

For a majority of cis-het men participants (10/15) and two cis-LBQ women, discovering that a woman they have interest in is transgender would automatically cause the woman to no longer be desirable. Two of the four cis-het men who were completely open to dating trans women had both dated trans women previously. One of them, Musiteli, had been in a relationship with a woman he did not know to be trans until well into the relationship. Another, Randall, was attracted to cis/trans women but was open to otherwise gendered partners. Two other cis-het men participants—Ky and Mike, a cis-het, White man—were potentially open to dating a trans woman. For Ky, it depended on whether the woman followed a cisnormative narrative of knowing that she was a girl at a young age and felt "trapped" in the "wrong body." For both Mike, Musiteli, and Ky, it depended upon which genitals the woman had and how "well" she passed as cisgender.

All four highlight patterns found in a recent survey of mostly cisgender respondents that those few (12 percent of the sample) who were open to dating a trans person were more likely to hold university degrees and less likely to be religious.[5] Additionally, bisexual, queer, pansexual and other individuals who were not gay or straight were most open to dating trans people. That those who were open to trans people were more likely to hold university degrees is most likely the case due to greater exposures to difference through education and discussion of such topics at college events and in college classrooms. Less religiosity would remove the influence of dogma and ideas of trans identity being a sin, and not being heterosexual or gay would decrease the likelihood that one's attractions are based on genitalia or gender. Neither Musiteli nor Randall had a formal education beyond high school; however, Musiteli was currently enrolled in trade school and had taken it upon himself

Table 4.1   Cis-Het Men Open to Dating Trans Women

Name[1]	Gender	Sexual Orientation	Age	Income	Race & Ethnicity	Religion	Education
Chris	Man	Bi[4]	36–46	Below/Near Poverty	Black	N/A	Less Than High School
Ky	Man	Heterosexual	18–24	Below/Near Poverty[2]	Black	N/A	Master's
Mike	Man	Heterosexual	18–24	Low	White	N/A	Bachelor's
Musiteli	Man	Heterosexual	18–24	Low	Black	Atheist	Bachelor's
Randall	Man	Heteroflexible[3]	25–35	Low	White	N/A	High School Diploma

[1]Names used are pseudonyms chosen by participants at time of interview.

[2] Below/Near Poverty (Less than $20,000); Low Income ($20–44,999); Middle Income ($45–139,999); Upper Middle Income ($140–149,999); High Income ($150–199,999); Highest Tax Brackets ($200,000+)

[3]Mostly attracted to women, occasionally attracted to men

[4]Only attracted to transgender women

to study topics ranging from sociology to business to the physical and life sciences informally via the internet. Randall was heteroflexible; thus, he was not strictly heterosexual or gay. All four were either agnostic, atheist, or simply not religious. One other participant, Chris, a cis-het, Black man, was attracted only to trans women. Chris identified as bisexual because of his attraction to trans women. Despite being attracted to and having relationships with trans women, Chris still referred to trans women as men.

CIS-LBQ PARTICIPANT'S OPENNESS TO DATING TRANS WOMEN

Cis-LBQ women's openness to dating trans women was more varied than cis-het men's. Rather than a strict binary of open or closed, cis-LBQ women's responses lay along a spectrum. Only one woman, Sheila, was entirely closed off to the idea of dating a transgender woman. When asked if she would date a woman who was trans, she responded, "I know I wouldn't date her, being that she's transgender." I asked her if it mattered whether they had undergone gender affirmation surgery, and she breathed in and said, "So me being me, I would wanna see it, like [breaths in again] I gotta see it. We gotta talk about this." However, ultimately, she felt she would not be able to turn off her brain, making it difficult for her to be with a trans woman regardless of surgery status.

Six women were open to exploring with a woman who has a penis, but they were unsure if they would enjoy it. Among those four was Cookie who felt that she could romantically be with a trans woman but might need to be polyamorous to fulfill her desire for a vulva elsewhere. Most were of these six were in there late 20s and early 30s, with one 20-years-old and one in her late 30s. Most had prior interactions with trans women. Only two participants who were not entirely open to trans women had never interacted on a recurring basis with people they knew to be trans. This included Sheila, who was entirely closed to dating trans women, and Jessica, who was only open if the woman had genital surgery. It is possible that having prior exposure to trans women made most of the women more open to exploring dating or having sex with a trans woman.

Eight cis-LBQ women were entirely open to a relationship with a trans woman. Two had completed college, five were in college, and one had never finished high school. All but one of the women had friends or family who were trans, with three knowing between three and five trans people and three knowing more than six. They were predominantly between the ages of 18–24, and only two were religious, but they explained that it was primarily for cultural reasons. Women participants, across the board, were more educated than men participants. However, it is possible that this group of participants' greater

Table 4.2   Cis-LBQ Women Not (Entirely) Open to Trans Women

Name[1]	Open to Trans Women?	Sexual Orientation	Age	Income	Race & Ethnicity	Religion	Education	Trans Interaction[3]
Alyx		Bi	18–24	Below/Near Poverty[2]	White	N/A	Some College	1–2
Amy	Open to exploring	Lesbian	36–46	Low	White Latina	N/A	Some College	0
Cookie	Open to exploring	Homoflexible[4]	25–35	Middle Income	Black	SBNR	Master's	11+
Jessica	If she's had surgery	Lesbian	25–35	Middle Income	Black	Christian	High School Diploma	0
Kylee	If she's had surgery	Lesbian	18–24	Below/Near Poverty	Black	N/A	Some College	3–5
LaLa	Open to exploring	Lesbian	18–24	Below/Near Poverty	Black	N/A	Some College	1–2
Liz	Open to exploring	Lesbian	25–35	Low	Latina	SBNR	Bachelor's	0
Sabrina	Open to exploring	Lesbian	25–35	Middle Income	Black	SBNR	Bachelor's	1–2
Sheila	No	Bisexual	25–35	Low	Black	Christian	Some College	0

[1] Names used are pseudonyms chosen by participants at time of interview.
[2] Below/Near Poverty (Less than $20,000); Low Income ($20–44,999); Middle Income ($45–139,999); Upper Middle Income ($140–149,999); High Income ($150–199,999); Highest Tax Brackets ($200,000+)
[3] Participants were asked at the end of the interview how many recurring interactions they have had with trans people, and particularly trans women, including friends, family members, (former) partners, and coworkers.
[4] Mostly attracted to women, occasionally attracted to men

Table 4.3   Cis-LBQ Women Open to Trans Women

Name[1]	Open to Trans Women?	Sexual Orientation	Age	Income	Race & Ethnicity	Religion	Education	Trans Interaction[4]
Alyshah	Yes	Lesbian	18–24	Below/Near Poverty[2]	Black	SBNR[3]	Some College	0
Amanda	Yes	Bi	25–35	Below/Near Poverty	Black	Christian	Less Than High School	3–5
Janelle	Yes	Queer	18–24	Middle Income	Black	Christian	Some College	1–2
Rachel	Yes	Lesbian	18–24	Low	White	N/A	Bachelor's	3–5
Renee	Yes	Lesbian	36–46	Low	Black	SBNR	Bachelor's	3–5
Peaches	Yes	Bi/Queer	18–24	Below/Near Poverty	Mixed—Black/White	SBNR	Some College	11+
Shantelle	Yes	Gay	18–24	Highest Tax Brackets	White	N/A	Some College	6–10
Vincent	Yes	Lesbian	18–24	Middle Income	White	N/A	Some College	6–10

[1]Names used are pseudonyms chosen by participants at time of interview.
[2] Below/Near Poverty (Less than $20,000); Low Income ($20–44,999); Middle Income ($45–139,999); Upper Middle Income ($140–149,999); High Income ($150–199,999); Highest Tax Brackets ($200,000+)
[3]Spiritual But Not Religious
[4]Participants were asked at the end of the interview how many recurring interactions they have had with trans people, and particularly trans women, including friends, family members, (former) partners, and coworkers.

frequency of connections to trans family members, friends, and coworkers made them more likely to be open to dating trans women. While those who were open to exploring with trans women also had recurring interactions with trans people, this group had a much larger transgender social network.

What It Means to Be with a Trans Woman

In large, what shaped cis men participant's openness to dating trans women was how they felt they would be viewed by others for doing so. When I asked Gee whether being with a trans woman would change how he sees himself, he responded, "I'm always going to be a heterosexual, and I know I'm a man." Gee had no desire to be with a trans woman but felt that he knew himself well enough that he was secure in his identity even if that his desire changed. However, I then asked him if dating a trans woman would change how others saw him. Gee explained, "They probably would be like, 'Is he a little bit less straight? Is he gay? Is he bi?' Because I know I would see them that way, and I would ask those questions." Gee had no desire to be with a woman "that has ever been a man" and repeatedly referred to trans women as men, using he/him pronouns for pictures of women that did not pass as cisgender. For Gee, to be with a trans woman meant that one was not truly with a woman.

While for some, it did not matter how others viewed them, Gee explained that he would feel bothered if others viewed him as anything other than het-erosexual. Gee stated, "Yeah, 'cause I don't want a man coming up to me on the street and being into me and hitting on me and being gay with me, because then Ima have to set him straight." I asked Gee what he meant by setting someone straight. Gee simply stated, "It's going to depend on how aggressive they are," and he did not explain any more with further probing. For Gee, being symbolically rendered as other than heterosexual meant that he was recognized as a potential date or hookup for gay/bisexual/queer men. Rather than simply taking a compliment from a man flirting with him or responding that he is heterosexual, Gee felt that he would have to "set him straight." The man's queerness, in this instance, is an affront to Gee's being. Thus, Gee's "setting him straight" becomes conceptualized as an act of self-defense. Fur-ther, Gee's worries about being perceived as other than a heterosexual man and experiencing other men hitting on him was not only about his sexual orientation but about his gender identity, as well. When I asked Gee about the murders of Black trans women, he responded:

> Well yeah, I could see that, I wouldn't kill them, but I could see why men would do that. Like there's a fear, you know, and that's a threat to your masculinity. You'd feel violated in a certain way. I know men who would do that. I wouldn't do that, but I know men who would.

Gee conceptualized dating and/or being with a trans woman as an assault upon his manhood and his masculinity. Being with a trans woman would mean that others may see him as gay or bisexual rather than straight, lowering him in a hierarchy of masculinities to what Connell terms "subordinate masculinities." Connell notes, "Oppression positions homosexual masculinities at the bottom of gender hierarchy among men."[6] Thus, even if a gay/bisexual man embodies an otherwise hegemonic masculinity, their non-heterosexual identity functionally depreciates their masculinity and manhood. Trans women's embodiment of a "pariah femininity"[7] is contaminating to cis-heterosexual men's masculinity, and violence against trans women enables cis-heterosexual men to move back up this hierarchy out of a subordinate masculinity.[8] While Gee, here, stated that he himself would not commit such violence, he exemplified Connell's conceptualization of "complicit masculinities."[9] Gee would not enact the violence, but he continues to benefit through his allegiance to other cis-heterosexual men and his willingness to justify their actions.

In the Introduction, I quoted Elektra from *Pose* stating, "They don't kill us because they hate us. They kill us because they hate what it means to love us." Gee explained repeatedly throughout the interview that he did not hate LGBT people. He was more accepting of cisgender LBQ women, because he had a fetish about being with a woman who wants to be with another women. However, he was tolerant of cisgender GBQ men and trans people. What is at question here, though, is not whether he can accept others existence. For Gee, trans women existing and him being seen as attracted to trans women are two different things. To be with a trans woman would render him less masculine, less heterosexual, and less of a man.

Similar to Gee, 14/15 cis-het men participants conflated gay-ness and trans-ness throughout their interviews. Musiteli did not presently conflate gay-ness and trans-ness but had in the past. Ci-LBQ women did not do so, which makes sense as they are gay/bi but are not transgender. Indeed, cisgender LGBQ people have historically fought to distinguish themselves from transgender people to make themselves more palatable to cis-het people.[10] The distinction between gay-ness and trans-ness remains more clearly drawn for cisgender LGBQ people than it is for cis-het individuals.

For example, Henry felt that people who dated trans women were not entirely heterosexual. Henry was not attracted to trans women, repeatedly explaining that "I'm just not into that." Henry, though, distinguished between cis-passing and non-passing trans women. When I asked Henry if being with a trans woman, in particular woman C, a "cis-passing," Asian American trans woman, would change how others see him, he responded:

Uh I don't, I don't think so, only because like I didn't think she was a trans woman, so no one else would dare to just be like, oh that's a trans woman, you

Figure 4.1   Woman C.

know, I mean like, if I didn't know, I know like blindly people are just like oh look at that pretty woman, you know what I mean? So, I don't think it would change or make any difference. I think if it were obvious like some of the other pictures, it definitely would change my surroundings and who I hang out with and who I associate with.

For Henry, a "cis-passing" woman did not de-heterosexualize, emasculate, or otherwise alter his being and identity. She was merely another woman unmarked by trans-ness, allowing him to remain un-marked by trans-ness. I asked Henry, though, in what ways his situation and how he was viewed would change if the woman were not "cis-passing." He said:

In the ways where people would, wouldn't want to associate with me, you know, because one, I'm gay, you know, that's already a thing, if you're gay, some people don't wanna associate, and then two, the simple fact that she's trans is like, like me and my friends were discussing, me and a close friend, he's homosexual, but he told me that there are levels to being gay, and I didn't, you know, I didn't quite get it, because I'm not in the gay community, but you know, you have your gays and you have your uh bisexuals and you have your uh trans, I mean at the very bottom, which I mean, you know, in the gay community, put trans people at the bottom, so I think knowing that, it's almost like, it's like almost, and this is a bad analogy, really, really bad analogy, but imagine if, like how back in the days when slaves kind of like, they knew they were slaves but most White men or some White men fell in love with slaves even though they were like the bottom of the bottom at the time, so it would be almost the same. Yeah. Ridicule from everyone, you know?

Henry's analogy, as poor as it is, equates interracial relationships in the antebellum United States with cisgender-transgender relationships in contemporary society. Dating a trans woman would symbolically lower him in a hierarchy of masculinities. While Connell conceptualizes gay men as embodying a "subordinate masculinity" and places them at the bottom of a hierarchy among men, Henry argued that being in a relationship with a trans woman would result in being even further below gay men in this gender hierarchy. To be trans, in this equation, is to be in excess of gay-ness. It is to be so gay that it renders one a spectacle, a target, and less than human. Gender, race, sex, and sexual orientation function as "regulatory ideals" which come to "[qualify] a body for life within the domain of cultural intelligibility."[11] Regulatory ideals are not simply categories that function to identify someone as Black or Asian American, gay or bisexual, transgender or cisgender. Rather, regulatory ideals function to delimit where the human stops and the Other begins. For Henry to be with a trans woman would result in some of the stigma placed on her as a trans woman "sticking," in the words of Goffman,[12] to him. He may be mocked, ridiculed, or further relegated into Other-ness, merely for loving someone who is excessively gay. Cis men dating trans women, thus, become hyper-subordinated within a hierarchy of masculinities.

In addition to conflating gay-ness and trans-ness, Henry conflates enslaved Blackness and trans-ness. It is important, analytically, that scholars do not collapse Blackness and trans-ness in a way that analogizes the two and ignores the intersecting experiences of Black trans people and erases the ways in which such "relationships" between White masters and Black enslaved peoples were, more often than not, nonconsensual. Henry understands that the analogy made is flawed. Yet, in his analogy is found a set of circulating symbols: differential conditions of life and death, fungibility, captivity, and fugitivity. Gender, produced out of the white supremacist enslavement of kidnapped African peoples and the genocide and internment of Indigenous peoples, "produce[d] 'gender-variant social formations as an excluded caste.'"[13] Blackness, trans-ness, and Black trans-ness are abjected from that which is human, that which is desirable, that which is loveable. Blackness, trans-ness, and Black trans-ness are surrounded by constellations of risk, violence, and death. In Henry's statement above, to love, desire, or be intimate with Black/trans people is to be touched by risk, violence, and death. Bey notes, "Gender is that which is made to attach to bodies of a domesticized space, predicated on the integrity of an ontology constituted by a White symbolic order."[14] To elude and disobey such a symbolic order is to make a tear in its fabrication, which does not go unnoticed by others who fit within and perpetuate its order. Henry is not so much unattracted to trans-ness as he is unattracted to the symbols that hover around trans-ness, which may hover around him if he finds himself in a relationship with a trans woman.

Cis-Het Women Policing Sexuality

Henry's fear of potential consequences for being attracted to trans women are not simply hypothetical. Other participants spoke of the ways in which other men may call them gay/bi, view them as less masculine, crack jokes about them and their hypothetical partner, or even, physically assault or murder another man for being with a trans woman. Such repercussions of dating a trans woman would come not only from other cis-het men but from cis-het women as well. Chris, a cis-bi, Black man spoke of his experiences being harassed by cis-het women and men for being attracted to trans women. Chris was solely attracted to trans women and identified himself to me as bisexual because of this. However, he also explained that he did not let many know he was attracted to or dated trans women. In previous relationships with trans women, he had met their friends, but he kept his world separate from the relationship. He explained why:

> I hear that every day, "I'm gay." I might sit down a [cis] woman to talk to her and somebody walk past me, "Ooh you gay. You talk to trans." I hear it every day. I walk down the street, I meet a lot of 'em [cis-het women], stop and talk to 'em, ask what they name is, but people who I know, they criticize me, "Why you fuckin around with that?"

At the time of our interview, Chris was involved in a program to prevent him from future re-arrest, as well as to help him find shelter, food, and the like. Chris had shelter, but he did not have a job and did not have any income. He spent a lot of time on the streets of downtown Atlanta, and in spending much time on the streets, interacted with others in the area who were also in similar situations. As some cis-het women came to find out he was attracted to trans women, he was harassed and made fun of. Cisgender men are not alone in policing hierarchies of masculinities. In an editorial follow-up to her work on homophobia, misogyny, and masculinities among young boys in high school, Pascoe writes of a conversation she had with a student who feared that his future son may want to play with dolls. He explained why he held this fear:

> When I was little, I loved playing with Barbies. My sister, she always told me to put 'em away. One day, she got so fed up; she dragged me outside, and shoved Barbies in all my pockets, and made me stand there while my friends laughed at me.[15]

While scholarship on masculinities has tended to focus on how cis men police one another's masculinities,[16] it is important to recognize the role cis-het women play in maintaining patriarchy and hegemonic masculinities/

femininities. Cisgender women do not benefit from the perpetuation of patriarchy, misogyny, and hegemonic masculinities; however, they too are socialized within a society that encourages young people to internalize gendered ideals. Schippers highlights that it is through social practice that masculinities and femininities are enacted and become hegemonic.[17] While she argues against conceptualizing non-hegemonic femininities as subordinate femininities because all femininities are subordinate to masculinity, there is a need for greater discussion of the ways in which cis women do subordinate and oppress trans femininities. Trans femininities, as pariah femininities, contaminate and infect the relations between masculinities and femininities. This results in some cis women mocking, degrading, and policing cis-het men's attractions to trans women. However, the policing of cis-het men's attractions to trans women is not meant to merely degrade the men but also to mock and denigrate trans women as the "improper" object of cis-het men's attractions.

While Chris was the only man I interviewed who intentionally dated trans women, two other cis-het men were open to dating trans women. However, they had not had long-term relationships with trans women that could lead others to become aware of their openness to trans women. A 2019 *Vice* article details the experience of one cis-het man whose girlfriend found out he was attracted to cis women and trans women. The article explains:

> At first, she cried and interrogated him: Was he gay? Was she just a prop for him to look straight? Why did he hide this from her? Then, she got mean. Over the course of a month, Owen said she used his sexuality as a weapon against him. According to Owen, she pitilessly mocked him, remarking on how disappointed he must be that she doesn't have a dick. He obviously "wanted to be a bottom," he recalled her saying; to "get a good fucking." Sometimes, when they were intimate, Owen said that she would climb on top of him and mockingly simulate fucking him in the ass.[18]

Much like Chris, the man involved in this situation was mocked, chided, and derided for being attracted to trans women in addition to cis women. He was assumed to be on the down low and to be using her as a beard, as she viewed trans women as men dressed in women's clothing. Monosexism[19] and cissexism intersect in this instance, with cis-het women assuming that a cis man can only like men or women, and if he likes women, it is assumed that "woman" only includes cisgender women.

Cis-het men were not alone, though, in feeling as though they would be perceived differently and may experience consequences for dating or being with a trans woman. Janelle, an eighteen-year-old, cis-queer Black woman, spoke of her hesitancy to introduce any woman she dated, whether cis or trans, to her given family. Janelle had only recently told her mother that she was queer, and her mother reacted poorly, citing Biblical fundamentalism as her "evidence" that Janelle had morally strayed. When I asked Janelle if being with a trans woman would change how others see her, she responded:

> Yeah probably . . . People are judgmental. They'd be like . . . I don't know just like people are judgmental and . . . and I don't know, just they, I don't think, I'm just thinking about like my family in specific. But I just gotta live my life for myself and not for others.

alithia: Okay what might your family say? Do you think they'd be more upset if you were with a trans woman than a cis woman?
Janelle: Yeah, maybe my mom actually will slit my throat.

Janelle, here, was being hyperbolic regarding her mother murdering her; however, her response echoes cis-het men's response. In Janelle's response, trans-ness is, again, conflated with an excess of queerness—an excess that would push away any familial relationship Janelle wanted to maintain. To be with a trans woman would mean that Janelle's family would rupture, which, for an eighteen-year-old, would be a profound shift in her life.

Cis-LBQ Women Policing Sexuality

In addition to cis-het women policing the relationships of cis-LBQ women, cis-LBQ women participants spoke of the ways in which cis-lesbian women police the boundaries of lesbian identity vis-à-vis trans women. In the White/White-passing participant focus group, I asked participants why they felt some cis-lesbian women might have a strong reaction to trans women being in lesbian spaces or claiming a lesbian identity. Vincent and Rachel responded:

Vincent: . . . I know some of us have had experiences with dating um like men and we kind of equate just like associate like if you identified as a man in the past or if you have or had a penis, well, it's, still kind of an intrusion like and some might have like traumatic experiences with it, not to say trans women don't belong in lesbian spaces, but if lesbians did feel threatened then that might be why.
Rachel: Yeah, I think that some lesbians feel that trans women don't belong in lesbian spaces because they're like quote not real women, um or they feel that like they're like men trying to infiltrate the like female spaces, which is just um outdated thinking and really inappropriate. Um [pause].
alithia: How come?
Rachel: Because like . . . if someone identifies as a woman, like they're a woman, and I don't think we should be questioning that, but I think some older lesbians are like more um cautious too or like more apprehensive about like accepting that.

Vincent, here, notes the ways in which the transphobia, in lesbian communities, may collapse around traumatic experiences with penises. 18.3 percent of cis women experience sexual assault/sexual violence in their lifetimes, with Black and Indigenous women experiencing higher rates of sexual victimization in their lifetimes.[20] As such, it would not be uncommon for numerous cis-lesbian women to have experienced sexual trauma at the hands of a cis man perpetrator. Nighty-eight percent of reported sexual assault/violence occurs at the hands of cis men. And, indeed, 37 percent of trans women experience sexual assault in their lifetimes, with Black, Indigenous, and Middle Eastern trans women experiencing higher rates of assault in their lifetimes.[21] Comparing the two rates, trans women experience double the likelihood of sexual assault in their lifetimes. Vincent explains, though, that the penis, rather than the cis man, functions symbolically as a perpetrator of trauma for some cis-lesbian women. As such, trans women, whether they have a penis or not, may be assumed to be potential threats of violence.

Additionally, Rachel attributed anti-trans attitudes to anachronistic, older, cis-lesbian women. Such an explanation functioned to dispel any association with transphobia from herself and other young lesbians and simultaneously explained transphobic attitudes as views that will eventually die away with older cis-lesbian women without needing any other shifts or changes within lesbian communities and spaces. Vincent and Rachel both explained the ways in which cis-lesbian spaces, communities, and/or identities may be policed by other cis-lesbian women. If it is assumed by some that trans women are not real women, can a cis-lesbian woman bring her trans lesbian girlfriend to a lesbian event, for example? How we understand and speak about gender can make precarious and fragile the material lives of trans women and those who love them, whether that individual be a cis-het man or a cis-LBQ woman.

CONCLUSION

What is at the core of this conversation for my participants is not simply whether a woman is trans or not, but whether a cis individual being with a trans woman may experience some of the barriers, harassment, and/or discrimination that trans people experience in their everyday lives. The symbols that circulate around a sociopolitical conceptualization of "trans woman" can come to stick to those that love and/or have sex with trans women. Violence becomes a way of shedding these symbols. This violence is not merely repressive of trans people, but it is also productive of cis-ness. As Westbrook, notes, "Violence genders, sexualizes, and racializes . . . violence itself produces and perpetuates gender, sexuality, and race as social systems."[22] Violence against Black trans women and the ways in which participants made sense of this violence produced an account of Black trans women and other trans women as assaultive, violating, and a threat. Simultaneously, violence against Black trans women may enable cis-het men to recuperate their position in a hierarchy of masculinities and produces and maintains cis-ness for cis-het men and cis-LBQ women.

A tension between desire for trans women and disgust of trans women exists in the lives of cis-het men participants. Cis-het men may find themselves physically attracted to trans women while simultaneously feeling disgusted or angered at the possibility that the woman they are into is not cisgender. In part, the affective dimension of anger and disgust arise out of the regulation of cis-het men's attractions and masculinities by other cis-het men, as well as by cis-het women. Manhood and hegemonic masculinities "must be validated by other men" in order to be actualized.[23] A lack of respect from other cis-het men can result in cis-het men losing some of the "power" that comes with their positionalities. For Black cis-het men participants, the consequences of being with a trans woman may be even more serious, as Black men's genders are hyper-regulated in US society.[24] Writing on the gendered and sexual geographies of Blackness, Bailey and Shabazz note, "If Black spatiality is excluded from the White world, then Black queer space . . . is placeless."[25] Black cis-het men's masculinities are already policed and questioned. If being with a trans woman means that a cis-het man lowers in the hierarchy of masculinities, then Black cis-het men are potentially at risk of further scrutiny, punishment, and racialized-gendered dispossession. As I detail as well in the next chapter, middle- and upper-income Black, cis-het men may differentiate themselves as "good" Black people in contrast to "bad" Black people (e.g., queer, trans, poor) in order to avoid being associated with the stigma of those deemed "bad." Page and Richardson, argue, for example, that "the racial penalties imposed on Blacks who violated white standards [historically]" have contributed "the cultural determinants producing Black anxiety about over-conforming or failing to conform to dominant standards."[26]

Collectively, the symbolic circuitry surrounding trans women comes to make *being with* trans women undesirable. To be with a trans woman comes to say something about the person with them. For cis-lesbian women and cis-het men participants, their lesbian identity and heterosexual identity respectively may come into question if they are with a trans woman, particularly a trans woman with a penis. Trans women's embodiment of pariah femininities contaminates the relations of masculinities and femininities, resulting in cis-het men feeling emasculated or enduring social punishment. For cis-LBQ women participants, the penis became the central obstacle, as so much of what it means to be gay, lesbian, or even heterosexual in US society revolves around partners having different or similar genitals. In the next chapter, I discuss how cis-het men and cis-LBQ women understand, explain, and/or justify the murders of Black trans women vis-à-vis such ruptures in heterosexuality and lesbian-ness.

NOTES

1. The Global Burden of Disease 2016 Injury Collaborators, 2018, "Global Mortality from Firearms."

2. Yapp and Picket, 2019, "Greater Income Inequality is Associated with Higher Rates of IPV."

3. Burnette, 2015, "Historical Oppression and IPV."

4. Ward, 2015, *Not Gay*, 35.

5. Blair and Hoskin, 2018, "Transgender Exclusion."

6. 1995, *Masculinities*, 28.

7. Schippers, 2007, "Recovering the Feminine Other."

8. Bourdieu, 1998, *Masculine Domination.* Pascoe, 2007, *Dude, You're a Fag.*

9. Connell and Messerschmidt, 2005, "Hegemonic Masculinity."

10. Chauncey, 1995, *Gay New York.* Vaid-Menon, 2015, "Trans is NOT the New Struggle!"

11. Butler, 1993, *Bodies that Matter.*

12. 1963, *Stigma.*

13. Page and Richardson, 2010, "On the Fear of Small Numbers." Cited from Snorton, 2017, *Black on Both Sides.*

14. 2019, "Black Fugitivity Un/Gendered," 56.

15. 2007, "'Dude, You're a Fag.'"

16. Connell, 1995, *Masculinities.* Bourdieu, 1998, *Masculine Domination.* Pascoe, 2007, *Dude, You're a Fag.*

17. 2007.

18. Tourjée, 2019, "What Happens When Your Girlfriend Finds Out You're into Trans Women."

19. Monosexism refers to the assumption that individuals are only attracted to one of two genders in a binary gender schema (Toft and Yip, 2018, "Intimacy Negotiated").

20. Black et al., 2011, "The National Intimate Partner and Sexual Violence Survey."

21. James et al., 2016, "The Report of the 2015 U.S. Transgender Survey."

22. 2021, *Unlivable Lives*, 28.

23. Bourdieu, 1998 [2002], *Masculine Domination.*

24. Bailey and Shabazz, 2014, "Gender and Sexual Geographies of Blackness."

25. Bailey and Shabazz, 2013, "Anti-Black Heterotopias."

26. Page and Richardson, 2011, "On the Fear of Small Numbers."

Chapter 5

"I Might Just Kill You"

The Murders of Black Trans Women

In August 2020, three trans women of color friends and social media influencers were attacked in Hollywood by a group of cisgender men while cisgender men and women onlookers laughed, berated, and egged on the men inflicting the physical violence. Joslyn, one of the women attacked, wrote on Instagram,

> He said if I was trans he would kill me. He then forced me to hold his hand while he looks [*sic*] for my friends to kill them for being trans. Meanwhile men and WOMEN screaming that I'm a man and telling him to beat me.[1]

Joslyn posted a video that onlookers had taken of the man threatening her and dragging her around the street. The onlooker filming captioned the video, "He mad she was a man . . ."

Unfortunately, anti-trans violence is not a rarity. When I first began my dissertation research, I was uncertain that cis-het men and cis-lesbian, bisexual, and queer (LBQ) women would tell me their true feelings about anti-trans violence and the murders of Black trans women. As I began interviewing participants, though, I was shocked at the nonchalance with which many reacted to the murders of Black trans women. After asking participants questions about what it would mean to desire or sexually/romantically be with a trans woman, I explained to them:

> Sometimes, men have sex with, flirt with, or interact in some way with a woman romantically/sexually, find out she's trans, and in response, the men will murder the woman, especially if she's Black. In court, some of these men argue that they were so distraught by finding out the woman was trans that they overreacted and didn't know what they were doing, resulting in her death. What are your thoughts in response to this argument?

After asking the question, I would reiterate that they can answer honestly and there would be no judgment however they answered. While no cis-LBQ woman participant said that they would kill a trans woman, knew people who would, or that they understood it, sixteen out of thirty-two participants described trans women as deceptive and as "hiding" the "truth" about who they are. Cis-het men participants were more diverse in their responses. Indeed, some found the murders heinous, while others openly stated they would kill a trans woman, knew men who would, or found the murders excessive but understandable.

In analyzing participant data regarding my question on the murders of Black trans women, I began to see four distinct categories in which participants' answers fell. These include those who found the murders extreme but understandable. Participants in this category would not murder someone themselves and did not feel they knew anyone who would. However, they were able to make logical sense of the murders of Black trans women. A second category of participants felt they, themselves, would commit such a murder or knew people who would. A third category of participants found the murders of trans women wrong. However, they simultaneously placed the blame of the murder on trans women for, what they perceived to be, a lack of honesty about one's trans identity. A final category differed greatly from these former three, in that, they re-conceptualized cisgender people as being at fault for the murders of Black trans women rather than placing the blame on trans women. In this chapter, I flesh out the reasons offered by participants as to why cis-het men kill Black trans women, including the ways in which participants decried and/or justified such violence. I highlight how trans-ness, itself, was conceptualized as an assault on innocent bystanders, and I discuss how more casual forms of cissexism intertwined with overt forms of cissexism, such as the murders of Black trans women.

EXTREME BUT UNDERSTANDABLE

Three out of thirty-two participants felt the murders of Black trans women were extreme reactions by cis-het men but were understandable situationally. The three were not hypermasculine or hyperfeminine in gender expression (see appendix table 9.2), nor did they have any known recurring interactions with trans people. As I show in the next section, as well, those who felt like the murders of trans women were, in some and/or all cases, justified knew few to no trans women. In addition to other demographics I have listed thus far, I additionally categorized perceived LGB acceptance of participants. I did not measure this in an empirical sense. Rather, my categorizations are meant to loosely assess how increased LGB antagonism potentially related

Table 5.1 **Extreme But Understandable**

Name[1]	Gender	Sexual Orientation	Age	Income	Race & Ethnicity	Religion	Education	Known Trans Interactions[3]
Jake	Man	Heterosexual	18–24	Low	Black	N/A	Bachelor's	0
Ky	Man	Heterosexual	18–24	Below/Near Poverty	Black	N/A	Master's	0
Sheila	Woman	Bisexual	25–35	Low	Black	Christian	Some College	0

[1] Names used are pseudonyms chosen by participants at time of interview.
[2] Below/Near Poverty (Less than $20,000); Low Income ($20–44,999); Middle Income ($45–139,999); Upper Middle Income ($140–149,999); High Income ($150–199,999); Highest Tax Brackets ($200,000+)
[3] Participants were asked at the end of the interview how many recurring interactions they have had with trans people, and particularly trans women, including friends, family members, (former) partners, and coworkers.

to cissexism and transmisogynoir. I categorized LGB acceptance as "inclusive," "slightly heteronormative," "moderately heteronormative," and "very heteronormative" (see table 9.2 in the appendix for categorical descriptions). One participant, Ky, was categorized as slightly heteronormative for his belief that some LGBT people may be queer or trans due to childhood sexual/mental trauma. However, the other two were overwhelmingly accepting and inclusive of cisgender LGB people. Their problem was not with same-gender sexual attraction. Their problem, instead, lay with trans people, trans surgeries, and what they saw as an "excess" of queerness presented through trans identity.

Sheila, consistently referred to trans women as men and used "he" pronouns for them throughout the interview. She told me that she had once had a trans woman coworker; however, she referred to her coworker as a "guy" and used "he" pronouns for her. When I asked Sheila how she felt regarding the murders of Black trans women, she responded:

Sheila: They lied.
alithia: Okay, why?
Sheila: Because, okay um. . .I don't say—trans as in full operation?
alithia: Either, both.
Sheila: Um I feel like full operation, that's a different story, still in process [pause].
alithia: How come?
Sheila: Full operation, because I feel that's a mental thing.
alithia: For the guy?
Sheila: Yeah, it's a mental thing for the guy, because [pause] in, in [pause] reality [pause] that's a woman. Like on paper, now, that's a woman. And in body form that's a woman. Um [pause] um so [pause] it's the fact that your mind can't get over the fact that that once had a penis, so in the moment if you flip, because [pause] because you couldn't control yourself or you didn't know what to do, emotionally you were so fucked up in that moment, like I could understand it. On a very small scale. But there are people who say they flipped after finding out with people still in process. Noooooo. The sex is too intimate for you to not have known. You knew. There's no way. No way. You knew.

For Sheila, the trans woman is perpetually tainted by the once penis. The man has in front of him what looks like a woman, speaks like a woman, is legally a woman *yet* the fact of this woman once having had a penis is emotionally disorienting. A survey of the websites of surgeons conducting trans surgeries and their results photo galleries displays the vulvas of numerous trans woman—vulvas that vary in size, shape, and hair like all other vulvas; vulvas that have labia, clitorises, clitoral hoods, vaginal canals; vulvas that are wet and vulvas that are dry. The fact, though, of the vulva having once been a penis and scrotum is intense enough to, despite this all, emotionally "fuck someone up" enough that "on a small scale," Sheila can understand why a man would commit such a murder.

In many ways, Sheila's response is reminiscent of the doctors and health care professionals Fausto-Sterling[2] and Davis[3] discuss who conduct nonconsensual surgeries on intersex babies. Such physicians, researchers, and surgeons believe that intersex children's bodies so disrupt the gender binary that they would experience enough harassment and psychic trauma that would "outweigh" the myriad risks and violence associated with the surgeries. Sheila's response highlighted that, while she does not feel murder is an acceptable response, that it is understandable that a man would feel so overwhelmed by a person whose existence defies binary sex/gender logic that he may react in a violent manner. Black trans women murdered by cis-het men face the very violence that doctors argue intersex surgeries can prevent. Trans-ness, as well as being intersex, becomes defined as an assault upon another's psyche.

Ky also felt that the reaction of murder is extreme in response to cis-het men "discovering" that a woman is transgender. Ky, like Sheila, believed murder is wrong and that everyone should be held accountable for committing murder. However, he also felt he could make sense of why a cis-het man would feel overwhelmed and urged to commit murder in this scenario. He stated:

> I mean, as far as feelings, people are entitled to their feelings. So I understand there are feelings, not understand, like I relate, but I can mathematically make sense of it, not for me, but for them. As far as an argument for like murder, I don't think it's very strong at all. I'm like, I'm sorry. You're not supposed to murder. I hate that this overwhelming urge came over you. And it resulted in the girl dying, but at the end of the day, you know, you can't murder somebody. So for me personally, it's a trash argument. Maybe I wouldn't give you like a crazy sentence for it. But, you know, you still murdered somebody; that's in no way taking you off the hook.

Despite the extremity of murder, all three participants in this category felt they could understand why someone would commit the crime. Jake, too, understood that "she—or he—fucked him [the cis-het man] up mentally, just like if a person killed your child . . . Like you could fuck somebody up with that." The "that" here that Jake was referring to at the end is the "hiding" of one's trans identity. For Jake, Sheila, and Ky, there is an element of trans-ness that is assaultive, duplicitous, and overwhelming. Just as one may feel the need to avenge their child's murder, they may feel the need to avenge a "violation" of their cisgender manhood and heterosexuality. The conceptualization of trans-ness as an assault renders a man's murder of a trans woman self-defense. Bourdieu highlights the role that fear plays for men and masculine individuals. For them, there is a "fear of losing the respect or admiration" of other men, which would result in a lack of social validation of one's manhood or masculinity.[4]

Ky explained this fear of losing the validation of one's manhood/masculinity in further explaining why men might kill trans women. Ky stated:

> You know, he's--maybe somewhere deep down he fears he might be gay. He's trying to run from that, see what I'm saying?. And now you know, he had it, he had sex with a trans and for him that trans might be like, yo, I know you say you're trans but you still a man in my mind, transitioned from male, you didn't tell me, you know, it can hurt his pride as a man . . . He's you know, having all kind of internal identity crises on the inside...And it even feels like this person did something to me . . . They did this to me, they're the reason I'm here, people with men's pride, you know, so high and so strong and angry with the beast to come out . . . these melting pot factors come together to kind of create mathematically speaking in a sense.

While Ky's response focused on a man potentially being gay and having internalized homophobia that results in an "identity crisis," it is important to highlight that, whether the man who murders is gay or not ultimately does not matter. The man who murders a trans woman, in being rendered gay, lowers in the hierarchy of masculinities to a "subordinate masculinity."[5] Masculinity, though, is a process, not a fixed identity. Pascoe, notes, one "moves out of faggotry by making another boy a fag."[6] From my analyses, I add that one can move out of faggotry by murdering a woman he finds out is trans.

While Jake, Sheila, and Ky did not advocate for murder or feel that it should occur, they also did not seek to rule it out as an understandable reaction. Trans-ness, in this way, was constructed as an attack against a person. A person, when attacked, "understandably" defends themself. To define trans-ness as an assault is to define the murders of Black trans women as a defense mechanism. In other words, participants argued that trans women cause their own murders. Cis-ness, while assumed natural, instead exists in this way as a fragile subjectivity, violated by the existence of someone who defies its logic. The three participants discussed here differed from the overt cissexism participants in the next section displayed. However, while they did not overtly advocate for or support the murders of trans women, the language used to "make sense" of the murders provides the foundation for the logic used by those who would kill.

"NOW THAT'S WHERE I MIGHT KILL YOU RIGHT THEN AND THERE."

In comparison to the three participants discussed in the previous section, four participants felt that there are scenarios in which they, or someone they know, would kill a trans woman. All four were cis-het, Christian, Black men, and repeatedly made reference to religious doctrine throughout the interviews and used heteronormative discourse when discussing LGB people. Mack, for example, emphasized that his fiancée was lesbian but chose to be with him because she was "saved through Christ." Additionally, three of the four were either very masculine in their expression or attempt to display their masculinity in more grandiose ways, such as Josh, who repeatedly emphasizes his "large dick" as a display of the power of his masculinity. Three of the four had never had any recurring interactions with people they knew to be trans. One of the four, Mack, had known trans women from his time in prison. None of the trans women he knew, though, were friends, family, otherwise intimate relations, and he still referred to them as men. This category of response was the only single gender category; in this case, cis-het men. In addition, it was the only category of response that was offered by an entirely Christian sub-sample and entirely Black men sub-sample.

The commonality between this category of participants and the former is that none of these participants had friends, family, or other intimates who they knew to be transgender. This lack of social contact with and proximity to trans people may have shaped their greater willingness to justify or commit murders of Black trans women. Several recent quantitative studies analyzing cisgender individuals' perceptions of trans people have found that those who closely know trans people are less likely to hold anti-trans sentiments.[7] In comparison to those in the previous category of individuals who found the murders extreme but understandable, those in this current category of individuals willing to commit the murders were all religious, with Christianity strongly shaping their views of the world and how they live their lives. Their high religiosity most likely also shaped this category of participants' willingness to commit murders of trans woman or to know individuals who would. Finally, as I will discuss further below, their masculinity as Black men in the US also factored into their responses.

Mack found a trans panic defense and the murders of Black trans women to be nonsensical if they resulted only out of a flirt, as in the case of Islan Nettles, who was murdered by a man after his friends mocked him for flirting with a trans woman.[8] While Mack felt that such a situation was extreme and was not a reason to murder someone, he responded otherwise regarding other situations. Mack told me:

> I ain't gonna front. If I had sex with a transgender and she told me after I had sex with her, that shit would make me mad as hell, and in that reaction I might just kill you, like, "Oh, I just shot you." Know what I'm saying? It happens, I might just have that strap like, 'Yo, that's just because I'm mad as fuck. Like I'm, I'm, I'm just that type of n***a. I'd kill anybody that fucks with me. Like the deception part. But if she's telling you, you ain't do anything, and y'all flirting, you ain't got to take it to the next step. Nah, give that n***a the book. I feel

Chapter 5

Table 5.2 "I Might Kill You"

Name[1]	Gender	Sexual Orientation	Age	Income	Race & Ethnicity	Religion	Education	Number of Recurring Known Trans Interactions[3]
Gee	Man	Heterosexual	36–46	Low	Black	Christian	Bachelor's	0
Iceberg	Man	Heterosexual	47+	Below/Near Poverty	Black	Christian	Some College	0
Josh	Man	Heterosexual	25–35	Middle Income	Black	Christian	Bachelor's	0
Mack	Man	Heterosexual	25–35	Middle Income	Black	Christian	Some College	3-5

[1] Names used are pseudonyms chosen by participants at time of interview.

[2] Below/Near Poverty (Less than $20,000); Low Income ($20–44,999); Middle Income ($45–139,999); Upper Middle Income ($140–149,999); High Income ($150–199,999); Highest Tax Brackets ($200,000+).

[3] Participants were asked at the end of the interview how many recurring interactions they have had with trans people, and particularly trans women, including friends, family members, (former) partners, and coworkers.

like yeah, he deserves the book. Because to me, ain't, 'I had a reaction.' 'Oh, oh I'm a transgender, oh shit' boom. Like . . . nah bro. What did she do to you? You know what I'm saying?

Here, Mack did not say, "If I had sex with a woman and she told me after that she was trans . . ." Instead, Mack said, "If I had sex with a *transgender*." For Mack, and five other participants, transgender was not an adjective to describe the type of woman A is. Instead, transgender functioned as a noun, referring to a separate gender or type of person. If one recognizes, though, that the woman they are sleeping with is indeed a woman, then there can be no deception, as she is not lying about her womanhood. The discursive description of trans women as deceptive only holds if one believes a trans woman is not, in essence, a woman.

Iceberg, also felt that there were certain scenarios in which killing a trans woman was understandable. He, too, distinguished between different situational encounters with trans women like Mack. For Iceberg, if the woman physically "passes" as a cisgender woman and has a vulva, then "she a woman, because . . . who would know?" As highlighted in Chapters One and Two, the idea that some trans individuals "pass" and others "appear to

Figure 5.1 Woman A.

be trans" necessitates problematization for several reasons. First, there is no "one look" of trans people or cis people. Trans women and cis women may have large or small hands, curvy or more square-shaped upper bodies, and facial hair or a smooth face. Trans women and cis women vary greatly within group vis-à-vis vocal tone, height, weight, and gender expression, as just a few examples. Ultimately, one cannot know another individual's gender identity or sex assigned at birth without either knowing the individual or asking. Individuals may be (mis)recognized as particular genders;[9] however, that (mis)recognition is based off cultural schemas that change across time and place. Further, the categorization of some women as "cis-passing" and others as "visibly trans" presumes that one category is aesthetically superior to the other. While trans women who are perceived to be "cis-passing" by others may experience less direct violence than other trans women, the privileging of "cis-passing" trans women perpetuates cisnormative, White standards of beauty as noted in chapters 1 and 2.

While Iceberg would not feel deceived if he slept with a trans woman with a vulva who did not tell him she was trans, he did feel that other situations would lead him to feel deceived. I asked Iceberg:

alithia: What if she hasn't had the surgery, doesn't "look" trans—
Iceberg: —And got something hanging?
alithia: Yeah.
Iceberg: Hell nah [laughs.] Yeah that's a trick. Nah, we aren't doing that one. I couldn't do that one now. Now that's where I might kill you right then and there. Uh-uh no. No, you got it wrapped up, balls up, uh-uh no. But see I'm not going to be jumped like that. I wouldn't be jumped like that. I'm going to take the time, fixing to see.

For Iceberg, the penis is the tipping point. To be perceived by others as a woman, to say you are a woman, and to not disclose your genitalia is "a trick." Iceberg explicated what Dozier argued in their study of trans men doing gender. Dozier argued that, when individuals are interpreting others' gender and gender expression, what they are often guessing at are the genitals one has.[10] When one appears "as a woman," it is culturally assumed that they have a vulva. When one appears "as a man," it is culturally assumed that they have a penis. It is not a question that is oft asked, but to be a woman and not disclose the presence of your penis becomes duplicitous. Not only is the penis the tipping point, though, but the woman's trans-ness and her genitalia become something that she has "covered up" ("got it wrapped up") and something that is assaulting ("jumped like that") Iceberg. Ten participants (eight cis men and two cis women), like Iceberg, conflated trans-ness as a covering up of one's sex assigned at birth. When asked if they could tell who is trans and who is not, participants would say it is getting hard to tell, because, as Jake stated, "Some of them are getting really good at like covering it up." This conflation of trans womanhood and a covering up of one's "manhood" is at the crux of Iceberg's feeling tricked if a woman does not tell him she has a penis. Her gender expression functions, for Iceberg, to cover up the fact of her penis.

Gee also conflated trans womanhood with a covering up of one's "manhood" and conceptualized trans-ness as an assault.

> I could see that. I wouldn't kill them, but I could see why men would do that. Like there's a fear, you know, and that's a threat to your masculinity. You'd feel violated in a certain way. I know men who would do that. I wouldn't do that, but I know men who would.

Trans-ness, again, was conceptualized as something that assaults, harms, and threatens. It is, in this way, not a state of being nor a description of one's gender. Trans-ness, instead, functioned for men like Gee as a weapon. As such, the murders of Black trans women become a defense mechanism. Cis-ness, masculinity, and heterosexuality come to necessitate the murders of Black trans women to protect themselves when threatened by attraction to a trans woman.

As discussed in the Introduction, Elliot and Lyons highlight, "The function of a phobic object is to specify and contain a generalized threat."[11] Cis-het men's fear of violation, in part, collapses around the penis, as in the case of Iceberg, Mack, Josh, and other men and women interviewed. The penis is socially constructed as a weapon, as having the power to violate. This is not surprising, given the historical and cultural construction of penises and penetration as a form of power. Bersani notes how Ancient Greeks, radical feminists, and various gay men communities have, at different times, conceptualized penetration, writing, "To be penetrated is to abdicate power."[12] In Iceberg, Mack, and Josh's responses, the presence of a penis on a woman comes to be viewed as a sort of social penetration resulting in a threat to a man's masculinity, power, and honor. Iceberg, Mack, Josh, and other cis-het men participants all, presumedly, have penises. However, their own penises do not necessarily elicit any threat of violation to themselves. Instead, it is the presence of a second penis on an individual whom they desire that evokes the threat and anxiety of violation. The threat of the second penis is also shaped by the conceptualization of hegemonic masculinities and femininities as different yet complementary. If a man's power or masculinity diminishes upon being attracted to a trans woman, then enacting violence against and murdering trans women may aid in recuperating and building back up his masculine, heterosexual subjectivity, as masculinity and manhood are accomplished, in part, when men "rise to the challenge of the opportunities available to [them] to increase [their] honor."[13]

The cis-het men participants in this section relayed their perceptions of the murders of Black trans women to me with complete ease and nonchalance. Their body language remained the same at this point of the interview as during other parts. Their responses also highlight the ease with which they would absolve a man of murdering a trans woman. A conceptualization of trans-ness as an assault and the collapsing of their cissexism around the penis both function to dehumanize a trans woman. She is not a woman but a penis; not a woman but a weapon.

Racialized Cis-ness

While those who felt the murders of Black trans women were extreme but understandable, and those who said they, or those they knew, would murder a trans woman were all Black, there were also Black participants who sought to challenge cissexism and transmisogynoir, and I will discuss them in subsequent sections. My sample is also predominantly Black, so participants in all categories are more likely to be Black than to be another race. White men and non-Black men of color are not somehow less transphobic than Black men.

Additionally, who men date and racial segregation of neighborhoods is important within this analysis. Both Gee and Jake preferred Black women as partners. While Josh and Iceberg flirted with me as a White woman and their preferences in women included women who look like "Kim Kardashian," they lived in a predominantly Black part of Atlanta, meaning they were more likely to interact with other Black people. Due to racial segregation of neighborhoods and US heterosexual and same-gender relationships being predominantly intra-racial.[14] Black cis-het cissexist men are more likely to murder Black trans women and White cis-het cissexist men are more likely to murder White trans women.

Further, as scholars like Elijah Anderson have detailed, cis-het, Black men who live in disinvested parts of the city, as Josh and Iceberg did, "understand that violence against any one of them means less to the authorities than violence against white people."[15] Josh and Iceberg both lived in segregated, impoverished areas in Atlanta, and Mack had previously been incarcerated and was part of a gang as a teenager and young adult. Class,[16] more than other factors, shapes adherence to differing types of masculinities,[17] and "race is, itself, an economic factor."[18] Working-class and oppressed men face challenges and opposition to their masculinities: from the criminal legal system, the workplace, peers, family members, and other men with whom they interact. These challenges to their masculinity tell them that they are not properly masculine; that is, that they are not masculine enough or too masculine. In response to over-policing of their neighborhoods, mass incarceration, economic disinvestment, and experiences of discrimination, working-class,

Black men may cultivate hypermasculinity as a defense mechanism.[19] Hyper-masculinity and violence become defense mechanisms to foster physical pro-tection, but even more so, to protect one's reputation and respect in the eyes of other men.[20] Again, Anderson is instructive here, noting:

> In the local community, the civil law and its agents have limited credibility, and over time confidence in the law has been seriously eroded. "Street justice" fills the void, becoming an important principle of local social relations. And matters of reputation or street credibility become all the more important, serving as a form of social coin. But "street cred" cannot be attained once and for all; it is high maintenance and must be husbanded, nurtured, and replenished from time to time . . . through actual deeds, which must be performed repeatedly to earn the desired effect: respect.[21]

It is also possible, that desiring trans women can result in further surveillance of cis-het, Black men by the police or social discipline from other Black people who, due to centuries of racialized punishment, perceive nonconformity as a collective threat.[22] One method some use to reduce police suspicion is to exag-gerate heterosexual relationships and ensure that cis-het women partners are around.[23] Black trans women, also hyper-surveilled and policed, may be viewed as a threat to this goal. Further, scholars have highlighted how middle-class Black men and women regulate gender and sexual difference through "appeals to normativity" as a way of distinguishing oneself as the "good" Black person in comparison to the "bad" (e.g., queer, trans, poor) Black person.[24] Combined, these structural, racial, and interpersonal factors produce a racialized and classed cis-ness, in which cis-ness may function differently, or arise out of different conditions than, a White and/or middle-class cis-ness. These factors do not justify the murders of Black trans women, but they must be addressed as part of efforts in ameliorating and ending the murders of Black trans women.

"MURDER IS WRONG, BUT . . . I FEEL LIKE A TRANSSEXUAL SHOULD JUST GO IN AND SAY, 'I'M A MAN.'"

In the previous section, I explicated the justifications cis-het men gave as to why they or other men would kill a trans woman. While such statements are overtly cissexist and bluntly accepting of transmisogynoir, I detail in this show how more subtle and covert transphobic responses provide the foun-dation from which cis-het men like the participants in the previous section draw when discussing and/or committing such murders. While only seven out of thirty-two participants felt the murders of trans women made sense, another nine strongly felt that the murders were unjustified, but continued to discursively perpetuate the cissexist arguments that the other seven utilized to

Table 5.3   "That's Not Okay But . . ."

Name[1]	Gender	Sexual Orientation	Age	Income	Race & Ethnicity	Religion	Education	Number of Recurring Known Trans Interactions[3]
Adam	Man	Heterosexual	25–35	Low[2]	Middle Eastern	Muslim	Some College	0
Amanda	Woman	Bi	25–35	Below/Near Poverty	Black	Christian	Woman	3–5
Chris	Man	Bi[4]	36–46	Below/Near Poverty	Black	N/A	Less Than High School	11+
D	Man	Heterosexual	25–35	Below/Near Poverty	Black	N/A	Some College	1–2
Liz	Woman	Lesbian	25–35	Low	Latina	SBNR	Bachelor's	0
Mike	Man	Heterosexual	18–24	Low	White	N/A	Bachelor's	0
Randall	Man	Heteroflexible[5]	25–35	Low	White	N/A	High School Diploma	11+
Renee	Woman	Lesbian	36–46	Low	Black	SBNR	Bachelor's	3–5
Spiderman	Man	Heterosexual	36–46	Below/Near Poverty	Black	Christian	High School Diploma	1–2

[1] Names used are pseudonyms chosen by participants at time of interview.

[2] Below/Near Poverty (Less than $20,000); Low Income ($20–44,999); Middle Income ($45–139,999); Upper Middle Income ($140–149,999); High Income ($150–199,999); Highest Tax Brackets ($200,000+)

[3] Participants were asked at the end of the interview how many recurring interactions they have had with trans people, and particularly trans women, including friends, family members, (former) partners, and coworkers.

[4] Only attracted to transgender women

[5] Mostly attracted to women, occasionally attracted to men

justify the murders. All seven felt the murders of trans women to be wrong, cruel, and unjustified. However, I highlight here how their responses and positions were not that radically different from those in the previous two sections.

Chris, for example, repeatedly explained to me that he felt women do not want anything from a man other than his money. He, in particular, felt this way about cis. Black women, who he outright refused to date. His sentiments regarding Black women included Black trans women; however, he was open to dating a Black trans woman. His only long-term relationship had included a fifteen-year relationship with a Black trans woman. One of the issues they had was that she engaged in sex work. He explained, "They wants to go to work, but they don't wanna go to work. That's why a lot of them [trans women] are out there [doing sex work on the street]." This sentiment and his experience with his previous girlfriend influenced his response regarding the murders of Black trans women. He did not feel that cis-het men are justified in murdering Black trans women. However, he stated:

> I feel like a transsexual should just go in and say, "I'm a man, I got a penis, I'm a transsexual," just don't tell a man a lie just to get the man money. Because you want the man money, because they do that too. A lot of 'em get killed.

While Chris was solely attracted to trans women, had known myriad trans women, and had been in a relationship with a trans woman, he still did not refer to trans women as women. Chris repeatedly conflated his attraction to trans women as being part of "the gay life," and he referred to trans women, in the comment above, as men or as "a transsexual" rather than as a woman/ trans woman. Chris, like other participants in this category, conceptualized nondisclosure of trans identity as deceit. Further, Chris's argument that trans women "deceived" cis-het men in order to get their money blames the victims of anti-trans violence. Rather than cis-het men being blamed for the murder, trans women become blamed for engaging in sex work.

Randall also utilized the very language that participants in the previous two categories used to justify the murders of Black trans women. Randall had gone on two dates with trans women but had never had a long-term relationship with any trans person. He also knew other trans and nonbinary people. He had grown up in a highly religious, Southern Baptist household, and he had worked to unlearn a lot of the homophobia and transphobia he was taught. When I asked him about the murders of Black trans women and the justification cis-het men provide for their actions, he responded:

> Um, I can't relate to that at all. It sounds like bullshit to me. Um, I can under- stand, like I said earlier, being, like feeling like your consent was violated, but that's like...the extent and it's and it's, that's a different level of consent violation

than like, like a violent way or something you know? So, like, I think that is just, just comes from a place of, of homophobic hatred.

Randall's language is the same language used by the men in previous two categories, such as Gee, who explained that a man may feel violated. Indeed, it is the same language used by cis-het men who have killed Black trans women, as Westbrook and Schilt detail.[25] In addition, it is important to ask what one is consenting to when they have sex with a woman and what precisely is the violation? If a man consents to have sex or be in a relationship with a woman, her being trans does not alter the fact that he consented to a relationship with a woman. To argue otherwise is to insinuate that a trans woman is somehow less "woman." Her statement that she is a woman and the man's belief that she is a woman then becomes a lie or mis-construal of the facts. Further, what participants in this category may be conceptualizing as deceit may better be understood as a secret not yet told. Bok notes, "While all deception requires secrecy, all secrecy is not meant to deceive."[26] To deceive is to pretend to be something that one is not. Trans individuals, though, are not pretending to be something they are not. Rather, they are simply living as who they are. Instead, trans individuals who do not disclose trans identity may keep secret their identity in order to protect themselves from harm.

Finally, Randall collapses anti-trans sentiment and anti-trans violence into a form of "homophobic hatred," as did most participants. Most participants, though (twenty-five out of thirty-two), were not interpersonally homophobic. The majority of participants did not utilize a homophobic discourse, shared that they had utmost acceptance for cisgender, LGB people, and had intimate and close relationships with cisgender, LGB people. Homophobia and transphobia, heterosexism and cissexism, are deeply connected, and indeed, cis-het men who justified the murders of Black trans women utilized homophobic logic. However, eighteen out of the twenty-five participants who did not justify the murders simultaneously utilized or perpetuated cissexist discourse, as Randall did here.

Liz, for example, did not utilize homophobic or biphobic language throughout the interview, nor did she have any overt contempt for LGB people. However, when I asked Liz about cis-het men feeling overwhelmed by a woman being trans and reacting by killing the woman, Liz responded:

> Being overwhelmed is the result of being uninformed. Yeah, it's definitely being uninformed, because if you, yeah, I'm not going to say it's not going to be a little shocking that you thought it was like woman, a woman who was born woman, and then you find out it's transgender.

Liz's statement was in no way overtly cissexist. Indeed, Liz found such murders to be horrendous and was visibly upset during this portion of the interview. Liz advocated for cisgender people learning more about trans-ness to reduce ignorance. However, she also understood feeling shocked upon learning that a woman is transgender. Cissexism is so institutionalized within society that it only seems natural and inevitable that one would be jolted by the "discovery" that someone is transgender. Indeed, cisnormative conceptualizations of trans-ness, socially and within the law, link trans identity with deception and criminality.[27] Thus, it is not surprising that Liz and others do so even when otherwise advocating for trans people's safety and rights.

I asked Liz how she would feel if she learned a partner was transgender after having already been on dates or had sex with this woman. Liz stated:

> If you are a man and you feel like a woman, you wanna be a woman, or other way around, it's just like, just be brave and face it. Don't hide it. Yeah, so why would you hide something like that from me? Yeah, so I would be upset.

Liz found it of the utmost importance that trans people out themselves to others, and she compared this to cisgender, gay men who keep their gay-ness a secret from others. To be out and open about one's gender or sexuality was to be "brave." To be otherwise was to be cowardly and deceptive.

Similar to Liz, Randall, and Chris, other participants like D, a cis-het, Black man, placed the blame of being murdered on Black trans women. However, D took their responses a step further. When I asked D, "If we want to keep men from killing trans women, what do you think would help," he responded:

D: Uh just to make sure that they know. It should be like a law so you can like ask first before um trying to pursue.
Alithia: So, it should be allowed that you meet a girl and then you ask her?
D: Yeah.
Alithia: And then what would happen like if, if that was a law, and then she lied, what would happen?
D: Then would be like going to court.
Alithia: And she would be in trouble?
D: Right.

D's response, here, was like that of Ky who felt that the murders of Black trans women were extreme but understandable. While Ky argued cis-het men who murder should receive a lesser sentence in the case of nondisclosure, D felt that trans women, themselves, should be criminalized. While this present category of participants did not seek to justify the murders of Black trans women, they perpetuated the conceptualization of trans women as embodying a "terrorizing trans-ness."[28] Trans-ness, for these participants, was a covering up of one's "true nature," and a lack of disclosure was a violating concealment.

One need not openly advocate for or support the murders of Black trans women to actively perpetuate these murders. More casual cissexism, as found in the responses of participants in this category, becomes imbedded in everyday discourse, making it seem more natural and "commonsense" to men like Gee, Mack, Josh, and Iceberg that they then would react and kill a woman. Further, the conceptualization of nondisclosure as deceptive becomes more complicated when one considers nonbinary and gender-nonconforming individuals. If a cis-het man or cis-lesbian woman sleeps with someone they perceive to be a woman, and this individual was assigned female at birth but identifies as nonbinary, is there a deceptive violation? Or does deceptive violation only occur when one's sex organs do not match their gender expression? In this case, a conceptualization of trans-ness as deceptive and violating relies upon a gender essentialist idea that one is born a man or a woman and ultimately remains a man or a woman despite how they look. Participants in this category argued trans women are women, trans men are men, and nonbinary people are nonbinary. However, in simultaneously arguing that nondisclosure is deceptive, they reified a gender essentialist logic that participants in the previous two categories relied upon in making sense of the murders of Black trans women. In this section, I have highlighted how the disavowal of anti-trans violence does not separate one from the same logic and discourse used by those who commit the violence. Instead, participants in this category were connected to those in the previous two categories through the language used to discuss trans women's decisions regarding their identities, openness, and relationships.

"IT'S REALLY FUCKED UP THE WORLD WE LIVE IN"

A final category of participants felt the murders of Black trans women were horrendous. These participants did not utilize cissexist discourse or logic in their responses to the murders, although nine out of sixteen did in other parts of the interview, as I discussed in chapter 3. The respondents in this category included 13/17 cis-women I interviewed and were predominantly lesbian. The predominance of cis-lesbian women in this category corresponds with prior research finding correlations between those harboring prejudice against gays, lesbians, and bisexuals and those having prejudice against transgender peoples, as well as a higher frequency of anti-trans sentiment among cisgender men.[29]

Participants in this category primarily turned to cultural explanations for why cis-het men commit these murders. These participants argued that cis-het men murder Black trans women because of the ways cis-het men are socialized and the way people in the United States are socialized. Cultural influences like toxic masculinity, religious belief, a binary gender system, thus,

Table 5.4 "The Murders Are Wrong"

Name[1]	Gender	Sexual Orientation	Age	Income	Race & Ethnicity	Religion	Education	Number of Recurring Known Trans Interactions[3]
Alyshah	Woman	Lesbian	18–24	Below/Near Poverty[2]	Black	SBNR[3]	Some College	0
Alyx	Woman	Bi[4]	18–24	Below/Near Poverty	White	N/A	Some College	1–2
Amy	Woman	Lesbian	36–46	Low	White Latina	N/A	Some College	0
Cookie	Woman	Homoflexible[4]	25–35	Middle Income	Black	SBNR	Master's	11+
Henry	Man	Heterosexual	25–35	Below/Near Poverty	Black	Christian	Some College	0
Janelle	Woman	Queer	18–24	Middle Income	Black	Christian	Woman	1–2
Jessica	Woman	Lesbian	25–35	Middle Income	Black	Christian	Woman	0
Kylee	Woman	Lesbian	18–24	Below/Near Poverty	Black	N/A	Some College	3–5
LaLa	Woman	Lesbian	18–24	Below/Near Poverty	Black	N/A	Some College	1–2
Musiteli	Man	Heterosexual	18–24	Low	Black	Atheist	Bachelor's	3–5
Peaches	Woman	Bi/Queer	18–24	Below/Near Poverty	Mixed—Black/White	SBNR	Some College	11+
Rachel	Woman	Lesbian	18–24	Low	White	N/A	Bachelor's	3–5
Ryan	Woman	Lesbian	36–46	Low	Black	SBNR	Bachelor's	1–2
Sabrina	Man	Heterosexual	18–24	Below/Near Poverty	Asian American	Hindu	Some College	1–2
Shantelle	Woman	Lesbian	25–35	Middle Income	Black	SBNR	Bachelor's	6–10
Vincent	Woman	Lesbian	18–24	Middle Income	White	N/A	Some College	6–10

[1] Names used are pseudonyms chosen by participants at time of interview.

[2] Below/Near Poverty (Less than $20,000); Low Income ($20–44,999); Middle Income ($45–139,999); Upper Middle Income ($140–149,999); High Income ($150–199,999); Highest Tax Brackets ($200,000+)

[3] Participants were asked at the end of the interview how many recurring interactions they have had with trans people, and particularly trans women, including friends, family members, (former) partners, and coworkers.

[4] Mostly attracted to women, occasionally attracted to men

result in cis-het men feeling embarrassed, emotionally insecure, and out of control when encountering individuals who do not fit within cultural schemas of gender. Alyshah, for example, explained:

> That is toxic masculinity, right there . . . it has to be some kind of insecurity within yourself . . . to try to kill someone to retaliate because they said this to you [that they are transgender] . . . If it happens, it happens. You accept the fact, but a lot of times, men, they try to just justify their actions by saying I was feeling this. I was feeling that. No, you're insecure. That's what it is. You didn't want to face the fact that you, [that] this happened. And so now you're blaming her, and you want to kill her for it, and it has nothing to do with her. It's about you.

Alyshah was currently a college student and had taken several sociology courses. Originally coined in the mythopoetic men's movement toxic masculinity has since come to signify extremely misogynistic, homophobic, cissexist, and hypermasculine attributes, behaviors, and believes.[30] For Alyshah, a man reacts with such violent force as murder when a culture has so deeply ingrained in him what it means to be a man and a woman that he cannot face what it means for him to be attracted to someone who disobeys binary logic. Scholars like Salter and Harrington have critiqued the use of the term "toxic masculinity," because it ignores the diversity of masculinities that exist and the ways other forms of masculinity also perpetuate misogyny, homophobia, and/or cissexism.[31] In addition to participants like Alyshah who used the concept of toxic masculinity to explain men's actions, other participants highlighted that the socialization of cis boys/men is at fault for the murders of Black trans women.

Amy, for example, felt that the ways men are socialized in the United States and abroad were at fault for raising generations of men who were emotionally arrested. Amy explained:

> Throughout history, we have trained our boys to...think that...they're the top, like they rule the world . . . the world revolves around them. We've trained them not to have emotions, because men [grunts and flexes]. Um we have like stunted them emotionally, I would argue, intellectually, physically, um we've created this monster, you know, generationally . . . It's like . . . just because I'm a passionate person, it doesn't make it okay for me to take it out on other people. Like you are still responsible for your own actions, I don't care who you are and what you've been through.

Men are not supposed to cry, feel love struck, or otherwise feel "feminine" emotions. However, Amy noted that men are trained to feel entitled, egoistic, and strong. Men, thus, are not, according to Amy, taught to process feelings and emotions or how to respond in ways that are not aggressive or violent.

When men, then, come to find themselves in an otherwise foreign (to them) situation upon meeting someone who does not fit within what they've been taught about gender and sexuality, they may not know how to handle the numerous feelings racing through them. Indeed, Bourdieu highlights the overwhelming role that fear plays in the lives of men as masculinity and manhood are accomplished through validation by other men/masculine individuals.[32] Thus, such fear may play a role in the resulting violence that ensues when desiring trans women.

Musiteli, felt that there needs to be attention placed on cis-het men and why they murder in order to prevent further murders. If we do not attend to the logic, emotions, and decision-making of men, we cannot address the root issue. Musiteli explained, "I guess the issue is men. Um . . . and . . . it would be, this, I guess this de-masculization that they feel, that they feel de-masculinized whenever they find out that they've been with a trans woman." As I pointed out in Chapter Four, stigma sticks to bodies, and trans women's embodiment of what Schippers terms pariah femininities contaminates the relations between masculinities and femininities.[33] The stigma of trans-ness lowers cis-het men in the hierarchies of masculinities, and it is through violence that they shed that stigma and recuperate their masculinity.

Vincent and Rachel also felt that cis-het men kill out of anger and fears of being "made gay" and/or emasculated. They explained in the focus group:

Vincent: I think 'cause they get angry. I mean the men that kill these trans women, they're probably like . . . afraid to be seen as gay like in anyway by anybody, and then they get angry about it. Like it's a defense mechanism, but it's still awful and wrong obviously.

Rachel: Yeah, I think they feel that it's like a threat to their masculinity and their like identity. Um and . . . yeah so they, they react with anger.

Vincent and Rachel highlight, again, the threat that cis-het men may feel trans women pose to their masculinity, their manhood, and their heterosexuality. Salamon elucidates how this construction of trans femininities as aggressive and assaultive is a racial-gender construction. Salamon explicates this in the murder of Latisha King. Throughout the trial, "descriptions of Latisha [a teenager] as 'aggressive' demonstrate a phobic relation to race as well as, and as intertwined with, gender and sexuality . . . Latisha was characterized as disruptive, as unruly."[34] During the trial of Latisha's murder, witnesses, the prosecutor, and the defense did not refer to her Black-ness. Instead, it was decided pre-trail that race was not a defining component of the crime. Similarly, my participants did not point to the role of Black trans women's Black-ness as a part of the equation resulting in their trans-ness being characterized as so aggressive as to injure a man's gender-sexual subjectivity. Race, though, was a part of the equation.

In addition to the construction of US masculinities and the socialization of cis-het men, participants pointed to the role that media play in the murders of Black trans women. Media images circulate of trans women as a joke or of trans women as "gay men" attempting to "trick" heterosexual men. These images portray trans women to create a cultural reaction of embarrassment, ridicule, and emasculation when a cis-het man finds himself attracted to a woman who happens to be trans. When I asked participants about the murders of Black trans women, several referenced *The Jerry Springer Show* that aired from 1991 to 2018.

Stuart Heritage, writing for The Guardian, described the talk show: "In episodes with titles such as I'm Pregnant by a Transsexual! and Lesbolicious, Springer would introduce a guest, hear their complaints, bring on an aggressor and watch as they verbally and physically attacked each other."[35] A google search of the show's episodes bring up numerous trans-related episodes, including "Transgender Triangles," "I Had Sex with a Tranny," "Do You Want Me or My Transsexual Brother," "Dating a Man, Woman, & Transgender Roast," "Transsexual Shockers," "Cheated with Transgender Stripper," and more. The show's salacious episodes averaged 1.7 million viewers in 2018 and was popular enough to bring the host, Jerry Springer, "a $30 million, five-year contract in 2000."[36]

Rachel pointed out that her progressive, women's college student center's televisions aired shows like Jerry Springer. Rachel stated, "I would walk into the student center and there would be like these weird shows where they would literally . . . invite trans women on the show just to argue with each other." Media images of trans women center trans-ness as a spectacle of deception. While media representation of trans characters and stories has increased in recent years, such media representation remains complicated, with some shows detailing the nuance, diversity, and complexity of trans experiences and others continuing to portray flat and limited storylines that perpetuate problems evident in *The Jerry Springer Show*.[37] In an interview with the producers of the Netflix documentary, *Disclosure*, viewers are provided a glimpse of the film in which actress, activist, model, and producer, Laverne Cox, states, "According to a study from GLADD, 80 percent of Americans don't personally know someone who is transgender. Most of the information that Americans get about who transgender people are, what our lives are and are about, comes from the media."[38] Media portrayals, past and present, continue to influence the ways cisgender people feel about and conceptualize trans people and trans lives. Such media representations create controlling images[39] of trans women that frame cissexism as a "natural and normal" facet of everyday life.

Controlling images shaped not only how trans-ness is conceptualized as deceptive and duplicitous, but also how Black women, including Black trans women, are viewed in society. I asked all participants to define femininity, and I asked whether race shapes or differentiates femininity. Several participants, primarily Black women, highlighted controlling images of Black women as masculine and aggressive and White women as feminine. As Sabrina noted, "I think a lot of people would say . . . African American women are a little bit more aggressive . . . because we've had the stereotype around us of bad attitudes." Participants also highlighted that Black men are constructed as, or as Cookie put it, "are made to be and appear more masculine." She explained why this is:

> Probably the same reason a lot of Black women are pushed into being more masculine or more independent, um at one point in time even now, pretty much we're kind of forced to um literally talk about Willie Lynch and, you know, us being taken from our men and us being, you know, men being beaten in front of our wives or kids, whether it's the welfare system, and, you know, in order to for us to get services, you know, they couldn't be in a house, we had to fend for ourselves and, you know, absent fathers and the prison system. I think it's a lot. A lot that plays into that so deeply rooted stuff. Some deeply rooted trauma.

Trans women, as a group, are constructed as assaultive, harmful, and aggressive. Black women are constructed as more masculine than White women. Black men are constructed as hypermasculine and more virile than White men. What then, does it look like, for a cis-het man to be attracted to a Black trans woman who is deemed hyper-aggressive, hypermasculine, and dangerous as a Black person, a Black person assigned male at birth, a Black woman, a trans person, and a Black trans woman? In this way, cultural socialization of children, the media narratives that circulate of trans women, a rigid, White, gender binary system, and legacies of white supremacy in the United States funnel into the conceptualization of the murders of Black trans women as a cis-het man's defense mechanism. Participants in this category explained the idea of the murders as a defense mechanism as the thought process of a cis-het man that needs to be changed, healed, and altered.

When I asked Cookie what needs to change for the murders of Black trans women to end, she responded:

> The issue isn't the community, the issue is the people that's fuckin 'killing them [laughs,] you know what I'm saying? So, it's like you shouldn't have to like divulge that. Um the person should just care enough to just want to know you and learn you, but we all know that that's not people, you know, and everybody

just kind of comes to the table with the same thoughts, feelings ideas . . . Um I don't know. We need to do a better job with normalizing as a community, we need to do a better job with educating and protecting. Um we need to do a better job of punishing people when they take this action, because there's not always people on the other side of the law that like, care enough about the gay guy or the trans woman or the lesbian woman to actually make an example when someone's, you know, life is taken, or dignity is taken, or whatever. Um you gotta set the example. . . . Because if you kill somebody because they love differently, they live differently or whatever, and they just kind of get off, is that really going to deter other people from doing it? You know, um, I think I think something has to give because this shit's crazy [crying].

Participants like Cookie took an entirely different stance on the murders of Black trans women than participants in the three prior categories. Rather than placing the blame on Black trans women, conceptualizing trans-ness as deceptive or duplicitous, or feeling as though trans women deserve this treatment, these participants placed the blame on cis-het men. They highlighted the need for a shift in how society understands gender and sexuality, as well as processes of accountability to keep cis-het men from continuing to murder. Cookie highlighted that the law does not protect those experiencing oppression. Instead, through either a lack of empathy or out of a desire to cause harm to those oppressed, those in power enact laws that continue to harm marginalized people and often refuse to enact laws meant to protect.[40] While the three other categories of participants exemplified the necropolitics of cisness (i.e., the production of cis-ness out of violence and death), this category of participants explicated and argued against it.

Further, this category of participants also elucidated the role of social norms, discourse, and controlling images. Bourdieu notes, "Symbolic domination . . . is exerted not in the pure logic of knowing consciousness but through the schemes of perception, appreciation, and action that are constitutive of habitus."[41] The construction of a White, cis habitus normalizes social degradation, dehumanization, and pathologization of Black trans women. This habitus comes to shape how cisgender individuals perceive Black trans women and other trans women of color, resulting in participants in the previous three categories conceptualizing the murdered women as deceptive and violating. While the majority of participants would not commit such murders, half of all participants were able to make sense of these murders due to their positionality within a White, cis habitus. Further, as I highlighted in chapter 3, nearly all participants perpetuated cissexist discourse at varying points in the interview; thus, even those who were strongly pro-trans remained shaped by their socialization within a White, cis habitus.

CONCLUSION

Participants of all demographics (race, age, income, gender, sexual orientation, and so forth) were scattered across the four categories, because cis-ness is not something produced only by certain people or certain bodies. Cis-ness is a political, discursive, and social manifestation that shapes how individuals see the world, provides a justification for cissexist violence, and institutionalizes (or makes "natural") a binary ontology of gender. Cis-ness and cissexism were produced out of capitalism and colonialism,[42] and thus are projects of a larger political economic system rather than acts of individual hatred. While the material components of cissexism would die away under a new social order (i.e., socialism),[43] the aspects of cis-ness that individuals have internalized under the current social order (i.e., white supremacist, cis-heteropatriarchal capitalism) have to be unlearned and actively worked against.

Cisgender people, cis-het men in particular, can be deeply affected by challenges to the gender binary and ruptures in popular understandings of masculinities and femininities. Violence enables such cis-het men to regain their status in the hierarchy of masculinities, and maintains cis-ness as a political, discursive, and social manifestation. The lack of accountability for cis-het men who murder and commit violence against Black trans women sends the message that the law and society hold trans women in low regard. Cis-het masculinity is sustained and recuperated through violence, and cis-ness is protected from further contamination vis-à-vis pariah femininities, as the source of "contamination" is no more.

As highlighted earlier, the racialization of cis-ness may lead to different reasons for cissexist violence among working class, Black men than among other cis-het men. Disinvestment in poor, Black neighborhoods across US urban centers has facilitated "overwhelming challenges" to poor and working-class Black men. Displays of hypermasculinity and more overt reliance on a gender binary and gender essentialism can function as "a kind of last resort in asserting power and producing masculinity" for working-class men who experience other forms of gendered-classed power inequities.[44] Further, Black, cis-het men who are "upwardly mobile" may use "every means available to distance themselves from the 'bad' Black male" and other Black individuals who carry the stigma of racial, gender, and sexual difference.[45]

Race, gender, socioeconomic status, and social contact each played differential and overlapping roles vis-à-vis participants' responses to the murders of Black trans women. Further, cultural discourse shapes how individuals come to make sense of the world around them. There is a limited cultural discourse from which cis people make sense of trans people. This limited discourse includes trans people as sick, as a joke, as deceptive and dishonest, and as harmful to individuals and society. This discourse becomes utilized by cis-het men and cis-LBQ women, as I detailed in this chapter, to justify and/ or perpetuate the murders of Black trans women. While few (seven out of thirty-two) participants felt that the murders were understandable or that they or people they knew would commit such a murder, the majority of participants provided the foundation for the logic that those who kill or those who understand the killings then use to justify such murders. In the next chapter, I conclude by describing what can be done to challenge the necropolitics of cis-ness.

NOTES

1. Damshenas, 2020, "Trans Influencers Savagely Beaten."
2. 2000, *Sexing the Body.*
3. 2015, *Contesting Intersex.*
4. Bourdieu, 1998, *Masculine Domination*, 52.
5. Connell, 1995, *Masculinities.*
6. 2007, *Dude, You're a Fag.*
7. King, Winter, and Webster, 2009, "Contact Reduces Transprejudice." Kooy, 2010, "Knowledge and Attitudes Toward Trans Persons."
8. McKinley, 2016, "Man's Confession in Transgender Woman's Death."
9. Pfeffer, 2017, *Queering Families.*
10. 2005, "Beards, Breasts, and Bodies."
11. 2017, "Transphobia as Symptom," 364.
12. 2010, *Is the Rectum a Grave?* 19.
13. Bourdieu, 1998, *Masculine Domination*, 51.
14. Pew Research Center, 2017, "Intermarriage in the U.S."
15. 2008, *Against the Wall*, 18; Messerschmidt, 2019, "The Salience of 'Hegemonic Masculinity.'"
16. Class, throughout, is used as a proxy for income, education, wealth, and the composition of one's neighborhood vis-à-vis those same factors. This is a misunderstanding of class, but I use it throughout to reflect how it is used within academic parlance.
17. Ravenell et al., 2006, "African American Men's Perceptions of Health." Royster et al., 2006, "Hey Brother, How's Your Health." Warfa et al., 2006, "Comparison of Life Events." Watkins et al., 2007, "Using Focus Groups." and Watkins et al., 2010, "A Meta-Study of Black Male Mental Health and Wellbeing."
18. Engels, 1894, "Engles to Borgius."
19. Anderson, 2008, *Against the Wall.* Watkins et al., 2010, "A Meta-Study of Black Male Mental Health & Wellbeing." Rios, 2011, *Punished.* Stuart and Benezra, 2018, "Criminalized Masculinities."
20. Harris, 2000, "Gender, Violence, Race, & Criminal Justice." Rios, 2011, *Punished.*
21. 2008, *Against the Wall*, 11.

22. Page and Richardson, 2009, "On the Fear of Small Numbers."

23. Stuart and Benezra, 2018, "Criminalized Masculinities."

24. Page and Richardson, 2009, "On the Fear of Small Numbers."

25. 2013, "Doing Gender, Determining Gender."

26. 1998, *Secrets*, 7. Cited from Ashley, 2018, "Genderfucking Non-Disclosure," 357.

27. DeGagne, 2021, "Protecting Cisnormative Private and Public Spheres."

28. Clarkson, 2020, "Terrorizing Transness."

29. Norton and Herek, 2013, "Heterosexuals' Attitudes Toward Transgender People." Kanamori and Xu, 2020, "Factors Associated with Transphobia."

30. Salter, 2019, "The Problem with a Fight Against Toxic Masculinity." Harrington, 2020, "What is 'Toxic Masculinity'?"

31. Salter, 2019, "The Problem with a Fight Against Toxic Masculinity." Harrington, 2020, "What is 'Toxic Masculinity,' and Why Does it Matter?"

32. 1998.

33. 2007, "Recovering the Feminine Other."

34. 2018, *The Life and Death of Latisha King*, 20.

35. 2020, "How the Jerry Springer Show Splashed Around in Humanity's Worst Excesses."

36. O'Connell, 2018, "'Jerry Springer' Future Uncertain."

37. zamantakis and Sumerau, 2019, "Streaming Transgender."

38. Netflix. "Why I Made Disclosure: The Story Behind the Netflix Documentary." Retrieved 26 August 2020 from https://www.youtube.com/watch?v=WGaTwxS92hw.

39. Collins, 1990, *Black Feminist Thought*.

40. DeGagne, 2021, "Protecting Cisnormative Private and Public Spheres."

41. 1998, 37.

42. Rodney. 1972, *How Europe Underdeveloped Africa*.
Lugones, 2007, "Heterosexualism and the Colonial/Modern Gender System." Mogul, Ritchie, and Whitlock, 2011, *Queer (In)Justice*. Driskill, 2016, *Asegi Stories*. Gossett, 2016, "Žižek's Trans/gender Trouble."

43. Rojo del Arcoíris, 2022, "Towards a Queer Marxism."

44. Pyke, 1996, "Class-Based Masculinities."

45. Anderson, 2008, *Against the Wall*. Page and Richardson, 2011, "On the Fear of Small Numbers."

Conclusion

What to Do about Cis-ness?

In writing this book, I aimed to push past what I viewed as the limits of sociological theory, and, in particular, the sociology of gender, sex, and sexualities. As noted at the start of this book, Schilt and Lagos traced the three main domains of the Sociology of Trans Studies in 2017. These three domains included:

> Research that explores the diversity of transgender peoples' identities and social locations, research that interrogates transgender peoples' experiences within institutional and organizational contexts, and research that presents quantitative approaches to transgender peoples' identities and experiences.[1]

Each of these foci of contemporary Sociology of Trans Studies has important functions to play in decentering cis-ness from sociological scholarship; empirically and theoretically exploring the experiences, needs, lives, and desires of trans people; and quantifying and elaborating the institutional and systemic barriers experienced in everyday life by trans people. However, it is necessary to either build within Trans Studies a study of cis-ness or to counteract it with a critical cis-ness studies. Several scholars are calling for such an examination of cis-ness, in addition to a critical endosex[2] studies. Jennifer Hites-Thomas, an instructor of sociology and anthropology at Pacific University of Oregon, hosted a panel at the 2023 Society for the Study of Social Problems asking, "How are cisitude [cis-ness] and endosex embodiment socially, historically, and medically constructed? How do race, nation, sexuality, and technology intersect in the production of cisitude and endosex bodies?" In November 2022, Jackson King, author of *Tesosterotica*, tweeted, "Enough of transgender studies. It's time for cisgender studies," asking, among other questions, "Why do they feel threatened by the gender of others if theirs is so factual and secure?"

143

A turn to a critical cis-ness studies would ask, as I have done in this book, "What is cis-ness? How is it produced and maintained? What are its ramifications? How do "good" cisgender "allies" perpetuate cis-ness in everyday interactions?" Further, such a field may ask, "What to do about cis-ness," as this chapter does. Indeed, what to do about cis-ness? What to do about a political, discursive, and social manifestation produced out of colonialism and capitalism? How does one challenge something that is not "out there," away and separate from "us," but is instead something within each of us—something that manifests differently across individuals, groups, and nations? Part of what I have aimed to do in this book to counteract cis-ness is to name it, define some of its contours, and elaborate its expression.

Culture and discourse justify and reify violence daily in subtle and explicit ways. I spent the majority of 2021 and 2022 writing and editing *Thinking Cis* By the end of 2021, at least fifty-three trans, nonbinary, and/or gender-nonconforming people lost their lives to intimate partner violence, racist and cissexist violence, or the slow death of living in an oppressive society.[3] Simultaneously, 122 bills were introduced in state legislatures across the United States seeking to limit the rights of trans/nonbinary people vis-à-vis healthcare, education, sports, and access to public accommodations. An additional ninety-eight anti-LGBTQ bills were introduced that attempt to provide increased religious protections for employers and individuals in health care, education, and other settings if they choose to discriminate against LGBTQ individuals.[4] By December 2022, at least thirty-two trans people were killed (twenty-six of whom were Black, Latina, and/or Indigenous trans women),[5] twenty-five anti-trans state bills were considered and/or signed into legislation.[6] Black trans women, trans women of color, and other trans, nonbinary, and/or gender-nonconforming people continue to exist in a heightened state of risk and precarity. The United States is in an ongoing attack on trans women and girls and a decades long debate of where trans people fit in society, if at all. This ongoing debate—a cultural, discursive, and ultimately physical debate—at the state and national levels reflects the same process occurring in communities across the country.

Society is changing. Trans people have, to some extent, greater legal protections than in decades past. At the same time, these raced and gendered shifts are so small and fleeting under a government of White, patriarchal, capitalist elites that we might say they aren't shifts at all but rather concessions won through decades of struggle that are quickly being torn away from the people before we ever progress even further forward. As they have long done, right wing politicians place the blame for contemporary economic and political crises on racially, gender, and otherwise minoritized populations. A supposed democratic conspiracy against hardworking families and Christians is claimed to be leaving "young children sterile, infertile, and sexually underdeveloped for life."[7] A TV advertisement paid for by the National Republican Senatorial Committee overlays the words "different" and "dangerous" on an image of Mandela Barnes, a Black lieutenant governor of Wisconsin, with Alexandria Ocasio Cortez, a Latina representative for the Bronx, Rashida Tlaib, a Palestinian representative for western Detroit, and Ilhan Omar, a Black representative for Minnesota[8]. A *New York Times* article headline reads, "They paused puberty, but at what price?" fanning the flames on an ongoing attack on transgender healthcare across the country.[9]

Such rhetoric is not new, nor is it isolated to an elite class of politicians and their campaign teams. While, to my knowledge, my participants did not actively murder anyone, their responses to trans women's bodies and murders and discussion of intimacy with trans women provide attempted justifications for the material reality in which Black trans women find themselves. In part, this is evidenced in participants' conceptualization of trans-ness as a "covering up" of the natural body and as a performance that one either does "well" or "poorly." This explicates that trans women are not only viewed as not women or something other than women but also that their womanhood is viewed as a guise. This conceptualization then justifies cis-het men feeling "tricked" or "duped" when finding out that a woman they are attracted to and/ or with is transgender. While sociologists highlight that gender, as a social construct, is a performance, it is important to simultaneously recognize that, among my participants, cisgender people's genders were not conceptualized as a performance while trans people's genders were. If cisgender people's genders were also recognized as performances or if transgender people's genders were affirmed and validated as real, then there would be no basis to cis-het men feeling "tricked" or defending murder through "trans panic" defenses.

A set of sociopolitical symbols circulated around "trans-ness" conceptually for cis-het men and cis-les/bi women participants. Their potential desires for a trans woman momentarily broke this circuitry causing shock, confusion, or panic, and violence (physical and/or emotional/verbal) helped fix things back into a binary logic (natural/unnatural, man/woman, straight/gay, male/female, desirable/disgusting). In order words, cis-ness functioned necropolitically. Violence becomes the justified vehicle for the symbols that circulate around "trans-ness" to not stick to cis people, preventing them from having to question gender/sexuality and/or experience some of the shame and harassment that trans people themselves experience. Trans people, thus, become stuck in a double bind of what scholars term the paradox of visibility.[10] If trans people are "out" and open about their trans-ness, they may experience violence. However, if they are not "out" and open about their trans-ness, then they are perceived to be "tricking" others, which may also result in violence.

Cisgender conceptualizations of trans bodies further highlight the construction of differential pariah femininities and subordinate masculinities. Pariah femininities contaminate the relations between femininities and masculinities. "Pariah trans femininities" contaminate the relations between masculinities and femininities, are viewed as fundamentally uncomplimentary to hegemonic and dominant masculinities, and are perceived as assaults upon one's manhood or lesbian identity. This results in cis-het men who are attracted to trans women embodying a "hyper-subordinated masculinity." Violence against Black trans women becomes the vehicle for cis-het men to recuperate their masculinity and regain their status within a hierarchy of masculinities, and cis-LBQ women become complicit in this violence by rendering trans women as tricksters. Cis-ness, thus, is a necropolitical force. Cis-ness relies upon anti-Black trans violence and the murders of Black trans women to sustain itself.

It is not possible to thoroughly analyze and make sense of cis-ness without attention to the ways in which it was birthed out of the racist and capitalist colonization, enslavement, and genocide of Black and Indigenous Peoples and is simultaneously perpetuated through anti-Black racism. Not only was this evident in cis-het men participants' ranking the photo of a White, cis-passing trans woman as more desirable than photos of other women, but it was also evident in how they spoke of the range of women presented in the photos with the White, "cis-passing" woman being viewed as warm, kind, non-threatening, and nurturing in comparison to photos of more "visibly trans" women of color which were described with harsher features, such as "sharp" facial structure, strong, mean, and "ratchet." Race, class, and gender intersected in how women were viewed not only in terms of desire but also in terms of "passability." The racialization of "passing" as cisgender elucidates, in part, why trans women of color may be more vulnerable to being seen as trans and thus targeted for anti-trans violence.

Western ontologies of "body reasoning"[11] remain prevalent shaping the ways in which individuals are interpreted in society. When individual's interpretations of other's bodies do not line up with preconceived notions of sex/gender, they are left without the cultural tools to make sense of the individual in front of them resulting in panic, confusion, and violence. The body and the symbols that attach value to some bodies and not to others are central to cis-ness. Trans bodies are excess or surplus to the binary logic of cis-ness, and, thus, they are not only undesirable but unnecessary. It is this lack of value attached to trans bodies and trans people that allowed many participants to justify, understand, and/or make sense out of the murders of Black trans women.

Hope is not lost, though. In fleshing out cis-ness as multidimensional, I discussed those participants who engaged in a more critical cis-ness. These participants highlighted that the perpetuation of cis-ness is not an inevitability. Instead, they demonstrated that cis individuals can act in agentic ways to actively support trans people. In doing so, they worked to actively challenge the necropolitics of cis-ness by acknowledging the vulnerability and precarity that Black trans women and other trans people of color experience, by marking cis-ness as pathological, problematic, and violent, and by recognizing and working against the ways in which desire shapes and is shaped by sociopolitical power. Ultimately all people, cis and trans, are socialized within a society in which thinking cis is perpetuated as the norm, yet participants who engaged in critical cis-ness elucidated the potential of cis individuals to work to continually unlearn cis-ness and to act against cissexism.

BUILDING AN AGENDA FOR FUTURE RESEARCH

In this book, I focused on cis-het men and cis-les/bi women participants to analyze the discourse of those groups that are most likely to come into intimate contact with trans women. However, there is needed analysis around the role that cis-het women and cis-gay/bi men play in transmisogynist and transmisogynoirist violence. One participant, Chris, noted the harassment he experienced from cis-het women regarding his desires for trans women. He was the only participant who mentioned this and only one of two cis-het men participants who had dated a trans woman. However, he highlighted a potential factor to consider in the social conditions that give rise to racialized cissexism. If cis-het women mock, denigrate, and/or refuse to date cis-het men who desire women of any sex assigned at birth, then it is feasible that cis-het women contribute to the perpetuation of toxic masculinity, which numerous participants spoke of when asked about the murders of Black trans women. Further, while only one participant spoke of this, the harassment of a group of trans women of color in L.A. (see chapter 5) and cis women onlookers cheering on cis-het men threatening the lives of these women highlights that Chris was not an anomaly.

Additionally, it is necessary to more deeply analyze the role that cis-gay/bi men play in the violence that Black trans women and other trans women experience. In 2016, Milo Yiannopoulos, a conservative, White, cis-gay man and cultural commentator, mocked a trans woman student while speaking at her university. He remarked:

> This quote unquote non-binary trans woman forced his way into the women's locker rooms this year. He got into the women's room the way liberals always operate, using the government and the courts to weasel their way where they don't belong . . . I have known some passing trannies in my life...The way that you know he's failing is I'd almost still bang him. It's just . . . it's just a man in a dress, isn't it?[12]

Yiannopoulos highlighted that simply because LGBT people are lumped categorically does not mean that they share experiences, nor does it mean that they are in solidarity with one another. Yiannopoulos not only deadnamed and misgendered this student, but he also perpetuated the same discursive construction of trans-ness as a "covering up" of the natural body that cis-het men and cis-les/bi women participants did in my interviews. Yiannopoulos is not alone in doing so. The UK-based LGB Alliance formed in 2019 to defend cisgender, lesbian, gay, and bisexual men and women from the "threat" of trans activism. The group has since spread to numerous nations across the globe, including the US, and continues to work to ensure that cisgender lesbian women and cisgender gay men have access to cis-woman only and cis-man only spaces. Thus, future research should attend to the unique ways in which cis-het women and cis-gay/bi men similarly and differently perpetuate transmisogynoir/transmisogyny.

While I was not able to analyze domestic violence, intimate partner violence, and anti-sex worker violence, each of these forms of violence deserve greater attention vis-à-vis the murders of Black trans women. Yerke and DeFeo[13] explicate that nearly 50 percent of transgender people are likely to experience intimate partner violence. Further, many of the known murders of Black trans women and other transgender people occur at the hands of cis-het men they know or have met through intimate settings. Bianca Muffin Bankz, a young, Black trans woman, was murdered in her apartment by her friend, Moses Allen, who committed suicide after killing her[14]. Later this same year, Fifty Bandz, a twenty-one-year-old, Black trans woman, was murdered by Michael Joshua Brooks, who had been "hiding their romance and had repeatedly threatened bodily harm against her."[15] As I edited *Thinking Cis*, Jeffrey JJ Bright, a sixteen-year-old trans boy of color, and his sibling, Jasmine Cannady, a twenty-two-year-old, nonbinary person of color, were both murdered by their mother. Each of these stories are not anomalies, but instead, when looking the Human Rights Campaign's annual list of murdered trans, nonbinary, and/or gender-nonconforming people, form a pattern of violence committed against trans people by the very people meant to love them.[16] While some research has analyzed the violence and harassment trans women experience doing sex work,[17] these studies could be further expanded to include larger sample sizes, quantitative analyses, and a deeper analysis of the connection of the murders of Black trans women to engagement in sex work. Additionally, few large-scale surveys and/or qualitative analyses of trans/nonbinary people's experiences of IPV, as well as interviews of those who kill intimate partners, have been conducted. Finally, no study to the best of my knowledge has analyzed the murders of Black trans women as committed by given-family members. Each of these various dimensions of the murders of Black trans women need deeper attention in sociology to piece together a larger picture of the sociopolitical and cultural conditions that give rise to this violence.

While I focused on how cis individuals make sense of, perpetuate, and/or justify the murders of Black trans women, similar research also needs to be conducted vis-a-vis the murders of Black trans men and nonbinary people. Murders of trans people of color are, in large part, murders of Black trans women. However, it is necessary to analyze whether differing conditions and discourse foster violence against variously racialized trans men and nonbinary people.

Finally, I find it important to highlight a need for more analysis of the ways in which "trans-attracted" cisgender men perpetuate violence against trans women. In my interview with Chris, he told me at one point, "Y'all are easier to get than women." Here, Chris simultaneously conceptualized trans women as easy to seduce and as something other than women. While Chris was attracted only to trans women, he repeatedly misgendered trans women and referred to them as men and as part of the "gay life." However, what I find more important to attend to that needs further analysis is the conceptualization of trans women as "easier to get." When we, as trans women, are perceived of as "easier to get," is it out of an assumption that we are simply more open to relationships, that we are more sexually active than cisgender women, that we are more desperate and, thus, manipulatable because of said desperation? If it is the latter, then how does that figure into the violence that trans women experience? Studies of cisgender men who seek out trans women sex workers have found that trans women are sought out by these men because they are perceived of as "free of intimacy, attachment, and obligation . . . disposable."[18] This conceptualization correlated, in these studies, with high rates of violence against trans women sex workers. Thus, if similar conceptualizations of trans women are found among cisgender men in general, then does this conceptualization facilitate higher rates of intimate partner violence, domestic abuse, and murder? Unfortunately, I am unable to answer this question. More analysis of cisgender men who seek out trans women as sexual/romantic partners needs to take place.

MITIGATING AND DISMANTLING CISSEXIST VIOLENCE

To return to the title of this conclusion, "What to do about cis-ness?" In concluding, I want not only to point to future directions for research but also future and ongoing efforts to mitigate and dismantle cissexist violence among political and community organizers across the United States. The 2021 American Sociological Association Annual Conference theme of "Emancipatory Sociology" called for sociologists to "push the limits of knowledge to point us toward relief from gender discrimination and sexual harassment, racism, ableism, heteronormativity, devastating class inequalities and epistemological and methodological blindness [*sic*],"[19] and it is in this vein that I write this concluding section.

Cis-ness, as I have argued, is necropolitical. That is, it relies on violence and death. Thus, I turn to work on anti-violence interventions in sociology, public health, women's and gender studies, and ethnic studies and look at examples of such work in practice. Violence does not just include violence inflicted on an individual by another individual. Cis-ness is produced, as well, through state violence, and high rates of interpersonal violence in the United States are fueled by systemic racism, (trans)misogyny, capitalism, and other systems that fuel inequities. Thus, anti-violence interventions to mitigate and dismantle cis-ness must target the institutions that feed on and perpetuate violence.[20]

Such interventions would center the victims of racist, cissexist violence in determining how they are planned and carried out. These may include the provision of housing, food, jobs, universal basic income, and affordable and/ or free (physical and mental) health care, all of which would serve to eliminate high rates of poverty, homelessness, unemployment, and lack of health care among Black trans women and other trans women, and would provide them greater security and safety from violence by moving them out of places of high risk (such as the streets, homeless shelters, and so forth).

One form of intervention that is both abolitionist and targets the structural determinants that facilitate violence is violence interruption, a strategy of preventing violence before it happens by providing mediation and conflict resolution in the moments leading to shootings, gang violence, and other forms of violence. One study examined the effects of CeaseFire, a national violence interruption program implemented in the West Side of Chicago (West Garfield Park and West Humboldt Park), the South Side of Chicago (Englewood), East Baltimore (McElderry Park, Ellwood Park, Madison-Eastend), and South Baltimore (Cherry Hill). The intervention provided mediators with cell phones, vehicles ("often used to remove . . . wood-be shooter[s] from the scene of a brewing conflict"), bright orange uniforms to easily identify them, and training in conflict mediation, resolution, and mitigation.[21]

Chicago CRED (Create real economic destiny) uses a "multifaceted approach to reducing gun violence"[22] Chicago CRED hires and trains street outreach workers who are on call 24/7 to provide violence interruption and conflict mediation, in addition to regular community engagement. However, beyond preventing violence in the moments immediately prior to it, they target structural and social determinants of violence by providing trauma counseling, life coaching, career mentorship, career training, paid internships, and training in the soft skills necessary to find work, and advocacy, coalition building, and leadership development across the city.

READI Chicago, a project built out of the University of Chicago's Crime Lab, employs cognitive-behavioral therapy techniques in group sessions for men in neighborhoods with the highest rates of violence, legal, mental health, and substance use treatment services, and employment transition services. Thus far, the study has found participants to be less likely to be shot or to shoot others, to be victims or perpetrators of homicide, and to have lower arrest rates than non-participants in the same neighborhoods.[23]

The National Network's Intimate Partner Violence (IPV) Intervention (NNIPVI) utilizes some of these same tools in order to specifically target IPV. Through the training and staffing of victim advocates who link victims of IPV to resources, services, and information, works in the community to develop social norms that sanction IPV, and prevents violence in the moments of conflict. Further, they communicate clearly and strongly to individuals who have committed IPV previously and to all in the community what consequences there will be for future violence. Analyses of the NNIPVI's work have found reductions in injuries to victims of IPV and IPV recidivism.[24]

The same types of interventions could be developed and deployed across the United States, providing the greatest financial and capacity-building resources to areas with the highest rates of anti-trans violence (e.g., Louisiana, New York, Texas, Puerto Rico). Such an intervention might build upon the work of these various violence interruption services to provide job training and transitional services, free, or at minimum affordable, housing, cell phones with pre-programmed emergency numbers for violence interrupters in their neighborhoods, health care, and education (including GED prep and testing, community college, and higher education) to Black, Indigenous, and other trans people of color and low-income trans people. Workshops, forums, and other forms of popular education could be held in communities with high rates of anti-trans violence, educating the community, developing social bonds, and instilling norms against violence, alongside posters, bus ads, and murals demanding an end to violence and highlighting the consequences of anti-trans violence for perpetrators. Prior perpetrators of anti-trans violence along with prior victims could be hired, provided counseling, and trained—separately—to work within their communities as violence interrupters and victim advocates respectively.

However, such services must be financially supported and backed by cities, counties, states, and the federal government. Without funds, this work is impossible. Anti-violence work carries high risk for those engaged in it. Hureau et al. surveyed violence interrupters in Chicago, finding that 12 percent were shot while engaged in violence interruption work in the past year.[25] For the past year, activists, organizers, and advocates have worked to secure funding from the state of Illinois to implement Passports for Peace, a violence interruption program, in South Shore Chicago, the neighborhood I live in, where 44 percent of residents earn less than $25,000 a year, nearly 20 percent of housing remains vacant, one of the lowest life expectancy rates in the city, and an average of 1.8–3.3 shoot victims per 1,000 residents annually.[26,27] While Passports for Peace was granted $450,000, they have yet to receive the funds months after having been awarded it. In the meantime, two residents who committed to the program have been killed, four have been shot, and one has been charged with murder.[28]

While the United States does not, en masse, fund such programs, continues to overfund police departments across the nation, and underfunds social work and social services, it is possible to create a new system of safety. Such systems are being developed in socialist nations like Cuba. In 2021, Cuba developed and implemented *La Estrategia Integral de Prevención y Atención a La Violencia de Género y La Violencia en el Escenario Familiar* (The Comprehensive Strategy of Prevention of and Attention to Gender-Based and Familial Violence).[29] Within this nine-year-long strategy, the state, society, and all individuals hold equal responsibility for violence and its prevention. The strategy includes the development of state-funded mass popular education and a communication strategy to raise awareness of violence, to target the social and cultural foundations of gender-based violence, and to counter stereotypes that justify or minimize gender-based violence; the support and further development of local and regional community organizations working to prevent violence already, services for children and adolescents, and victims services; the development of rehabilitative systems of accountability for those who commit such violence; and the further codification of laws criminalizing violence against women (including and specifically naming transgender women).

Organizers and scholars co-writing *Socialist Reconstruction: A Better Future for the United States* point to the development of new services and programs that would be instituted and guaranteed under a socialist government, including "universal childcare, health care, education, housing, and meaningful work."[30] Such services would provide needed resources to disinvested communities facing high rates of violence. Guaranteed housing and social services would ensure that trans and cis women escaping violent situations would not face homelessness or poverty. Education, media, and public-health campaigns would be developed and implemented on a mass scale to target violence and shift cultural discourses on it.

It is possible to shift discourses around violence, to target the social and structural determinants of violence, and to provide the material investment in long impoverished communities necessary to decrease violence. The programs I've highlighted and the possibilities inherent in different nations highlight that violence is not inevitable. It is my hope that *Thinking Cis* provides a deeper understanding and analysis of the conditions that give rise to racist, cissexist violence, and in doing so, can provide a basis for future research to develop a blueprint for a more just society. Black trans activist, Miss Major Griffin-Gracy, once stated, "I'd like for the girls to get a chance to be who they are. For young transgender people to go to school, learn like everyone else does, and then get out there and live their lives, not afraid or thinking that the only solution for them is death." It is time that we, sociologists, and all people analyze the conditions that prevent this goal from being attained, co-develop and evaluate strategies to target identified conditions, and engage in scholarly and activist work necessary to ensure Miss Major's dream becomes reality.

NOTES

1. 2017, 146.
2. Endosex refers to individuals who are not intersex. Intersex individuals do not fit within Western, medical definitions of "male" or "female." Endosex individuals have chromosomes, hormones, and physical characteristics that "align" with their sex assigned at birth (i.e., endosex males have XY chromosomes, higher testosterone levels than estrogen, a penis that was greater than one inch in length at birth with a urethral opening at the tip of the glans, and testicles; endosex females have XX chromosomes, higher estrogen levels than testosterone, a vulva, a vagina, a clitoris that was under 3/8 of an inch at birth, a uterus, and breasts).
3. Human Rights Campaign, 2021, "Fatal Violence Against the Transgender and Gender Non-Conforming Community in 2021."
4. ACLU, 2021, "Legislation Affecting LGBT Rights Across the Country."
5. Human Rights Campaign, 2022, "Fatal Violence Against the Transgender and Gender Non-Conforming Community in 2022."
6. Freedom for All Americans, 2022, "Legislative Tracker: All Anti-LGBTQ Bills."
7. Dorn, 2022, "Ex-Trump Aides Behind Scare Ads."
8. 2022, "WI: Waukesha."
9. Twohey and Jewett, 2022, "Pusieron pausa a la pubertad."
10. Tourmaline, Stanley, and Burton, 2017, *Trap Door.*
11. Oyěwùmí, 1997, *Inventing Women.*
12. McNamara, 2016, "Milo Yiannopoulos Harassed a Transgender Student at Her School."
13. 2016, "Redefining Intimate Partner Violence."
14. Hennie, 2021, "Transgender Woman Shot to Death."
15. Clifton, 2021, "Two Black Trans Women Were Reportedly Murdered."
16. See: https://www.hrc.org/resources/fatal-violence-against-the-transgender-and-gender-non-conforming-community-in-2021.
17. For example, Bianchi et al., 2014, "Sex Work Among MSM and Trans Women." Ristock et al., 2017, "Impacts of Colonization."

18. Reback, Larkins, and Clark, 2018, "Motivations for a Casual or Occasional Sexual Encounter."

19. See: asanet.org/annual-meeting-2021/theme-and-program-committee.

20. Armstead, Wilkins, and Nation, 2019, "Structural and Social Determinants of Inequities in Violence Risk."

21. Whitehill, Webster, Frattaroli, and Parker, 2014, "Interrupting Violence."

22. Chicago CRED, 2022, "A Radical Reduction in Gun Violence is Within Reach."

23. N.A., 2022, "READI Chicago."

24. Sechrist and Weil, 2016, "Evaluation of the OFDVI in High Point, NC."

25. Hureau et al., 2022, "Exposure to Gun Violence."

26. Chicago Metropolitan Agency for Planning, 2022, "South Shore."

27. City of Chicago, 2020, "Our City, Our Safety."

28. Evans, 2022, "As South Shore Anti-Violence Program Waits, Members Are Getting Shot."

29. La Federación de Mujeres Cubanas, 2021, "Estrategia Integral."

30. Aslamy et al., 2022, *Socialist Reconstruction*, 158.

Appendix 1

Methods and Methodologies

Interviews were conducted face-to-face at a location of the participant's choosing. Sixteen interviews took place at coffee shops across Atlanta, with about one-third occurring in downtown Atlanta, one-third in nearby Decatur, and another third outside the perimeter of the city. Eight interviews occurred at a college or university, including at Georgia State University, in a private room or office. Two participants, I interviewed in my car. The first, Iceberg, was unable to get transportation to the coffee shop at which we originally planned to do the interview. I debated whether or not to continue the interview due to safety risks on my part as a trans woman. However, I ultimately decided to drive to him and interview him from my car, as I felt it necessary to engage participants where they were and to not erect class barriers through transportation. Iceberg then offered to help me with another participant and asked me to pick him up and drive him to where another participant was. This second participant was interviewed in my car as well. Finally, six interviews were recruited through the Atlanta Pre-Arrest Diversion Program and took place in their center. Interviews lasted an average of sixty minutes, with a range of 30 minutes (with one interview being cut short for safety reasons) to 100 minutes. Because of the time duration of the interviews, I compensated participants fifteen dollars each at the end of the interview.

In terms of participant demographics, the sample was predominantly of color with only 19 percent non-Latinx White (see table 9.1 in appendix 2). Twenty-two (69 percent) of participants were Black, including one individual who was Black and Portuguese, one who was Haitian, one who was Moor, and nineteen African American. One participant (3 percent) was Middle Eastern/Iraqi American. Two (6 percent) were Latina, including one White Latina and one non-White Latina. One participant was Indian/Asian American (3 percent). Six (19 percent) were non-Latinx White. Just slightly over

155

half (seventeen out of thirty-two) participants were cisgender women, and the remainder cisgender men. I additionally self-coded participant gender expression to assess how varying intensities of masculinities, femininities, and other expressions potentially related to their discussions of transgender women (*see* table 9.2 in appendix 2). Fourteen of the fifteen cisgender men participants were heterosexual, with one heteroflexible—this participant, however, had only ever had relationships with women. Seven of the seventeen (41.2 percent) cisgender women participants were bisexual/queer with primary attractions to women, one (6 percent) was homoflexible (however she had only had relationships with women), and the other nine (52.8 percent) were lesbian. Fourteen participants (44 percent) were between the ages of 18–24, twelve (37 percent) were 25–35, five (16 percent) were 36–46, and one (3 percent) was over 47. Half (16) had either completed some college or were currently in the process of working on a bachelor's degree. Nine (29 percent) had a bachelor's degree, two (6 percent) had a Master's degree, three (9 percent) had a high school diploma, and two (6 percent) had never completed high school.

Recruitment

The thirty-two participants were recruited from the Metro Atlanta area due to my physical proximity. I posted flyers in coffee shops, libraries, and universities, on social media, and placed flyers randomly on cars at the Memorial Street Kroger in Stone Mountain, the Moreland Avenue Kroger in Atlanta, and the Buford Highway Kroger in North Atlanta, the College Park Walmart, the Riverside Walmart, the West End Kroger, and the Midtown Whole Foods as a way of ensuring wide reach and the ability to recruit from a diverse pool of potential participants. I also utilized snowball sampling and passed out flyers at community events. Interview participants were also provided with miniature flyers and asked to share information regarding the study with friends.

Moore emphasizes that "frequenting a range of physical spaces where members of the group are thought to spend time" helps in building samples of marginalized groups.[1] As such, in addition to spaces like coffee shops, and libraries, I utilized cars at grocery stores as a method of reaching a larger span of people. The Memorial Street Kroger, College Park Walmart, Riverside Walmart and West End Kroger are in largely African American/Black and/or working-class customer neighborhoods and surrounding suburbs; whereas, the Moreland Avenue Kroger in the gentrified Atlanta "Edgewood" neighborhood and Midtown Whole Foods are in largely White, middle-class customer neighborhoods. The Buford Highway Kroger is within the Buford Highway Corridor with the ability to recruit Latinx and Asian/Asian American individuals into the study as well. While my sample is primarily of color, only one Latinx participant and one Asian American participant participated.

PHOTO ELICITATION

Dona Schwartz explains that photos are able to elicit response and interpretation from the respondent and are able to be analyzed by the researcher in understanding the geography of a particular area. Photos, Schwartz explains, are a "receptacle from which individual viewers withdraw meaning."[2] I utilized photos in my study in order to ask my participants to detail the meaning that becomes ascribed to particular bodies. Photos of particular bodies allowed me to make more concrete what may otherwise seem and feel very abstract to participants. Participants could verbally detail an open preference for all bodies, but in asking them to rate photos in order of least desirability to most desirability, the option to state complete neutrality was removed and required, instead, deeper introspection and reflection of the participant.

Several scholars have utilized photo ranking in analyzing perceptions of desirability vis-à-vis trans people.[3] Most of these, though, analyzed gender in isolation from other intersecting identities/axes of power. Gerhardstein and Anderson and Broussard and Warner both had majority White samples of young, college students analyze vignettes/photos. Broussard and Warner presented students with vignettes that depicted how the gender-nonconforming person physically looked. The vignettes, though, were racially unmarked, and thus, most likely assumed White by the majority of participants. Gerhardstein and Anderson utilized photos of a (presumed cisgender) White man and (presumed cisgender) White woman and manipulated facial appearance to make them look "more transgender/gender-nonconforming." Mao et al.,[4] though, included photos of Asian, Black, Latinx, and White men and women and asked for similar rankings as the other three. All were focused merely on differences in desirability. Collectively, though, all three detailed similar rankings of trans women as undesirable and cisgender women as more open to friendships/partnerships with transgender men. The similar patterns highlight the potential of photos to elicit meaning from participants regarding transgender people.

CODING

In analyzing data, I conducted an initial, qualitative coding, coding over segments of a single transcript numerous times to assess what the data were presenting to me. After initial coding, I sorted through the hundreds of codes to collapse codes into similar, overarching categories and assessed patterns in the codes. Through this, I arrived at thirty higher level codes that I then either connected, such as "hair as filthy" and "racialized preferences," or left as is. Each higher level code then had subsequent "child" codes. In what follows, I focus on specific themes that fill gaps in the current literature, that felt particularly necessary to attend to, such as the symbolic violence of trans murders, and which spanned the interviews of numerous, if not all, participants. My higher level codes included "desiring natural women," "appeals to commonsense logic," "cis discourse," "desiring trans women," "preferring sameness," "preferring difference," "trans-ness as an assault," "trans women are women," "critical cis-ness," and "tainted by the penis." After higher level coding and during writing, I conducted axial coding on higher level codes like "ending the murders of trans women" in order analyze racialized, gendered, and classed patterns in participant discourse.

METHODOLOGIES

I frame my work within feminist and queer methodologies that emphasize reflexivity, the partiality of all knowledge, and researcher accountability to our participants. My aim was not to conduct a study generalizable to all cisgender people. Rather, my aim was to theoretically expand academic discourse on cis-ness to have more in-depth understandings and analyses of how cis-ness functions. All perspectives are partial; however, the aim of research should be to enable "the connections and unexpected openings situated knowledges make possible."[5] I seek to begin weaving some of the webs of connection between cis-ness, whiteness, maleness, and lesbian-ness to foster further research in this area. I work, additionally, to foster dialogue between my participants and I, as well as between my participants during the focus group, to allow the "ruling relations"[6] of cis-ness to emerge without force or assumption.

Further, I interrogate gender-race-sexuality as interconnected, co-constructed, and co-maintained systems of oppression.[7] This does not mean that the distinctness of white supremacy, patriarchy, cissexism, and heterosexism are lost. Instead, an intersectional analysis highlights the heterogeneity of lived experiences, as individuals and social groups are differentially positioned within the interpersonal, structural, and cultural domains of power. While intersectionality has been critiqued for a focus on the interpersonal/interactional level of thought vis-à-vis identity, intersectional thought has also worked to understand production of intersectional vulnerabilities through the interworking of institutions and systems. In analyzing interview and focus group data through an intersectional lens, I sought to interrogate the ways in which the participants' construct discourse that is simultaneously racialized, sexed, gendered, and sexualized. In doing so, I aimed to understand the ways in which such discourse works to maintain systems of oppression that render trans women of color vulnerable.

Additionally, I explicitly mark when I am referencing trans women of color (and more explicitly if I am referencing Black, Latina, Asian/Asian American, and/or Indigenous trans women), as well as when I am referencing White trans women. A lack of specificity otherwise would collapse all of (trans) womanhood into a singular, universal ontology, denying differences of race, class, ability, and so forth.[8] Further, the lack of explicit specificity allows White (trans) womanhood to stand as the reference point for all of (trans) womanhood, contributing not only limitations to my analysis, but perpetuating white supremacy within my analysis.[9]

NOTES

1. 2018, "Challenges, Triumphs, and Praxis," 171.

2. Schwartz, 1992, *Waucoma Twilight,* 121.

3. For example: Gerhardstein and Anderson, 2010, "There's More Than Meets the Eye." Broussard and Warner, 2018, "Gender Nonconformity is Perceived Differently."

4. 2018, "How Gender Identity and Transgender Status Affect Perceptions of Attractiveness."

5. Haraway, 2004, "Situated Knowledges," 93.

6. Smith, 1987, *The Everyday World as Problematic.* Naples, 2003, *Feminism and Method.*

7. Smith, 2006, "Heteropatriarchy and the Three Pillars of White Supremacy." Lugones, 2007, "Heterosexualism and the Colonial/Modern Gender System." Crenshaw, 2012, "From Private Violence to Mass Incarceration."

8. Gill-Peterson, 2018, *Histories of the Transgender Child.*

9. hooks, 1981, *Ain't I a Woman.* hooks, 1984, *Feminist Theory.*

Appendix 2

Participant Demographics

Table 9.1 Participant Demographics

Name[1]	Gender	Sexual Orientation	Age	Income	Race & Ethnicity	Religion	Education
Adam	Man	Heterosexual	25–35	Low[2]	Middle Eastern	Muslim	Some College
Alyshah	Woman	Lesbian	18–24	Below/Near Poverty	Black	SBNR[3]	Some College
Alyx	Woman	Bi[4]	18–24	Below/Near Poverty	White	N/A	Some College
Amanda	Woman	Bi	25–35	Below/Near Poverty	Black	Christian	Less Than High School
Amy	Woman	Lesbian	36–46	Low	White Latina	N/A	Some College
Chris	Man	Bi[5]	36–46	Below/Near Poverty	Black	N/A	Less Than High School
Cookie	Woman	Homoflexible[6]	25–35	Middle Income	Black	SBNR	Master's
D	Man	Heterosexual	25–35	Below/Near Poverty	Black	N/A	Some College
Gee	Man	Heterosexual	36–46	Low	Black	Christian	Bachelor's
Henry	Man	Heterosexual	25–35	Below/Near Poverty	Black	Christian	Some College
Iceberg	Man	Heterosexual	47+	Below/Near Poverty	Black	Christian	Some College
Jake	Man	Heterosexual	18–24	Low	Black	N/A	Bachelor's
Janelle	Woman	Queer	18–24	Middle Income	Black	Christian	Some College
Jessica	Woman	Lesbian	25–35	Middle Income	Black	Christian	High School Diploma
Josh	Man	Heterosexual	25–35	Middle Income	Black	Christian	Bachelor's
Ky	Man	Heterosexual	18–24	Below/Near Poverty	Black	N/A	Master's
Kylee	Woman	Lesbian	18–24	Below/Near Poverty	Black	N/A	Some College
LaLa	Woman	Lesbian	18–24	Below/Near Poverty	Black	N/A	Some College
Liz	Woman	Lesbian	25–35	Low	Latina	SBNR	Bachelor's

Name	Gender	Sexual Orientation	Age	Income	Race	Religion	Education
Mack	Man	Heterosexual	25–35	Middle Income	Black	Christian	Some College
Mike	Man	Heterosexual	18–24	Low	White	N/A	Bachelor's
Musiteli	Man	Heterosexual	18–24	Low	Black	Atheist	Bachelor's
Peaches	Woman	Bi/Queer	18–24	Below/Near Poverty	Mixed—Black/White	SBNR	Some College
Rachel	Woman	Lesbian	18–24	Low	White	N/A	Bachelor's
Randall	Man	Heteroflexible[7]	25–35	Low	White	N/A	High School Diploma
Renee	Woman	Lesbian	36–46	Low	Black	SBNR	Bachelor's
Ryan	Man	Heterosexual	18–24	Below/Near Poverty	Asian American	Hindu	Some College
Sabrina	Woman	Lesbian	25–35	Middle Income	Black	SBNR	Bachelor's
Shantelle	Woman	Gay	18–24	Highest Tax Brackets	White	N/A	Some College
Sheila	Woman	Bisexual	25–35	Low	Black	Christian	Some College
Spiderman	Man	Heterosexual	36–46	Below/Near Poverty	Black	Christian	High School Diploma
Vincent	Woman	Lesbian	18–24	Middle Income	White	N/A	Some College

[1] Names used are pseudonyms chosen by participants at time of interview.

[2] Below/Near Poverty (Less than $20,000); Low Income ($20–44,999); Middle Income ($45–139,999); Upper Middle Income ($140–149,999); High Income ($150–199,999); Highest Tax Brackets ($200,000+)

[3] Spiritual But Not Religious

[4] Bisexual, primarily attracted to women and does not date cisgender men

[5] Only attracted to transgender women

[6] Mostly attracted to women, occasionally attracted to men

[7] Mostly attracted to women, occasionally attracted to men

Appendix 3

Additional Participant Demographics and Focus Group Participant Demographics

Table 9.2   Additional Participant Demographics

Name	Level of Religiosity[1]	Gender Expression[2]	LGB Acceptance[3]	Number of Recurring Known Trans Interactions[4]
Adam	Low	Very Masculine	Inclusive	0
Alyshah	N/A	More Feminine	Inclusive	0
Alyx	N/A	More Feminine	Inclusive	1–2
Amanda	Medium	Very Feminine	Inclusive	3–5
Amy	N/A	None of the Above	Inclusive	0
Chris	N/A	More Masculine	Inclusive	11+
Cookie	N/A	None of the Above	Inclusive	11+
D	N/A	More Masculine	Inclusive	1–2
Low	Low	Very Masculine	Moderately Heteronormative	0
Henry	Low	More Masculine	Inclusive	0
Iceberg	Medium	More Masculine	Moderately Heteronormative	0
Jake	N/A	More Masculine	Inclusive	0
Janelle	Medium	Very Feminine	Inclusive	1–2
Jessica	Low	Very Feminine	Slightly Heteronormative	0
Josh	Medium	Very Masculine	Very Heteronormative	0
Ky	N/A	More Masculine	Slightly Heteronormative	0
Kylee	N/A	More Masculine	Inclusive	3–5
LaLa	N/A	More Masculine	Slightly Heteronormative	1–2
Liz	N/A	None of the Above	Inclusive	0
Mack	Medium	Very Masculine	Slightly Heteronormative	3–5
Mike	N/A	More Masculine	Inclusive	0
Musiteli	N/A	More Masculine	Slightly Heteronormative	3–5
Peaches	N/A	More Feminine	Inclusive	11+
Rachel	N/A	More Feminine	Inclusive	3–5

(continued)

Name	Level of Religiosity[1]	Gender Expression[2]	LGB Acceptance[3]	Number of Recurring Known Trans Interactions[4]
Randall	N/A	More Masculine	Inclusive	11+
Renee	N/A	More Feminine	Inclusive	3–5
Ryan	High	More Masculine	Inclusive	1-2
Sabrina	N/A	More Feminine	Inclusive	1-2
Shantelle	N/A	More Feminine	Inclusive	6–10
Sheila	For Cultural Reasons Only	More Feminine	Inclusive	0
Spiderman	Low	Very Masculine	Very Heteronormative	1–2
Vincent	N/A	More Masculine	Inclusive	6–10

[1] "Level" of Religiosity is not to empirically assess religiosity but rather to display self-coded differences in level of religious expression. Participant religiosity was categorized based off a "point system." Participants accrued a "point" for each of the following: having a temple/alter at home; attending church/temple regularly; praying regularly; holding to scriptures dogmatically. Participants accrued a half point for each of the following: praying occasionally; attending church/temple occasionally. These were selected based of what participants offered as descriptions of "how religious" they are. Low religiosity: ½-1; Medium: 1.5–2.5; High: 3–4. "N/A" is used for participants who were not religious.

[2] I self-coded gender expression in order to tease apart the ways in which varying "intensities" of masculinities and femininities potentially shaped how participants viewed and reacted to trans women. I coded based off how participants described themselves *and* how I perceived them. This is in no way meant to be representative or generalizable, but instead to detail connections between gender expression and reactions to trans women. Adam, for example, described himself as very masculine, and indeed he express his gender in very masculine ways. He wore a "men's" suit, "men's" dress shoes, had a beard, wore cologne, spread his legs wide, and commented on my looks and single-ness. LaLa described herself as none of the above, but she wore more "masculine" clothing—a loose hoodie, loose pants, "men's" shoes—spread her legs wide and described her aesthetic as comfortable, so I rated her more masculine. Cookie had "feminine" and "masculine" attributes. She was warm, smiling, her legs and arms together rather than spread apart, and she mentioned that she, at times, wears heels. But she also had locs, wore "men's" clothing, and described herself as fluid. I placed her in none of the above rather than androgynous, because she didn't appear to me or describe herself as androgynous.

[3] LGB Acceptance was not measured in an empirical sense but rather to loosely assess how increased LGB antagonism potentially related to transphobia. Participant LGB acceptance was assessed on a "point system." Participants accrued points for each of the following: not wanting "it" in their face; having a lesbian/bi woman fetish; bi exclusionism; intolerance for gay men; referring to LGB identities as "choices"; believing religion could "save" an LGB person and convert them back to heterosexuality; believing trauma causes LGB identity; referring to AIDS as a divine punishment for "homosexuality." These factors were simply categorized based off participants' discussions of LGB people and the phrases they used to refer to LGB people. Inclusive: 0 points; Slightly Heteronormative: 1–3 points; More Heteronormative: 4–6 points; Very Heteronormative: 7–8 points.

[4] Participants were asked at the end of the interview how many recurring interactions they have had with trans people, and particularly trans women, including friends, family members, (former) partners, and coworkers.

Table 9.3 Focus Group Participant Demographics

Name	Gender	Sexual Orientation	Age	Income	Race & Ethnicity	Religion	Education
Adam	Man	Heterosexual	25-35	Low[2]	Middle Eastern	Muslim	Some College
Alyx	Woman	Bi	18-24	Below/Near Poverty	White	N/A	Some College
Amy	Woman	Lesbian	36-46	Low	White Latina	N/A	Some College
Rachel	Woman	Lesbian	18-24	Low	White	N/A	Bachelor's
Vincent	Woman	Lesbian	18-24	Middle Class	White	N/A	Some College

[1]Names used are pseudonyms chosen by participants at time of interview.

[2] Below/Near Poverty (Less than $20,000); Low Income ($20–44,999); Middle Class ($45–139,999); Upper Middle Class ($140–149,999); High Income ($150–199,999); Highest Tax Brackets ($200,000+)

References

ACLU. 2021. "Legislation Affecting LGBT Rights Across the Country." Retrieved from https://www.aclu.org/legislation-affecting-lgbt-rights-across-country.

Adam, Seth and Matt Goodman. 2015. "Number of Americans Who Report Knowing a Transgender Person Doubles in Seven Years, According to a New GLAAD Survey." *GLAAD*. Retrieved from https://www.glaad.org/releases/number-americans -who-report-knowing-transgender-person-doubles-seven-years-according-new.

Adams, M., Mickaela Bee, Ash Stephens, Toni-Michelle Williams, Janetta Johnson, Ola Osaze, and Sean Saifa Wall. 2020. "Ending the War on Black Trans People." *M4BL*. Retrieved from https://m4bl.org/events/ending-the-war-on-black -trans-people/.

Ahlm, Jody. 2017. "Respectable Promiscuity: Digital Cruising in an Era of Queer Liberalism." *Sexualities* 20, no. 3: 364–379. DOI: 10.1177/1363460716665783.

Ahmed, Sara. 2000. *Strange Encounters: Embodied Others in Post-Coloniality*. New York: Routledge.

Ahmed, Sara. 2004. *The Cultural Politics of Emotion*. New York: Routledge.

Ahmed, Sara. 2006. "Orientations: Toward a Queer Phenomenology." *GLQ: A Journal of Lesbian and Gay Studies* 12, no. 4: 543–574. DOI: 10.1215/10642684-2006-002.

Ahmed, Sara. 2006. *Queer Phenomenology*. Durham: Duke University Press.

Aizura, Aren Z. 2014. "Trans Feminine Value, Racialized Others and the Limits of Necropolitics." In *Queer Necropolitics*, edited by J. Haritaworn, A. Kuntsman, and S. Posocco, 129–148. New York: Routledge.

Almaguer, Tomas. 1993. "Chicano Men: A Cartography of Homosexual Identity and Behavior." In *The Lesbian and Gay Studies Reader*, edited by H. Abelove, M.A. Barale, and D.M. Halperin, 255–273. New York City: Routledge.

Althusser, Louis. 1972. *Lenin and Philosophy and Other Essays*. New York City: New York University Press.

Amante, Chase. n.d. "12 Ways to Spot a Transsexual (Signs She's a He)." Retrieved from http://www.girlschase.com/content-12-ways-spot-transsexual-signs-shes -he.

Anderson, Elijah. 2008. *Against the Wall: Poor, Young, Black, and Male*. Philadelphia: University of Pennsylvania Press.

Armstead, Theresa L., Natalie Wilkins, and Maury Nation. 2019. "Structural and Social Determinants of Inequities in Violence Risk: A Review of Indicators." *Journal of Community Psychology* 49, no. 4: 878–906. DOI: 10.1002/jcop.22232.

Ashley, Florence. 2018. "Genderfucking Non-Disclosure: Sexual Fraud, Transgender Bodies, and Messy Identities." *Dalhousie Law Journal* 41, no. 2: 339–378.

Aslamy, Sohrob, Ben Becker, Brian Becker, Richard Becker, Hannah Craig, Jane Cutter, Jodi Dean, Hannah Dickinson, et al. 2022. *Socialist Reconstruction: A Better Future for the United States*. San Francisco, CA: Liberation Media.

Assunção, Muri. 2022. "Friends Hold Vigil for 19-Year-Old Trans Woman Fatally Shot by her Father." *Daily News*. Retrieved from https://www.nydailynews.com/news/crime/ny-kathryn-katie-newhouse-asian-american-transgender-woman-shot-father-killed-20220405-w2ae67h6lrfflo4mifbnmzktyq-story.html.

Bailey, Marlon M. and Rashad Shabazz. 2013. "Gender and Sexual Geographies of Blackness: Anti-Black Heterotopias (Part 1)." *Gender, Place & Culture: A Journal of Feminist Geography* 21, no. 3: 316–321. DOI: 10.1080/0966369X.2013.781305.

Bailey, Marlon M. and Rashad Shabazz. 2014. "Gender and Sexual Geographies of Blackness: New Black Cartographies of Resistance and Survival (Part 2)." *Gender, Place & Culture: A Journal of Feminist Geography* 21, no. 4: 449–452. DOI: 10.1080/0966369X.2013.786303.

Bame, Yael. 2017. "21% of Americans Believe that Being Transgender is a Mental Illness." *YouGov*. Retrieved from https://today.yougov.com/topics/relationships/articles-reports/2017/05/17/21-americans-believe-identifying-transgender-menta.

Barbir, Lara A., Anna W. Vandevender, and Tracy J. Cohn. 2016. "Friendship, Attitudes, and Behavioral Intentions of Cisgender Heterosexuals Toward Transgender Individuals." *Journal of Gay & Lesbian Mental Health* 21, no. 2: 154–170. DOI: 10.1080/19359705.2016.1273157.

Barthes, Roland. 1980. *Camera Lucida: Reflections on Photography*. New York City: Hill & Wang.

Bartky, Sandra Lee. 1988. "Foucault, Femininity, and the Modernization of Patriarchal Power." In *Feminism and Foucault: Reflections on Resistance*, edited by I. Diamond and L. Quinby, 25–45. Boston: Northeastern University Press.

Bartlett, Katharine T. 1994. "Only Girls Wear Barrettes: Dress and Appearance Standards, Community Norms, and Workplace Equality." *Michigan Law Review* 92, no. 8: 2541–2582. DOI: 10.2307/129002.

de Beauvoir, Simone. 1949 [1973]. *The Second Sex*. New York: Vintage Books.

Bergner, Daniel. 2019. "The Struggles of Rejecting the Gender Binary." *The New York Times*. Retrieved from https://www.nytimes.com/2019/06/04/magazine/gender-nonbinary.html.

Bersani, Leo. 2010. *Is the Rectum a Grave? And Other Essays*. Chicago: University of Chicago Press.

Bettcher, Talia Mae. 2007. "Evil Deceivers and Make-Believers: On Transphobic Violence and the Politics of Illusion." *Hypatia* 22, no. 3: 43–65. DOI: 10.1111/j.1527-2001.2007.tb01090.x

Bettie, Julie. 2002. *Women Without Class: Girls, Race, and Identity*. Berkeley: University of California Press.

Bey, Marquis. 2019. "Black Fugitivity Un/Gendered." *The Black Scholar: Journal of Black Studies and Research* 49, no. 1: 55–62. DOI: 10.1080/00064246.2019.154.8059.

Bianchi, Fernanda T., Carol A. Reisen, Maria Cecilia Zen, Salvador Vidal-Ortiz, Felisa A. Gonzales, Fabián Betancourt, Marcela Aguilar, and Paul J. Poppen. 2014. "Sex Work Among Men Who Have Sex with Men and Transgender Women in Bogotá." *Archive of Sexual Behaviour* 43: 1637–1650.

Blair, Karen L. and Rhea Ashley Hoskin. 2018. "Transgender Exclusion from the World of Dating: Patterns of Acceptance and Rejection of Hypothetical Trans Dating Partners as a Function of Sexual and Gender Identity." *Journal of Social and Personal Relationships* 36, no. 7: 2074–2095. DOI: 10.1177/0265407518779139.

Bode, David, Dean A. Seehusen, and Drew Baird. 2012. "Hirsutism in Women." *American Family Physician* 85, no. 4: 373–380.

Bok, Sissela. 1998. *Secrets: On the Ethics of Concealment and Revelation*. London: Vintage Books.

Bonilla-Silva, Eduardo. 2014. *Racism without Racists: Color-Blind Racism and the Persistence of Racial Inequality in America*. Lanham: Rowman & Littlefield.

Bourdieu, Pierre. 1998 [2002]. *Masculine Domination*. Redwood City: Stanford University Press.

Brooks, Laken. 2020. "The Pigments of Patriarchy and Femme Trans Exclusion in the History of the 'All Natural' Makeup Movement." In *Makeup in the World of Beauty Vlogging: Community, Commerce, and Culture*, edited by C.D. Little, 127–142. Washington, DC: Lexington Books.

Broussard, Kristin A. and Ruth H. Warner. 2018. "Gender Nonconformity is Perceived Differently for Cisgender and Transgender Targets." *Sex Roles* August: 1–20.

Burnette, Catherine. 2015. "Historical Oppression and Intimate Partner Violence Experienced by Indigenous Women bin the United States: Understanding Connections." *Social Service Review* 89, no. 3. doi: 10.1086/683336.

Butler, Judith. 1990. *Gender Trouble*. New York: Routledge.

Butler, Judith. 1993. *Bodies that Matter: On the Discursive Limits of Sex*. New York: Routledge.

Butler, Judith. 2004. *Undoing Gender*. New York: Routledge.

Byrd, A.D. and L.L. Tharps. 2014. "When Black Hair is Against the Rules." *The New York Times*. Retrieved from http://www.nytimes.com/2014/05/01/opinion/when-black-hair-is-against-the-rules.html?_r=0.

Caluya, Gilbert 2006. "The (Gay) Scene of Racism: Face, Shame, and Gay Asian Males." *Australian Critical Race and Whiteness Studies Association e-Journal* 2, no. 2.

Chauncey, George. 1995. *Gay New York: Gender, Urban Culture, and the Making of the Gay Male World 18990-1940*. New York: Basic Books.

Cheng, Anne Anlin. 2010. *Second Skin: Josephine Backer & the Modern Surface*. Oxford: Oxford University Press.

Chicago CRED. 2022. "A Radical Reduction in Gun Violence is Within Reach." Accessed 3 January 2023 from chicagocred.org.

Chicago Metropolitan Agency for Planning. 2022. "South Shore: Community Data Snapshot." Retrieved January 3, 2023 from https://www.cmap.illinois.gov/documents/10180/126764/South+Shore.pdf.

City of Chicago. 2020. "Our City, Our Safety: A Comprehensive Plan to Reduce Violence in Chicago." Retrieved January 3, 2023 from https://www.chicago.gov/content/dam/city/sites/public-safety-and-violenc-reduction/pdfs/OurCityOur-Safety.pdf.

Clarkson, Nicholas L. 2020. "Terrorizing Transness: Necropolitical Nationalism." *Feminist Formations* 32, no. 2: 163–182. DOI: 10.1353/ff.2020.0029.

Clary, Sasha. 2018. "Bottom Surgery: What You Need to Know." *Healthline.* Retrieved from https://www.healthline.com/health/transgender/bottom-surgery.

Clifton, Derrick. 2021. "Two Black Trans Women Were Reportedly Murdered in Florida and Louisiana." *Them.* Retrieved from https://www.them.us/story/two-black-trans-women-reportedly-murdered-florida-louisiana-alexus-braxton-fifty-bandz.

Collins, Patricia Hill. [1990] 2000. *Black Feminist Thought: Knowledge, Consciousness, and the Politics of Empowerment,* 2nd ed. New York: Routledge.

Collins, Patricia Hill. 2005. *Black Sexual Politics: African Americans, Gender, and the New Racism.* New York: Routledge.

Connell, R.W. [1995] 2005. *Masculinities,* 2nd ed. Berkely: University of California Press.

Connell, R.W. and James W. Messerschmidt. 2005. "Hegemonic Masculinity: Rethinking the Concept." *Gender & Society* 19, no. 6: 829–859.

Conron, Kerith J., Winston Luhur, and Shoshana K. Goldberg. 2021. "LGBT Adults in Large US Metropolitan Areas." *The Williams Institute.* Retrieved from https://williamsinstitute.law.ucla.edu/wp-content/uploads/MSA-LGBT-Ranking-Mar-2021.pdf.

Cox, Jonathan and Emily Merwin. 2016. "How Every Neighborhood in Metro Atlanta Voted in the 2016 Presidential Election." *Atlanta Journal Constitution.* Retrieved from https://www.ajc.com/atlanta-neighborhood-2016-presidential-election-results-map/?_gl=1*117ibsg*_ga*NzkwMjY2NTA2LjE2NjI0Mjc0NTc.*_ga_6VR7Y4BTY5*MTY2MjQzMDU1NS4yLjAuMTY2MjQzMDU1Ny4wLjAuMA.

Crenshaw, Kimberlé W. 2012. "From Private Violence to Mass Incarceration: Thinking Intersectionally About Women, Race, and Social Control." *UCLA Law Review* 59: 1420–1472.

Croson, Charlotte. 2001. "Sex, Lies and Feminism." *Off Our Backs* 31, no. 6 Retrieved from https://feminist-reprise.org/library/gender-patriarchal-construct/sex-lies-and-feminism/.

Damshenas, Sam. 2020. "Trans Influencers Savagely Beaten By Homophobes as Onlookers Did Nothing." *Gay Times.* Retrieved from https://www.gaytimes.co.uk/life/trans-influencers-savagely-beaten-by-homophobes-as-onlookers-did-nothing/.

Dank, Meredith, Pamela Lachman, Janine M. Zweig, and Jennifer Yahner. 2014. "Dating Violence Experiences of Lesbian, Gay, Bisexual, and Transgender Youth." *Journal of Youth and Adolescence* 43: 846–857. DOI: 10.1007/s10964-013-9975-8.

Davis, Georgiann. 2015. *Contesting Intersex: The Dubious Diagnosis.* New York: New York University Press.

Decena, Carlos Ulises. 2007. *Tacit Subjects: Belonging and Same-Sex Desire Among Dominican Immigrant Men.* Durham: Duke University Press.

DeGagne, Alexa. 2021. "Protecting Cisnormative Private and Public Spheres: The Canadian Conservative Denunciation of Transgender Rights." *Studies in Social Justice* 15, no. 3: 497–517.

The Department of Housing and Urban Development. 24 CFR Part 5 1-29 (2020).

Dinno, Alexis. 2017. "Homocide Rates of Transgender Individuals in the United States: 2010-2014." *American Journal of Public Health* 107, no. 9: 1441–1447. DOI:10.2105/AJPH.2017.303878.

Dorn, Sara. 2022. "Ex-Trump Aides Behind Scare Ads Attacking Democrats Over Transgender Issues and Immigration." *Forbes.* Retrieved November 27, 2022 from https://www.forbes.com/sites/saradorn/2022/10/25/ex-trump-aides-behind-scare-ads -attacking-democrats-over-transgender-issues-and-immigration/?sh=2f2bb5972735.

Dozier, Raine. 2005. "Beards, Breasts, and Bodies: Doing Sex in a Gendered World." *Gender & Society* 19: 297–316.

Driskill, Qwo-Li. 2016. *Asegi Stories: Cherokee Queer and Two-Spirit Memory.* Tucson: University of Arizona Press.

DuBois, W.E.B. 1903. *The Souls of Black Folk.* Mineola: Dover Publication.

Duggan, Lisa. 2003. *The Twilight of Equality?: Neoliberalism, Cultural Politics, and the Attack on Democracy.* Boston: Beacon Press.

Elliot, Patricia and Lawrence Lyons. 2017. "Transphobia as Symptom: Fear of the 'Unwoman'." *TSQ: Transgender Studies Quarterly* 4, no. 3–4: 358–383. DOI: 10.1215/23239252-4189874.

Ellison, Treva. 2017. "The Labor of Werqing It: The Performance and Protest Strategies of Sir Lady Java." In *Trap Door: Trans Cultural Production and the Politics of Visibility,* edited by Reina Gossett, Erica A. Stanley, and J. Burton, 1–22. Cambridge: The MIT Press.

Engels, Fredrick. 1894 [1968; 2000]. "Engels to Borgius," in *Marx-Engels Correspondence 1894.* Accessed May 19, 2023 from Marxists.org.

Fact.MR. 2023. "Hair Removal Wax Market is Posed to Reach US$18.4 Billion by 2033: Fact.MR Study." *Global Newswire.* Retrieved 13 September 2023 from https://www.globenewswire.com/news-release/2023/09/08/2739866/0/en/Hair-Removal-Wax-Market-is-Poised-to-Reach-US-18-4-Billion-by-2033-Fact-MR-Study.html#:~:text=Rockville%2C%20Sept.,CAGR%20of%206%25%20through%202033.

Fahs, Breanne. 2011. "Dreaded 'Otherness': Heteronormative Patrolling in Women's Body Hair Rebellions." *Gender & Society* 25, no. 4: 451–472. DOI: 10.1177/0891243211414877.

Fausto-Sterling, Anne. 2000. *Sexing the Body: Gender, Politics, and the Construction of Sexuality.* New York: Basic Books.

Feagin, Joe. 2006. *Systemic Racism: A Theory of Oppression.* New York: Routledge.

Feingberg, Leslie. 1998. *Trans Liberation: Beyond Pink or Blue.* New York: Beacon Press.

Ferber, Abby L. 2010. "Constructing Whiteness: The Intersections of Race and Gender in US White Supremacist Discourse." *Ethnic and Racial Studies* 21, no. 1: 48–63. DOI: 10.1080/014198798330098.

Ferriman, David and J.D. Gallwey. 1961. "Clinical Assessment of Body Hair Growth in Women." *The Journal of Clinical Endocrinology & Metabolism* 21, no. 11: 1440–1447. DOI: 10.120/jcem-21-11-1440.

Frankenberg, Ruth. 1993. *White Women, Race Matters: The Social Construction of Whiteness.* Minneapolis: University of Minnesota Press.

Freedom for All Americans. 2022. "Legislative Tracker: All Anti-LGBTQ Bills." Retrieved from tps://freedomforallamericans.org/legislative-tracker/anti-lgbtq-bills/.

Garn, Stanley M. 1990. "Sex Differences and Ethnic/Racial Differences in Body Size and Body Composition." In *Body Composition and Physical Performance: Applications for the Military Services,* edited by B.M. Marriott and J. Grumstrup-Scott. Washington, DC: National Academies Press.

Gerhardstein, Kelly R. and Veanne N. Anderson. 2010. "There's More Than Meets the Eye: Facial Appearance and Evaluations of Transsexual People." *Sex Roles* 62: 361–373. DOI: 10.1007/s11199-010-9746.

Gill-Peterson, Jules. 2018. *Histories of the Transgender Child.* Minneapolis: University of Minnesota Press.

Glenn, Evelyn Nakano. 2002. *Unequal Freedom: How Race and Gender Shaped American Citizenship and Labor.* Cambridge, MA: Harvard University Press.

Global Burden of Disease 2016 Injury Collaborators. 2018. "Global Morality from Firearms, 1990-2016." *Journal of the American Medical Association* 320, no. 8: 792–814. doi: 10.1001/jama.2018.10060.

Goffman, Erving. 1963. *Stigma: Notes on the management of Spoiled Identity.* New York: Simon & Schuster.

Goodnough, Abby, Erica L. Green, and Margot Sanger-Katz. 2019. "Trump Administration Proposes Rollback of Transgender Protections." *The New York Times.* Retrieved from https://www.nytimes.com/2019/05/24/us/politics/donald-trump-transgender-protections.html.

Gossett, Che. 2016. "Žižek's Trans/gender Trouble." *The LA Review of Books.* Retrieved from https://lareviewofbooks.org/article/zizeks-transgender-trouble/#!.

Green, Eli R. 2006. "Debating Trans Inclusion in the Feminist Movement: A Trans-Positive Analysis." *Journal of Lesbian Studies* 10, no. 1/2: 231–248. DOI: 10.1300/j155v10n01_12.

Green, Gerald. 2022. "Support Urgent Immigrant Hunger Strike at Georgia Prison." *Liberation News.* Retrieved from https://www.liberationnews.org/support-urgent-immigrant-hunger-strike-at-georgia-prison/.

Greene, D. Wendy. 2012. "A Multidimensional Analysis of What Not to Wear in the Workplace: Hijabs and Natural Hair." *FIU Law Review* 8, no. 2.

Halberstam, Judith Jack. 1994. "F2M: The Making of Female-Masculinity." In *The Lesbian Postmodern,* edited by L. Doan, 210–228. New York: Columbia University Press.

Hall, Peter. 2018. "Boyertown Students Ask U.S. Supreme Court to Hear Appeal of Transgender Bathroom Challenge. *The Morning Call.* Retrieved from https://www.mcall.com/news/police/mc-nws-boyertown-transgender-bathroom-supreme-court-peitition-20181119-story.html.

Hamermesh, Daniel S. 2011. *Beauty Pays: Why Attractive People Are More Successful.* Princeton: Princeton University Press.

Haraway, Donna. 1985. "Manifesto for Cyborgs: Science, Technology, and Socialist Feminism in the 1980s." *Socialist Review* 80: 65–108.

Haraway, Donna. 1988. "Situated Knowledges: The Science Question in Feminism and the Privilege of Partial Perspective." *Feminist Studies* 14, no. 3: 575–599.

Haritaworn, Jin. 2012. *The Biopolitics of Mixing: Thai Multiracialities and Haunted Ascendancies*. Burlington: Ashgate.

Haritaworn, Jin., Adi Kunstman, and Silvia Posocco. 2014. *Queer Necropolitics*. New York: Routledge.

Harrington, Carol. 2020. "What is 'Toxic Masculinity,' and Why Does it Matter?" *Men & Masculinities*. DOI: 10.1177/1097184X20943254.

Harris, Angela P. 2000. "Gender, Violence, Race, and Criminal Justice." *Stanford Law Review* 52 (4): 777–807. DOI: 10.2307/1229430.

Hennie, Matt. 2021. "Transgender Teen Found in Midtown was Murdered, Activists Say. *Project Q*. Retrieved from https://www.projectq.us/transgender-teen-found-in -midtown-was-murdered-activists-say/.

Hennie, Matt. 2021. "Transgender Woman Shot to Death in Her Atlanta Apartment." *Project Q*. Retrieved from https://www.projectq.us/transgender-woman-shot-to -death-in-her-atlanta-apartment/.

Heritage, Stuart. 2020. "How The Jerry Springer Show Splashed Around in Humanity's Worst Excesses." *The Guardian*. Retrieved from https://www.theguardian .com/tv-and-radio/2020/apr/06/jump-the-shark-the-jerry-springer-show.

Herzig, Rebecca M. 2015. *Plucked: A History of Hair Removal*. New York City: New York University Press.

Hess, Amanda. 2017. "America is Struggling to Sort Out Where 'Violence' Begins and Ends." *The New York Times*. Retrieved from https://www.nytimes.com/2017/08/15/ magazine/america-is-struggling-to-sort-out-where-violence-begins-and-ends.html.

Hobson, Maurice J. 2017. *The Legend of the Black Mecca: Politics and Class in the Making of Modern Atlanta*. Chapel Hill: The University of North Carolina Press.

Holmes, Tamara E. 2019. "Feature: The Industry that Black Women Built." *Essence*. Retrieved from https://www.essence.com/news/money-career/business -black-beauty/.

hooks, bell. 1981. *Ain't I A Woman?* London: Pluto Press.

hooks, bell. 1984. *Feminist Theory: From Margin to Center*. New York City: South End Press.

Human Rights Campaign. 2017. "A National Epidemic: Fatal Anti-Transgender Violence in America in 2017." Retrieved from http://assets2.hrc.org/files/assets /resources/A_Time_To_Act_2017_REV3.pdf?_ga=2.173828966.452789393 .1662428047-99866844.1658524009.

Human Rights Campaign. 2018. "Violence Against the Transgender Community in 2018." Retrieved from https://www.hrc.org/resources/violence-against-the-trans- gender-community-in-2018.

Human Rights Campaign. 2021. "Fatal Violence Against the Transgender and Gender Non-Conforming Community in 2021." Retrieved from https://www.hrc .org/resources/fatal-violence-against-the-transgender-and-gender-non-conforming -community-in-2021.

Human Rights Campaign. 2022. "Fatal Violence Against the Transgender and Gender Non-Conforming Community in 2022." Retrieved from https://www.hrc .org/resources/fatal-violence-against-the-transgender-and-gender-non-conforming -community-in-2022.

Hureau, David, Theodore Wilson, Hilary Jackl, Jalon Arthur, Christopher Patterson, and Andrew Papachristos. 2022. "Exposure to Gun Violence Among the Population of Chicago Community Violence Interventionists (WP-22-12)." *Northwestern University Institute for Policy Research*. Retrieved January 3, 2023 from https:// www.ipr.northwestern.edu/our-work/working-papers/2022/wp-22-12.html.

Ingraham, Chrys. 2003. *Thinking Straight: The Power, Promise, and Paradox of Heterosexuality*. New York: Routledge.

International Center for Transgender Care. 2021. "Body Feminization Procedures." Retrieved from https://thetranscenter.com/transwomen/body-feminization -procedures/.

Intersex Society of North America. 2020. "Congenital Adrenal Hyperplasia." Retrieved from https://.org/faq/conditions/cah.

Jackson, Stevi. 2005. "Sexuality, Heterosexuality and Gender Hierarchy: Getting Our Priorities Straight." In *Thinking Straight: The Power, the Promise, and the Paradox of Heterosexuality*, edited by C. Ingraham, 39–62. New York: Routledge.

James, Sandy E., Jody L. Herman, Susan Rankin, Mara Keisling, Lisa Mottet, and Ma'ayan Anafi. 2016. "The Report of the 2015 U.S. Transgender Survey." *National Center for Transgender Equality*. Retrieved from https://transequality.org /sites/default/files/docs/usts/USTS-Full-Report-Dec17.pdf.

Johnson, Austin. 2016. "Transnormativity: A New Concept and Its Validation Through Documentary Film About Transgender Men." *Sociological Inquiry* 86, no. 4: 465–491. DOI: 10.1111/soin.2016.86.issue-4.

Joseph-Salisbury, Remi and Laura Connelly. 2018. "'If Your Hair is Relaxed, White People Are Relaxed. If Your Hair is Nappy, They're Not Happy': Black Hair as a Site of 'Post-Racial' Social Control in English Schools." *Social Sciences* 7, no. 219. DOI: 10.3390/socsci7110219.

Kanamori, Yasuko and Yonghong J. Xu. 2020. "Factors Associated with Transphobia: A Structural Equation Modeling Approach." *Journal of Homosexuality*. DOI: 10.1080/00918369.2020.1851959.

Kang, Miliann. 2010. *The Managed Hand: Race, Gender, and the Body in Beauty Service Work*. Berkeley: University of California Press.

Kho, Adeline, Sangeetha Thanapal, and Petra Dierkes-Thrun. 2015. "Chinese Privilege, Gender and Intersectionality in Singapore: A Conversation between Adeline Koh and Sangeetha Thanapal." *boundary 2*. Retrieved from https://www.boundary2.org/2015/03/chinese-privilege-gender-and-intersectionality-in-singapore-a -conversation-between-adeline-koh-and-sangeetha-thanapal/.

Kooy, Rachel E. 2010. "Knowledge and Attitudes Toward Trans Persons." Master's Thesis. Department of Counseling Psychology at Humboldt State University. https://scholarworks.calstate.edu/downloads/dn39x396c.

Kramer, Sarah. 2019. "Should Ideology Trump Biology in Schools?" *Alliance Defending Freedom*. Retrieved from https://www.adflegal.org/detailspages/blog -details/allianceedge/2019/01/07/should-ideology-trump-biology-in-schools.

La Federación de Mujeres Cubanas. 2021. "Estrategia Integral de Prevención y Atención a la Violencia de Género y la Violencia en el Escenario Familiar." Retrieved
January 3, 2023 from http://www.mujeres.cu/pdf/Estrategia_integral_de_preven-
cion_y_atencion.pdf.
Lambert, Bianca. 2020. "How Much It Costs to Maintain Natural Black Hair." *Huff-
Post*. Retrieved from https://www.huffpost.com/entry/costs-natural-black-hair_l
_5e441e19c5b6d0ea3811b813.
Lee, Joey. 2018. "East Asian 'China Doll' or 'Dragon Lady'?" *Bridges: An Under-
graduate Journal of Contemporary Connections* 3, no. 1: 1–6.
Long, Robyn. 2018. "Sexual Subjectivities within Neoliberalism: Can Queer and
Crip Engagements Offer an Alternative Praxis?" *Journal of International Women's
Studies* 19, no. 1: 78–93.
Lugones, Maria. 2007. "Heterosexualism and the Colonial/Modern Gender System."
Hypatia 22, no. 1: 186–209.
Lyon, Jacqueline. 2020. "Pajón Power: Styling Citizenship and Black Politics in
the Dominican Natural Hair Movement." *Ethnic and Racial Studies* 43, no. 12:
2120–2139. DOI: 10.1080/01419870.2019.1671601.
Mao, Jessica M., M.L. Haupert, and Eliot R. Smith. 2018. "How Gender Identity and
Transgender Status Affect Perceptions of Attractiveness." *Social Psychological
and Personality Science* 10, no. 6: 1–12. DOI: 10.1177/1948550618783716.
Marx, Karl. 1858. *The Grundrisse*. London: Penguin Books.
Mbembe, Achille. 2003. "Necropolitics." *Public Culture* 15, no. 1: 11–40. Translated
by Libby Meintjes.
McKinley Jr., James C. 2016. "Man's Confession in Transgender Woman's Death
is Admissible, Judge Rules." *The New York Times*. Retrieved from https://
www.nytimes.com/2016/04/02/nyregion/mans-confession-in-transgender-womans
-death-is-admissible-judge-rules.html.
McNamara, Brittney. 2016. "Milo Yiannopoulos Harassed a Transgender Student at
Her School." *Teen Vogue*. Retrieved from https://www.teenvogue.com/story/milo
-yiannopoulos-harassed-a-transgender-student-at-her-school.
Meadow, Tey 2018. *Trans Kids: Being Gendered in the Twenty-First Century*.
Berkeley: University of California Press.
Messerschmidt, James W. 2019. "The Salience of 'Hegemonic Masculinity'." *Men
and Masculinities* 22, no. 1. DOI: 10.1177/1097184X18805555.
Miller, Jordan F. 2018. "YouTube as a Site of Counternarratives to Transnormativity."
Journal of Homosexuality 66, no. 6: 815–837. DOI: 10.1080/00918369.2018.1484629.
Mills, C.W. 2007. "White Ignorance." In *Race and Epistemologies of Ignorance*, edited
by S. Sullivan and N. Tuana, 13–38. Albany: State University of New York Press.
Mock, Janet. 2017. "Being Pretty is a Privilege, But We Refuse to Acknowledge It."
Allure. Retrieved from https://www.allure.com/story/pretty-privilege.
Mogul, Joey, Andrea J. Ritchie, and Kay Whitlock. 2011. *Queer (In)Justice: The
Criminalization of LGBT People in the United States*. Boston: Beacon Press.
Moore, Lisa Jean and Mary Kosut. 2015. *The Body Reader*. New York City: New
York University Press.
Moore, Mignon R. 2006. "Lipstick or Timberlands? Meanings of Gender Presentation
in Black Lesbian Communities." *Signs* 32, no. 1: 113–139. DOI: 10.1086/505269.

Moore, Mignon R. 2011. *Invisible Families: Gay Identities, Relationships, and Motherhood Among Black Women*. Berkeley: University of California Press.

Moore, Mignon R. 2018. "Challenges, Triumphs, and Praxis: Collecting Qualitative Data on Less Visible and Marginalized Populations." In *Other, Please Specify*, edited by D. Compton, T. Meadow, and K. Schilt, 169–184. Berkeley: University of California Press.

Morris, Bonnie J. 2016. *The Disappearing L: Erasure of Lesbian Spaces and Culture*. New York: SUNY Press.

Morrison, Eleanor G. 2010. "Transgender as Ingroup or Outgroup? Lesbian, Gay, and Bisexual Viewers Respond to a Transgender Character in Daytime Television." *Journal of Homosexuality* 57: 650–665. DOI: 10.1080/00918361003712103.

Movement Advancement Project. 2022. "Georgia's Equality Profile." Retrieved from https://www.lgbtmap.org/equality-maps/profile_state/GA.

Moynihan, Daniel P. 1965. "The Negro Family: The Case for National Action." *Office of Policy Planning and Research*. United States Department of Labor.

Murphy, Ryan, Brad Falchuk, and Steven Canals. 2018. "Life's a Beach." *Pose*. Los Angeles: FX Productions.

Musser, Amber Jamilla. 2016. "Black Hair and Textures of Defensiveness." *Palimpsest: A Journal on Women, Gender, and the Black International*. 5, no. 1: 1–19. DOI: 10.153/pal.2016.0001.

Musser, Amber Jamilla. 2018. "Surface-Becoming: Lyle Ashton Harris and Brown Jouissance." *Women and Performance* 28, no. 1: 34–45. DOI: 10.1080/07 40770X.2018.1427333.

N.A. 2022. "READI Chicago: A Community-Based Approach to Reducing Gun Violence." *University of Chicago Urban Labs*. Retrieved January 1, 2023 from https://urbanlabs.uchicago.edu/attachments/f1a1e66c0c14b1e1b48d398d43054a9 1163360d5/store/548bc1f4652f976195c082320b00f290915e99267c0388ce9af ae332aa06/Final+READI+2+Pager+4.25.22.pdf.

Naples, Nancy A. 2003. *Feminism and Method: Ethnography, Discourse Analysis, and Activist Research*. New York: Routledge.

Nataf, Zachary I. 1996. *Lesbians Talk: Transgender*. London: Scarlet Press.

National Republican Senatorial Committee. 2022. "WI: Waukesha." Retrieved November 27, 2022 from https://www.youtube.com/watch?v=Zpo6j1ufjF4&t=22s.

O'Connell, Michael. 2018. "'Jerry Springer' Future Uncertain as Production Halts After 27 Years." *The Hollywood Reporter*.

O'Connor, K.M. and E. Gladstone. 2018. "Beauty and Social Capital: Being Attractive Shapes Social Networks." *Social Networks* 52: 42–47. DOI: 10.1016/j. socnet.2017.05.003.

Ohki, M., K. Naito, and P. Cole. 1991. "Dimensions and Resistances of the Human Nose: Racial Differences." *Laryngoscope* 101 , no. 3: 276–278. DOI: 10.1288/00005537-199103000-00009.

Opie, Tina R. and Katherine W. Phillips. 2015. "Hair Penalties: The Negative Influence of Afrocentric Hair on Ratings of Black Women's Dominance and Professionalism." *Frontiers in Psychology* 6. DOI: 10.3389/fpsyg.2015.01311.

Oyedemi, Toks. 2016. "Beauty as Violence: 'Beautiful' Hair and the Cultural Violence of Identity Erasure." *Social Identities* 22, no. 5: 537-553. DOI: 10.1080/13504630. 2016.1157455.

Oyěwùmí, Oyèrónkẹ́. 1997. *The Invention of Women: Making an African Sense of Western Gender Discourses.* Minneapolis: University of Minnesota Press.

Paechter, Carrie. 2018. "Rethinking the Possibilities for Hegemonic Femininity: Exploring a Gramscian Framework." *Women's Studies International Forum* 68: 121–128. DOI: 10.1016/j.wsif.2018.03.005.

Page, Enoch H., and Matt U. Richardson. 2009. "On the Fear of Small Numbers: A Twenty-First Century Prolegomenon of the U.S. Black Transgender Experience." In *Black Sexualities: Probing Powers, Passions, Practices, and Policies*, edited by J. Battle and S.L. Barnes, 57–81. New Brunswick, NJ: Rutgers University Press.

Pascoe, C.J. 2007. "'Dude, You're a Fag.'" *Inside Higher Ed.* Retrieved from https://www.insidehighered.com/views/2007/06/28/dude-youre-fag.

Pascoe, C.J. 2007. *Dude, You're a Fag: Masculinity and Sexuality in High School.* Berkeley: University of California Press.

Patel, Vrushali. 2017. "Sex, Gender, and Sexuality in Colonial Modernity: Towards a Sociology of Webbed Connectivities." In *Global Historical Sociology*, edited by J. Go and G. Lawson, 124–141. Cambridge: Cambridge University Press.

Patton, Tracey Owens. 2006. "Hey Girl, Am I More Than My Hair?: African American Women and Their Struggles with Beauty, Body Image, and Hair." *NWSA Journal* 18, no. 2: 24–51. DOI: 10.1353/nwsa.2006.0037.

Pearce, Ruth, Sonja Erikainen, and Ben Vincent. 2020. "TERF Wars: An Introduction." *The Sociological Review* 68, no. 4: 677–698. DOI: 10.1177/0038026120934713.

Peiss, Kathy. 1998. *Hope in a Jar: The Making of America's Beauty Culture.* Philadelphia: University of Pennsylvania Press.

Pew Research Center. 2017. "Intermarriage in the U.S. 50 Years After *Loving v. Virginia*." Retrieved from https://www.pewsocialtrends.org/2017/05/18/1-trends-and-patterns-in-intermarriage/.

Pfeffer, Carla A. 2017. *Queering Families: The Postmodern Partnerships of Cisgender Women and Transgender Men.* New York: Oxford University Press.

Pimentel, Alejandra Wundram and Mónica Leonardo Segura. 2018. "Paradoxes of Visibility: The Proposed Guatemlan Gender Identity Law." *TSQ: Transgender Studies Quarterly* 5, no. 1: 83–99. DOI: 10.1215/23289252-4291538.

Pooley, Karen. 2015. "Segregation's New Geography: The Atlanta Metro Region, Race, and the Declining Prospects for Upward Mobility." *Southern Spaces.* Retrieved from https://southernspaces.org/2015/segregations-new-geography-atlanta-metro-region-race-and-declining-prospects-upward-mobility/.

Proctor, Aungelique and Fox 5 Atlanta Digital Team. 2021. "Trans Woman Shot and Killed Outside Apartment in Brookhaven, Police Say." *Fox 5.* Retrieved from https://www.fox5atlanta.com/news/trans-woman-shot-and-killed-outside-apartment-in-brookhaven-police-say.

Pyke, Karen D. 1996. "Class-Based Masculinities: The Interdependence of Gender, Class, and Interpersonal Power." *Gender & Society* 10, no. 5: 527–549. DOI: 10.1177/089124396010005003.

Pyke, Karen D. and Tran Dang. 2003. "'FOB' and 'Whitewashed': Identity and Internalized Racism Among Second Generation Asian Americans." *Qualitative Sociology* 26, no. 2: 147–172.

Ravenell, Joseph E., Waldo E. Johnson, and Eric E. Whitaker. 2006. "African American Men's Perceptions of Health: A Focus Group Study." *Journal of the National Medical Association,* 98: 544–550.

Raymond, Janice. 1979. *The Transsexual Empire: The Making of the She-Male.* Boston: Beacon Press.

Reback, Cathy J., Sherry Larkins, and Kristy Clark. 2018. "Motivations for a Casual or Occasional Sexual Encounter with a Man and/or Transgender Woman Among Heterosexual Men: Toward a Better Understanding of Atypical Sexual Partnering." *Sexuality and Culture* (October): 1–16.

Richie, Cristina. 2018. "A Queer, Feminist Bioethics Critique of Facial Feminization Surgery." *The American Journal of Bioethics* 18, no. 12: 33–35. DOI: 10.1080/15265161.2018.1531161.

Rios, Victor M. 2011. *Punished: Policing the Lives of Black and Latino Boys.* New York: New York University Press.

Ristock, Janice, Art Zoccole, Lisa Passante, and Jonathan Potskin. 2017. "Impacts of Colonization on Indigenous Two-Spirit/LGBTQ Canadians' Experiences of Migration, Mobility, and Relationship Violence." *Sexualities* 1–18. DOI: 10.1177/1363460716681474.

Rodney, Walter. 1972. *How Europe Underdeveloped Africa.* London: Bogle-L'Ouverture Publications.

Rojo del Arcoiris. 2022. "Towards a Queer Marxism: A Manifesto." Accessed June 10, 2023 from https://rojodelarcoiris.com/2022/03/23/towards-a-%E2%98%ADueer-marxism-a-manifesto/.

Ross, Sabrina N. 2013. "The Politics of Politeness: Theorizing Race, Gender, and Education in White Southern Space." *Counterpoints:* 412: 143–159.

Royster, Michael O., Al Richmond, Eugenia Eng, and Lewis Margolis. 2006. "Hey Brother, How's Your Health?: A Focus Group Analysis of the Health and Health-Related Concerns of African American Men in a Southern City in the United States." *Men and Masculinities* 8, no. 4: 389–404. DOI: 10.1177/109718X04268798.

Rowling, J.K. 2020. "J.K. Rowling Writes about Her Reasons for Speaking out on Sex and Gender Issues." Retrieved from https://www.jkrowling.com/opinions/j-k-rowling-writes-about-her-reasons-for-speaking-out-on-sex-and-gender-issues/.

Rubin, Gayle. 1975. "The Traffic in Women: Notes on the 'Political Economy' of Sex." In *Toward an Anthropology of Women,* edited by Rayna R. Reiter, 157–210. New York City: Monthly Review Press.

Ryan, Caitlin L., Jasmine M. Patraw, and Maree Bednar. 2012. "Discussing Princess Boys and Pregnant Men: Teaching About Gender Diversity and Transgender Experiences within an Elementary School Curriculum." *Journal of LGBT Youth* 10, no. 1–2: 83–105. DOI: 10.1080/19361653.2012.718540.

Saczkowski, Thomas. 2011. "Narratives of Violence: The Relationship of Masculinity and Ableism." A Master's Thesis in Critical Disability Studies at York University.

Saguy, Abigail C., Juliet A. Williams, Robin Dembroff, and Daniel Wodak. 2019. "We Should All Use They/Them Pronouns…Eventually." *Scientific American*.

Salamon, Gayle. 2018. *The Life and Death of Latisha King: A Critical Phenomenology of Transphobia*. New York City: New York University Press.

Salter, Michael. 2019. "The Problem with a Fight Against Toxic Masculinity." *The Atlantic*. Retrieved from https://www.theatlantic.com/health/archive/2019/02/toxic-masculinity-history/583411/.

Sanchez, Travis, Teresa Finlayson, Christopher Murrill, Vincent Guilin, and Laura Dean. 2009. "Risk Behaviors and Psychosocial Stressors in New York City House Ball Community: A Comparison of Men and Transgender Women who have Sex with Men." *AIDS Behavior* 14: 351–358. DOI: 10.1007/s10461-009-9610-6.

Schilt, Kristen and Danya Lagos. 2017. "The Development of Transgender Studies in Sociology." *Annual Review of Sociology* 43: 425–443. DOI: 10.1146/annurev-soc-060116-053348.

Schilt, Kristen and Laurel Westbrook. 2009. "Doing Gender, Doing Heteronormativity: 'Gender Normals,' Transgender People, and the Social Maintenance of Heterosexuality." *Gender & Society* 23, no. 4: 440–464. DOI: 10.1177/0891243209340034.

Schippers, Mimi. 2007. "Recovering the Feminine Other: Masculinity, Femininity, and Gender Hegemony." *Theory & Society* 36: 85–102. DOI: 10.1007/s1186-007-9022-4.

Schuster, Stef M. 2017. "Punctuating Accountability: How Discursive Aggression Regulates Transgender People." *Gender & Society* 31, no. 4: 481–502. DOI: 10.1177/0891243217717710.

Schwartz, Dona. 1992. *Waucoma Twilight: Generations of the Farm*. Washington, DC: Smithsonian.

Sechrist, S.M., J.D.L. Weil, and T.L. Shelton. 2016. "Evaluation of the Offender Focused Domestic Violence Initiative (OFDVI) in High Point, N.C. and Replication in Lexington, N.C.: Executive Summary for Community Oriented Policing Services." Washington, DC: U.S. Department of Justice.

Seidman, Steven. 1996. *Queer Theory/Sociology*. Cambridge: Blackwell Publishers.

Shakhsari, Sima. 2014. "Killing Me Softly with Your Rights: Queer Death and the Politics of Rightful Killing." In *Queer Necropolitics*, edited by J. Haritaworn, A. Kuntsman, and S. Posocco, 93–110. New York: Routledge.

Sims, Jennifer Patrice, Whitney Laster Pirtle, and Iris Johnson-Arnold. 2020. "Doing Hair, Doing Race: The Influence of Hairstyle on Racial Perception Across the U.S." *Ethnic and Racial Studies* 43, no. 12: 2099–2119. DOI: 10.1080/01419870.2019.1700296.

Smith, Andrea L. 2006. "Heteropatriarchy and the Three Pillars of White Supremacy: Rethinking Women of Color Organizing." In *The Color of Violence: The INCITE! Anthology*, edited by A.L. Smith, B.E. Richie, J. Sudbury, and J. White, 68–73. New York: South End Press.

Smith, Dorothy E. 1987. *The Everyday World as Problematic: A Feminist Sociology*. Toronto: University of Toronto Press.

Smith, William A., Walter R. Allen, and Lynette L. Danley. 2007. "'Assume the Position…You Fit the Description': Psychosocial Experiences and Racial Battle

Fatigue Among African American Male College Students." *American Behavioral Scientist* 51, no.4. DOI: 10.1177/0002764207307742.

Snorton, C. Riley. 2009. "'A New Hope': The Psychic Life of Passing." *Hypatia: A Journal of Feminist Philosophy* 24, no. 3: 77–92. DOI: 10.1111/j.1527-2001.2009.01046.x.

Snorton, C. Riley. 2017. *Black on Both Sides: A Racial History of Trans Identity*. Minneapolis: University of Minnesota Press.

Snorton, C. Riley and Jin Haritaworn. 2013. "Trans Necropolitics: A Transnational Reflection on Violence, Death, and the Trans of Color Afterlife." *The Transgender Studies Reader*, 2nd ed., edited by S. Stryker and A. Aizura, 66–74. New York: Routledge.

Snyder, R. Claire. 2008. "What is Third Wave Feminism? A New Directions Essay." *Signs* 34, no. 1: 175–196. DOI: 10.1086/588436.

Sommerville, Siobhan B. 2000. *Queering the Color Line: Race and the Invention of Homosexuality in American Culture*. Durham: Duke University Press.

Spade, Dean. 2011. *Normal Life: Administrative Violence, Critical Trans Politics, and the Limits of the Law*. Brooklyn: South End Press.

Stearns, Peter N. 1999. *Battleground of Desire: The Struggle for Self-Control in Modern America*. New York City: New York University Press.

Steinbugler, Amy C. 2012. *Beyond Loving: Intimate Racework in Lesbian, Gay, and Straight Interracial Relationships*. New York City: Oxford University Press.

Stepanova, Elena V. and Michael S. Strube. 2017. "Attractiveness as a Function of Skin Tone and Facial Features: Evidence from Categorization Studies." *Journal of General Psychology* 145, no. 1: 1–20. DOI: 10.1080/00221309.2017.1394811.

Strauss, E.W. 1952. "The Upright Posture." *Psychiatric Quarterly* 26: 529–561. DOI: 10.1007/BF01568490.

Stryker, Susan. 2006. "(De)Subjugated Knowledges: An Introduction to Transgender Studies." In *The Transgender Studies Reader*, edited by S. Stryker and S. Whittle, 1–15. New York: Routledge.

Stuart, Forrest and Ava Benezra. 2018. "Criminalized Masculinities: How Policing Shapes the Construction of Gender and Sexuality in Poor Black Communities." *Social Problems* 65: 174–190. DOI: 10.1093/socpro/spx017.

Toft, Alex, and Andrew Kam-Tuck Yip. 2018. "Intimacy Negotiated: The Management of Relationships and the Construction of Personal Communities in the Lives of Bisexual Women and Men." *Sexualities* 21, no 1–2: 233–250. DOI: 10.1177/1363460716679793.

Tong, Rosemarie. 2014. *Feminist Thought: A More Comprehensive Introduction*. Boulder: Westview Press.

Tourmaline, Eric A. Stanley, and Johanna Burton. 2017. *Trap Door: Trans Cultural Production and the Politics of Visibility*. Cambridge: The MIT Press.

Towle, Evan B. and Lynn M. Morgan. 2002. "Romancing the Transgender Native: Rethinking the Use of the 'Third Gender' Concept." *GLQ: A Journal of Lesbian and Gay Studies* 8, no. 4: 469–497.

Trans Housing Coalition. 2022. "Who We Are." Retrieved from https://www.transhousingcoalition.org/our-story.

Twohey, Megan and Christina Jewett. 2022. "Pusieron la Pausa a la Pubertad, ¿A Qué Precio?" *The New York Times*. Accessed January 3, 2023 at https://www.nytimes.com/es/2022/12/14/espanol/bloqueadores-pubertad-adolescentes-trans.html.

Vaid-Menon, Alok. 2015. "Trans is NOT the New Struggle!" *Return the Gayze*. Retrieved from http://returnthegayze.com/2015/07/22/trans-is-not-thenew-struggle/.

Vitulli, Elias. 2010. "A Defining Moment in Civil Rights History? The Employment Non-Discrimination Act, Trans-Inclusion, and Homonormativity." *Sexuality Research & Social Policy* 7, no. 3: 155–167. DOI: 10.1007/s13178-010-0015-0.

Voss, Brandon. 2018. "Anti-Trans Lesbian Protest Allowed to Lead, Disrupt London Pride Parade." *New, Now, Next*. Retrieved from http://www.newnownext.com/anti-trans-lesbian-protest-terfs-lead-disrupt-london-pride-parade/07/2018/.

Wade, Lisa and Myra Marx Ferree. 2015. *Gender: Ideas, Interactions, Institutions*. New York: Norton.

Ward, Jane. 2010. "Gender Labor: Transmen, Femmes, and Collective Work of Transgression." *Sexualities* 13, no. 2. DOI: 10.1177/1363460709359114.

Ward, Jane. 2015. *Not Gay: Sex Between Straight White Men*. New York City: New York University Press.

Warfa, Nasir, Kamaldeep Bhui, Kwame Phillips, and Krishna Nandy. 2006. "Comparison of Life Events, Substance Misuse, Service Use and Mental Illness Among African-Caribbean, Black African, and White British Men in East London: A Qualitative Study." *Diversity in Health and Social Care* 3: 111–121.

Waring, Chandra D.L. 2013. "'They See Me as Exotic…That Intrigues Them:' Gender, Sexuality and the Racially Ambiguous Body." *Race, Gender, & Class* 20, no. 3–4: 299–317.

Watkins, Daphne C., B. Lee Green, Patricia Goodson, Jeff Guidry, and Christine Stanley. 2007. "Using Focus Groups to Explore the Stressful Life Events of Black College Men." *Journal of College Student Development*, 48: 105–118.

Watkins, Daphne C., Rheeda L. Walker, and Derek M. Griffith. 2010. "A Meta-Study of Black Male Mental Health and Wellbeing." *Journal of Black Psychology*, 36 (3): 303–330. DOI: 10.1177/0095798409353756.

Weeden, J. and J. Sabini. 2005. "Physical Attractiveness and Health in Western Societies: A Review." *Psychological Bulletin* 131, no. 5: 635–653. DOI: 10.1037/0033-2909.131.5.635.

Weinberg, Martin S. and Colin J. Williams. 2010. "Men Sexually Interested in Transwomen (MSTW): Gendered Embodiment and the Construction of Sexual Desire." *The Journal of Sex Research* 47, no. 4: 374–383.

Weinhold, Bob. 2006. "Epigenetics: The Science of Change." *Environmental Health Perspectives* 114, no. 3: A160–A167. DOI: 10.1289/ehp.114-a160.

West, Candace and Don H. Zimmerman. 1987. "Doing Gender." *Gender & Society* 1, no. 2: 125–151.

Westbrook, Laurel. 2021. *Unlivable Lives: Violence and Identity in Transgender Activism*. Berkeley: University of California Press.

Westbrook, Laurel and Kristen Schilt. 2013. "Doing Gender, Determining Gender: Transgender People, Gender Panics, and the Maintenance of the

Sex/Gender/Sexuality System." *Gender & Society* 28, no. 1: 32–57. DOI: 10.1177/0891243213503203.

Whitehill, Jennifer M., Daniel W. Webster, Shannon Frattaroli, and Elizabeth M. Parker. 2014. "Interrupting Violence: How the CeaseFire Program Prevents Imminent Gun Violence through Conflict Mediation." *Journal of Urban Health* 91, no. 1. DOI: 10.1007/s11524-013-9796-9.

Wild, Angela C. 2019. "Lesbians at Ground Zero: How Transgenderism is Conquering the Lesbian Body." *Get the L Out UK*. Retrieved from file:///Users/alithia/Downloads/LesbiansAtGroundZeroFindings.pdf.

Williams, Cristian. 2014. "TERF: What it Means and Where it Came From." *The Trans Advocate*. Retrieved from https://www.transadvocate.com/terf-what-it-means-and-where-it-came-from_n_13066.htm.

Willis, Raquel. 2021. "Across the South, a Trans Housing Movement Grows." *Vogue*. Retrieved from https://www.vogue.com/article/across-the-south-a-trans-housing-movement-grows.

Wilson, Mandy, Paul L. Simpson, Tony G. Butler, Juliet Richters, Lorraine Yap, and Basil Duncan. 2017. "'You're a Woman, A Convenience, A Cat, A Poof, A Thing, An Idiot'" Transgender Women Negotiating Sexual Experiences in Men's Prisons in Australia." *Sexualities* 20, no. 3: 380–402.

Winnubst, Shannon. 2012. "The Queer Thing About Neoliberal Pleasure: A Foucauldian Warning." *Foucault Studies* 14: 79–97.

Wittig, Monique. 1978 [1992]. *The Straight Mind*. New York: Beacon Press.

Yanagina, Yukari. 2020. "The Psychoanalysis of Murderous Violence at the Intersection of Race, Gender, and Sexuality." Lecture given at The Institute for Psychoanalytic Research and Training's IPTAR-Q, October 5, 2020.

Yapp, Emma, and Kate E. Pickett. 2019. "Greater Income Inequality is Associated with Higher Rates of Intimate Partner Violence in Latin America." *Public Health* 175: 87–89. doi: 10.1016.j.puhe.2019.07.004.

Yerke, Adam F. and Jennifer DeFeo. 2016. "Redefining Intimate Partner Violence Beyond the Binary to Include Transgender People." *Journal of Family Violence* 31: 975–979. DOI: 10.1007/s10896-016-9887-y.

Yildiz, Bulent O, Sheila Bolour, Keslie Woods, April Moore, and Ricardo Azziz. 2010. "Visually Scoring Hirsutism." *Human Reproduction Update* 16, no. 1: 51–65. DOI: 10.1093/humupd/dmp024.

Zamantakis, Alithia and J.E. Sumerau. 2019. "Streaming Transgender: Visualizing Continuity and Change in Transgender Media Representations." In *Gender & Pop Culture*, edited by Adrienne Trier-Bieniek, 25–42. Boston: Sense Publishers.

Zimmerly, Grace. 2013. "The Real Costs of Sex Reassignment Surgery." *The Yale News*. Retrieved from https://yaledailynews.com/blog/2013/03/05/zimmerly-the-real-costs-of-sex-reassignment-surgery/.

Index

Abjection, xx, 125–26
Abstract liberalism, 54–58, 75. *See also* liberalism; neoliberalism
accountable conduct, xv–xviii, 1, 19
alexithymia, 89–90

binary, 3; binarism, 54; Black/White, xxii; gender, xvi–xviii, xxi–xxii, 1–2, 63, 65, 67, 84, 92, 119, 132, 139; sexual, 92
Black feminist theory, 2, 9–10
Blackness, xxix–xxx, 4, 10, 20, 38, 46, 49, 108, 135–36; Black political consciousness, 11–12
body-reasoning, 1–2, 71, 78, 86, 146

capitalism, xxxii, 16, 94, 139, 150; capitalist class, xv–xvi, xxii, xxx, 144–45
cis-centricity, xxxi, 44, 59–60
cis-ness, xiv, xx–xxii, xxvii, 3, 19–20, 24, 54, 63–69, 84–96, 112–13, 120, 125, 139, 143, 145–47, 150, 158; critical cis-ness studies, xiv–xviii, 144; racialized, 126–27, 139
cisnormativity, 83, 89, 100, 124
cissexism, xv, xx–xxi, xxv, xxxi, xxxii, 2–3, 8–9, 40, 42, 49, 55, 60, 63–68, 75, 77, 83–84, 89–90, 95, 110, 116–18, 126–27, 130–32, 139, 144, 147, 150, 152; racialized, xxix–xxx, 147
class, xxviii–xxix, xxxi, 4, 8–9, 32–34, 94, 113, 126–27, 139, 149–50, 155, 158; status, xvi, xviii. *See also* socioeconomic status
colonialism, xv, xxii, xxxii, 13–14, 54, 64, 99, 108, 139, 146
colorism, 5, 42, 45–46, 49, 59–60, 83, 94
controlling images, 54, 137–38. *See also* intersectionality; misogynoir
critical race feminism, xviii. *See also* critical race theory
critical race theory, xviii, xxxii. *See also* critical race feminism

discourse, xiii, xiv–xviii, 16, 63, 67, 80, 96, 100, 139–40, 144–45, 147, 158
doing gender, xv–xviii, 1, 124–25
dyadism, 40, 119

Eurocentricity, xxxi, 24, 44, 59–60, 83, 94, 124
excess, 2–8, 13–20, 39–44, 57–58, 111, 118, 146

feminities, xxxi, 29–30, 34, 69; Black, 135–37; feminine bodies, 14, 39, 40;

www.ingramcontent.com/pod-product-compliance
Lightning Source LLC
Chambersburg PA
CBHW071051280326
41928CB00050B/2178